Library of
Davidson College

GREEK INSECTS

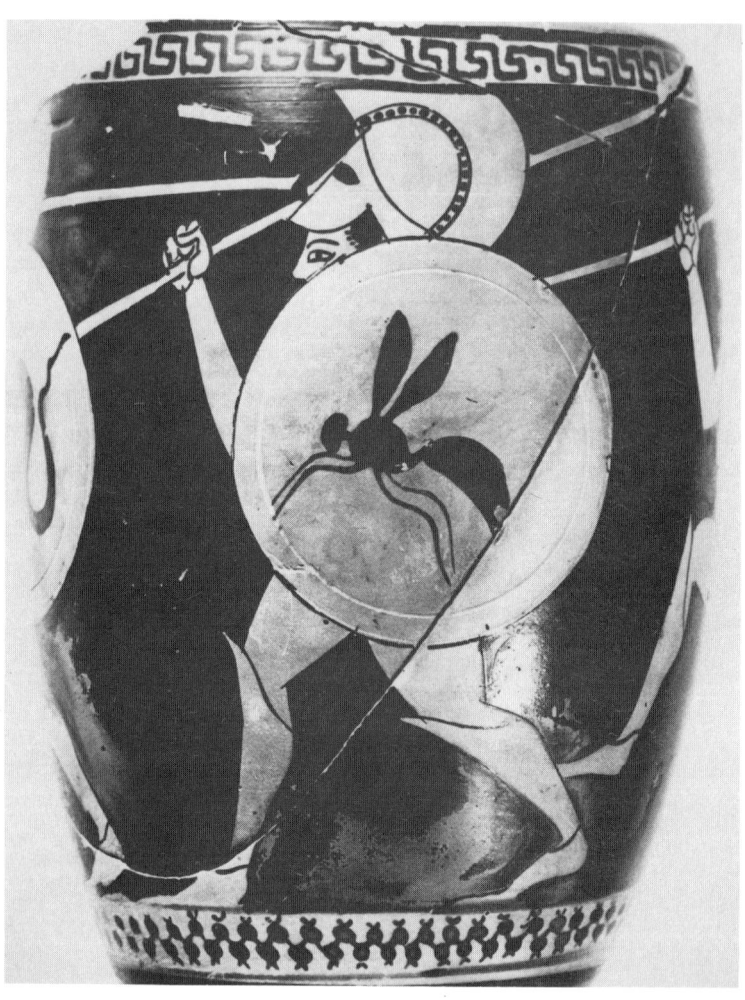

Flying wasp as a shield device on an early Attic red-figure lecythos by the Roundabout Painter (Athens, Agora Museum P24061: ARV^2 131): see H.A. Thompson, *Hesperia* 24 (1955) 63; the insect (for whose shape compare Fig. 17) might conceivably be a flying ant, but this seems less appropriate as a soldier's symbol (see p. 75). From the American School of Classical Studies at Athens: Agora Excavations.

Greek Insects

Malcolm Davies
&
Jeyaraney Kathirithamby

New York   Oxford
OXFORD UNIVERSITY PRESS
1986

© 1986 by Malcolm Davies & Jeyaraney Kathirithamby

Published in 1986 by
Gerald Duckworth & Co. Ltd.
The Old Piano Factory
43 Gloucester Crescent, London NW1

Published in 1986 in the United States by
Oxford University Press, Inc.
200 Madison Avenue, New York, New York 10016

Oxford is a registered trademark of Oxford University Press

All rights reserved. No part of this
publication may be reproduced, stored in a
retrieval system, or transmitted, in any
form or by any means, electronic, mechanical,
photocopying, recording, or otherwise, without
the prior permission of the publisher.

ISBN (U.S.) 0 19 520548-0

Printing (last digit): 9 8 7 6 5 4 3 2 1
Printed in Great Britain

Contents

Preface	vii
Abbreviations	xv
Introduction	1
The insect in Aesop's fables and Greek poetry	1
Aristotle and the scientific study of insects	16
Insects in Greek art	30
Glossary	
1. Ant	37
2. Bed bug	46
3. Bee/wasp	47
4. Beetle/cockchafer	83
5. Borers of wood	96
6. Butterfly/moth	99
7. Cicada	113
8. Cricket/grasshopper/locust	134
9. Flea	149
10. Fly	150
11. Gnat/mosquito	164
12. Leekbane	167
13. Louse	168
14. Praying mantis	176
Index of modern works	181
Index locorum	192
General index	201

The data collected and discussed by the ancient Greek entomologists have never been methodically examined, most probably because the topic never appealed either to historians of the sciences or to classicists ... A careful, thoroughgoing evaluation of the ancient texts and archaeological evidence would contribute not only to the history of the natural sciences, entomology in particular, but even to the history of the humanities, since, for the ancient Greeks at least, science and philosophy were kindred disciplines.

Liliane Bodson, *The Classical Outlook* (Oct./Nov. 1983) p.5

Preface

A proper study of ancient Greek insects should embrace not only the obvious questions of their identification, in modern terms of species and genera, but also such issues as the etymologies (both formal and popular) of the various insect names, the folk-lore, religious, and other significant associations of these creatures, and the differences in attitude towards them shown by the ancient and modern world. Doubtless our book will be found not completely proper either in these or in other respects; but we have done our best to approach the topic from as many angles as seemed fruitful and revealing.

First and foremost, the question of identification. Our original models for this book were those two famous studies *A Glossary of Greek Birds* (second edition, Oxford 1936) and *A Glossary of Greek Fishes* (Oxford 1947) by the incomparable D'Arcy Wentworth Thompson, a scholar whose combination of classical and zoological expertise rendered him uniquely qualified in the task he undertook, whose uniquely charming (if slightly archaic) style makes those books classics in every sense. But as we proceeded, we found that what was feasible for relatively large animals was far more difficult with such small creatures as insects, whose very inconspicuousness meant that they were less noticed and remarked upon, perhaps, indeed, taken less seriously, by Antiquity. Besides, though he never undertook a formal study of insects in the same manner as his treatment of fishes and birds, Thompson himself had recorded most of the obviously correct identifications (his own and those of earlier scholars) in various works (especially in the notes to his translation of Aristotle's *Historia Animalium*, but also, for example, in his contributions to the Greek Lexicon of Liddell, Scott & Jones). We had less to do here than originally anticipated and have therefore been able to spread ourselves on other no less fascinating topics.

But first some more general remarks on the principles that underlie the whole question of identifications of animals described in authors who lived so long ago. As P. Ansell Robin has observed (*Animal Lore in English Literature* (London 1932) p.4):

> Individual observation in natural history or, as we now call it, nature-study, has always been unreliable, and trained experts with ample opportunities are rare. Even at the present day there are many points still to be cleared up in the life-history of comparatively well-known animals, and authorities are sometimes at variance. In the past the difficulties of observation or the deficiencies of observers have been responsible for many errors. For example, those who brought news to Europe (in the sixteenth century) of the birds of paradise either had never seen them except on the wing, or had seen only birds from which the natives had removed the legs; they therefore reported that, having no legs, these birds never alighted, and that they were nourished by the 'dews of heaven'.

More recently Sir Ernst Gombrich has reminded us, in a famous passage from *Art and Illusion* (pp. 70ff.), how difficult an eighteenth-century English draftsman found it to free himself of 'preconceived prejudices' in depicting an African rhinoceros.

Descriptions of animals in ancient authors have their own special problems. Discussing 'Observation, Description and Imagination' in ancient poetry and the relative absence of 'the close and individual observation of something quite ordinary' from such poetry, Gordon Williams notes (*Tradition and Originality in Roman Poetry* (Oxford 1968) p. 669):

> There has been preserved a Greek papyrus containing four passages of poetry (*Tebtunis Papyri* i 1902.1: date about 100 B.C.), one of which is a description of dawn in the country. The type of description is 'exhaustive', first of birds and their behaviour, then of bees. It has been possible to recognise from this latter description a certain species of bees, Chalicodoma, which is native to Egypt. But this is not because accurate and individual observation can be seen in the passage; it is simply that certain features of these bees' behaviour, which could be learnt from an

Preface

encyclopaedia, are represented in a long series of compound adjectives.

In fact even this verdict may be excessively optimistic. The identification referred to (for which see below p. 52) largely depends on the adjectives which Williams mentions, and, like many words in many Greek texts, their meaning is not sacrosanct and unassailable, but ambiguous or perhaps even corrupt. If, for instance, *lipokentros* means 'stingless', and *pelourgos* and *askepeis* 'working in day' and 'without hive', the identification may be correct. It has been suggested, however, (by A.D. Knox in CR 39 (1925) 192) that *lipokentros* means 'leaving behind stings' (a much more normal usage) and that *pêlourgos* is corrupt for *pteleourgos* (an unattested but not unimaginable word: 'they used the resin to wax the floors of their hives') and *askepeis* for *askêthes* (to be referred to the following allusion to honey: the adjective is used of that substance in Antimachus fr. 20.2 Wyss). Such maddening uncertainties in interpretation are not infrequent in ancient texts. They must be accepted as a part of life.

On the issue of *etymology* we have been able to rely, for much of the time, upon one of the very few important and relatively recent studies of any aspect of insects in antiquity, Gil Fernández's *Nombres de Insectos en Griego Antiguo* (Madrid 1959) a work which fully deserved the honour of being regularly cited under the entries which concern insects in Pierre Chantraine's standard work *Dictionnaire Etymologique de la Langue Grecque*. Another important study in this area is R. Strömberg's *Griechische Wortstudien* (Göteborg, 1944).

Often the explanation of a name must remain hypothetical, of course. The study of popular etymologies of insect names, erroneous but widely held derivatives and explanations of puzzling forms, surely needs no defence. Anyone who has ever wondered, for instance, why the English named the cockroach after a bird and a fish, must see the fascination inherent in the study of this topic, which frequently involves processes of analogy no less unexpected than the above mentioned transformation of the original Spanish *cucuracha* (roach-fish[1]). It is not perhaps pretentious to suggest that insight into how minds work may be obtained by observing such similar phenomena.

[1] Cf. Howard Ensign Evans, *Life on a Little-Known Planet*[2] (1984), p. 49.

This is even more obviously the case when we come to an examination of the various superstitions, religious and other beliefs attached to insects in the ancient world. The bee and the butterfly are but the most obvious examples of creatures whose numinous associations should interest the anthropologist and others. On a slightly less profound level, it is at least entertaining (and perhaps instructive too) to ask, for example, why the ancient Greeks found the sound of the cicada so attractive (in strong contrast to the reactions of modern travellers from northerly climates). Has perception or taste changed so radically?

From studies such as these there is much to learn, and there are implications to be grasped too. The extreme anthropomorphisation of some insects by ancient writers may strike us as naive until we read Jean Henri Fabre's classic essay on 'the sacred beetle' (handily reprinted in Martin Gardner's anthology *The Sacred Beetle and other great essays in science* (Oxford 1985) pp. 72ff.) where we discover that well into the nineteenth century a similar fallacy obtained concerning the dung beetle, which was supposed to call on the help of his comrades if difficulties were encountered in rolling his ball of dung. Fabre's refutation is memorable (from *The Sacred Beetle* etc. p.84f. ≃ *Souvenirs Entomologiques* 1.14):

> It is no light matter to attribute to an insect a really astonishing grasp of a situation, combined with an even more amazing power of communication between individuals of the same species. Such an admission involves more than one imagines. That is why I insist on my point. What! Are we to believe that a Beetle in distress will conceive the idea of going in quest of help? We are to imagine him flying off and scouring the country to find fellow-workers on some patch of dung; when he has found them, we are to suppose that he addresses them, in a sort of pantomime, by gestures with his antennae more particularly, in some such words as these:
>
> 'I say, you fellows, my load's upset in a hole over there; come and help me get it out. I'll do as much for you one day!'
>
> And we are to believe that his comrades understand! And, more incredible still, that they straightaway leave their work, the pellet which they have just begun, the beloved pill exposed to the cupidity of others and certain to be filched in their absence, and go to the help of the suppliant! I am profoundly incredulous of such unselfishness ...

Preface

But that such a belief should have endured for so long shows we have no right to patronise Antiquity for its anthropomorphisation of ant or bee.

Like Thompson, we have restricted ourselves to the evidence of literature and art.[2] Unlike him, we have tended to exclude Roman writers and artists, except for the elder Pliny, whose dependence on Aristotle's *Historia Animalium* makes him a special case, to be quoted regularly. And later evidence has been brought in when (as with the symbolism of the butterfly, for instance) earlier evidence was inadequate on its own for a full understanding of the facts. Our original plan was to include all animals which the Greeks (as opposed to modern science) regarded as insects. This would have brought spiders, scorpions and millipedes within the scope of this work, and other creatures besides. However, when we had assembled material on the most commonly described of insects, we paused, looked about, and concluded (rightly or wrongly) that we had on our hands a book of adequate depth and dimensions. Should the response to the present work prove encouraging, we plan to extend our study to Greek 'insects' (as well as insects less often noticed in Greek antiquity). It is for this reason that we have chosen to list the insects in the way we have, for the alphabetic sequence of ant to mantis is easily continued with millipede, scorpion and spider, provided wasp is catalogued with bee and one or two other stratagems, independently urged by ancient Greek attitudes and assumptions, are adopted.

Before the actual glossary of insects we have placed a general discussion of the treatment of these animals in ancient literature, especially scientific literature, and art. This section is not intended to be in any way a substitute for the 'history of early entomology, chiefly Greek and Roman' desiderated and promised by Professor John Scarborough (*Melsheimer Entomological Series* no. 26 (1976) pp. 17ff.). Its much more modest aim is that of orienting the reader in potentially unfamiliar

---

[2] Some actual insects have survived from antiquity. For instance W.F. Jashemski, *The Gardens of Pompeii* (New York 1979) pp. 320ff. describes various types of carbonised material from the villa of L. Crassus Tertius at Torre Annuziata, including a brown scavenger beetle and an insect larva from the first century A.D. (photo-electron microscope depictions thereof in pls. 516-17). Furthermore, a bruchid, the strawberry weevil, has been discovered within ancient beans at Pompeii (see p. 242).

territory and in particular of drawing on recent research to provide a balanced view of Aristotle's achievement as entomologist that avoids extremes of eulogy and blame. 'The interests of a scientist or a philosopher are inevitably coloured by the mental atmosphere in which he lives', as W.K.C. Guthrie effectively reminded classical scholars some time ago (*In the Beginning: some Greek views on the origins of life and the early state of man* (London 1957) p. 34). 'It is not far-fetched to suppose that the prevailing tone of economic and social ideas in mid-Victorian England encouraged Darwin and others towards the idea of natural selection.' The same realisation applied to Aristotle produces a more plausible picture of the man (or some aspects of him) than some we have seen.

Thompson amassed large lists of relevant material which scholars over the years have found extremely useful. We have been rather more selective and have often saved space by quoting handy secondary literature. We have also refrained from quoting too many obscure and out of the way authors.

We have, however, quoted some comparative material and should, perhaps, have quoted more. When one reads (C.W. Hobley, *Bantu Beliefs and Magic* (London 1922) p. 252) that in Kitui 'the owner of the beehive cannot cohabit with his wife until he sees that a swarm of bees has settled in the hive and is building there. Two nights after he is satisfied that this is the case, he may resume his marital relations', it is impossible not to be reminded of similar ideas current in ancient Greece (see p. 70 n.31 below). When one hears (cf. E. Porter, *Cambridgeshire Customs and Folklore* (London 1969) p.50) that 'if you see a white butterfly, you know that a baby or a little child has just died', who does not think of the ancient Greek association between the soul and that insect?[3] The related idea of souls in the shape of insects[4] has world-wide currency.

[3] This particular superstition seems to have an abiding appeal. It was exploited by the American author Stephen Vincent Benét in his short story of 1922 entitled 'The Devil and Daniel Webster' (see e.g. *Folklore in American Literature* (ed. J.T. Flannigan and A.P. Hudson (New York 1958) p.44) where the Devil carries a human soul in his handkerchief 'like a moth, but it wasn't a moth ... just like a butterfly'; a scene that makes a striking impression still in the film adaptation ('All that Money can Buy' (1941)) of Benét's play on the same theme.

[4] Cf., for instance, V.N. Chernetsov ap. *Studies in Siberian Shamanism* (ed. H.N. Michael (1963)) p. 12f. on souls in the form of beetles, water-beetles and mosquitos. See further J.G. Frazer, *Golden Bough* General Index s.v. 'Insects, spirits of the dead thought to lodge in', and Bächtold-Stäubli, *Handwörterbuch des deutschen Aberglaubens* 2.1627, 4.906 etc.

Preface xiii

But enough of explanation and apology: *ad insecta transeamus: haec namque restant, immensae subtilitatis animalia.*[5]

Bibliographical note

There is little to record in the way of earlier studies of Greek insects. The three works most frequently referred to in our book are those studies (etymological rather than entomological) by Gil Fernández, Strömberg and Chantraine mentioned on p. ix above. General bibliographical surveys are provided by J. Scarborough, *Melsheimer Entomological Series* 26 (1976) pp. 17ff. and L. Bodson, *The Classical Outlook* 1983 Oct./Nov. p. 6. The classical scholar is warned that many of the articles on insects in *RE* (handily listed by Scarborough, p. 21) which the hurried and harassed non-specialist may consult, supply misleadingly impressive-looking and specific lists of identifications of ancient names with modern species that are perfectly arbitrary and based on no ancient evidence at all.

Note on illustrations

We have made the merest selection from the numerous fascinating ancient artefacts that depict insects. Since we are not primarily concerned with these as *objets d'art* in their own right we have not included details as to the actual size and proportion of the originals (or the extent to which our illustrations have enlarged or reduced them). We do, however, regularly supply references to secondary literature where the former class of information may be found. We are grateful to the various museums which sent us photographs of the artefacts together with permission to publish them. John Boardman, Andrew Burnett and Donna Kurz kindly helped in various ways with the obtaining of photographs, Maurice Chuzeville, John Haywood and R.L. Wilkins with the production of them.

---

[5] Pliny *NH* 10.212 (cf. ib.11.1).

Abbreviations

Latin titles of works by ancient authors[1]

AP	*Anthologia Palatina:* the Palatine Anthology: a collection of Greek epigrams of varying dates.
CP	*de Causis Plantarum*
GA	*de Generatione Animalium*
HA	*Historia Animalium*
HP	*Historia Plantarum*
NA	*de Natura Animalium*
NH	*Naturalis Historia*
PA	*de Partibus Animalium*

Classical journals (marked with an asterisk) and works of reference

ABV	*Attic Black-Figure Vases* (Oxford 1956) by J.D. Beazley
*AJA	*American Journal of Archaeology*
ARV^2	*Attic Red-Figure Vases*[2] (Oxford 1963) by J.D. Beazley
*Class. Phil.	*Classical Philology*
*CQ	*Classical Quarterly*
*CR	*Classical Review*
CVA	*Corpus Vasorum Atticorum*
DK	Diels and Kranz (edd.), *Fragmente der Vorsokratiker*

[1] For a fuller account of the works in question see pp. 13 and 26ff.

Abbreviations

FGE	*Further Greek Epigrams* (Cambridge 1981) edited by D.L. Page
F.Gr.Hist.	*Fragmente der Griechische Historiker* edited by F. Jacoby
GP	*Garland of Philip* (Cambridge 1968) edited by A.S.F. Gow and D.L. Page
*HSCP	*Harvard Studies in Classical Philology*
*JHS	*Journal of Hellenic Studies*
*Journ. Phil	*Journal of Philology*
*JRS	*Journal of Roman Studies*
K	Kock (ed.), *Comicorum Atticorum Fragmenta* (1880-1889)
LP	Lobel and Page (edd.), *Lesbiorum Poetarum Fragmenta* (Oxford 1955)
LSJ	Liddell, Scott and Jones (edd.), *Greek-English Lexicon* (Oxford 1968)
MW	Merkelbach and West (edd.), *Fragmenta Hesiodea* (Oxford 1967)
*Mnemos.	*Mnemosyne*
P	Page (ed.), *Poetae Melici Graeci* (Oxford 1962)
Pf	Pfeiffer (ed.), *Callimachi Fragmenta* (Oxford 1949)
PCG	*Poetae Comici Graeci* edited by R. Kassel and C. Austin (Berlin 1983)
*PCPS	*Proceedings of the Cambridge Philological Society*
*QUCC	*Quaderni Urbinati di Cultura Classica*
RE	*Real-Encyclopädie der klassischen Altertumswissenschaft*
*Rev. Phil.	*Revue de Philologie*
*Rh.Mus.	*Rheinische Museum*
Suppl. Hell.	*Supplementum Hellenisticum* (Berlin 1983) edited by H. Lloyd-Jones and P.J. Parsons
Tr.G.F.	*Tragicorum Graecorum Fragmenta* (Göttingen 1971–) edited by B. Snell, R. Kannicht, S.L. Radt
V	Voigt (ed.) *Sappho et Alcaeus: Fragmenta* (Amsterdam 1971)
W	West (ed.), *Iambi et Elegi Graeci* (Oxford 1971 and 1972)
*ZPE	*Zeitschrift für Papyrologie und Epigraphik*

To the memory of

Thambapillay Kathirithamby

1900–1976

Introduction

The insect in Aesop's fables and Greek poetry

It is traditional in surveys of this sort to begin with Homer; but, for reasons which will shortly become plain, it is more appropriate in the present case to start with Aesop's fables.[1] The texts of these, as we possess them, are late, but there is no reason to doubt that many of them derive from an earlier, ultimately pre-literate, stage of Greek culture.[2] Animals loom very large, of course, within this category of literature, and insects play their part in spite of, or, rather, precisely because of, their small size. This is true both of Greek fables and of their Oriental counterparts and prototypes.[3] Thus a Babylonian fable describes how 'when the gnat had settled on the elephant he said, "Brother, have I been a burden to you? [If so], I will go away,

---

[1] The most convenient general introduction to the whole problem of the Aesopic fable, its origins and nature, the date and identity of Aesop and other related questions, will be found in B.E. Perry's Loeb text and translation of Babrius and Phaedrus (1965), the two ancient poets who preserve (in Greek and Latin respectively) a large proportion of these fables. This work also includes a useful Appendix and Index that embrace Aesopic fables not treated by Babrius and Phaedrus. See further T. Karadagli, *Fabel und Ainos: Studien zur gr. Fabel* (*Beitr. zur kl. Phil.* 135 (1981)) passim. For a penetrating study of fable and the rôle of animals within it see K. Meuli, *W.F. Otto Festschrift (Schweizerisches Archiv für Volkskunde* 50 (1954)) pp. 65ff. = *Ges. Schr.* 2.731ff., esp. 69f. = 735f.

[2] It can sometimes be shown to be very likely that relatively early works of literature presuppose fables first attested only at a much later date: see e.g. Davies, *Hermes* 109 (1981) 248ff.

[3] On Oriental fables that closely resemble (and thus seem to have inspired) the Greek variety see Perry pp. xxviiiff; the various contributions to *La Fable* (*Entretiens sur l'Antiquité Classique* 30 (1984)) esp. M.L. West pp. 109ff.; and W. Burkert, *Sitzb. d. Heidelberg. Akad. d. Wiss. phil.-hist. Kl.* 1 (1984) 110ff..

over there by the pond." Said the elephant to the gnat, "I was not aware that you had settled on me. What are you anyhow? And if you have left, well, I didn't notice your departure either." [4] An almost identical story is preserved by the fabulist Babrius (late first century A.D.),[5] though in his version the gnat settles on the curved horn of a bull and magnanimously offers to move to a poplar tree on the bank of a river.[6] The similarities here are remarkably close and seem only explicable in terms of borrowing if not paraphrase. Another fable involving the self-importance of a tiny insect is familiar to English-speaking peoples because of Sir Francis Bacon's summary: 'The fly sate upon the axle-tree of the chariot-wheel and said, "What a dust do I raise!" [7] This too had an Oriental prototype, though here the analogy is not quite so close: 'The fox having urinated into the sea said, "The whole of the sea is my urine".'[8]

The above instances are concerned with deflating the self-importance of the minuscule.[9] Contrarily, other Aesopic fables endeavour to stress the truth that effective action and work are not necessarily indexes of size. The most famous encapsulation of this involves the lion and the mouse (Babrius *fab.* 107 (p. 136f. Perry)), but a comparable variant deals with an ant and a dove: a dove rescues an ant that is nearly drowning in a spring by dropping down a twig on to which the ant climbs. Later

---

[4] This fable is quoted by E. Ebeling, *Die babylonische Fabel und ihre Bedeutung für die Literaturgeschichte (Mitteilungen der altorientalischen Gesellschaft* 2.2 (1927)) p.50. We produce the translation given by Perry p. xxxii. See further M.L. West, 'Near Eastern material in Hellenistic and Roman literature', *HSCP* 73 (1969) 114f.

[5] On Babrius' life and date see Perry pp. xliviiff. Though he wrote in Greek it seems likely, as Perry pp. liiff. observes, that he enjoyed Roman nationality.

[6] Babrius *fab.* 84 (p. 102f. Perry). For another version of the fable of the gnat and the bull cf. Perry's Appendix 137.

[7] From the essay *Of Vainglory*. This version is actually of late origin: Lorenzo Bevilaqua (see *Notes and Queries* 202 (1957) 378), Abstemius 16 (Perry's Appendix 724). Cf. M.P. Tilley, *A Dictionary of the Proverbs in England in the Sixteenth and Seventeenth Centuries* (1950) D652.

[8] Quoted from E.I. Gordon, *Sumerian Proverbs: glimpses of everyday life in ancient Mesopotamia* (Philadelphia 1959) p.222.

[9] Other instances of this general motif include the fable in which a caterpillar bursts trying to equal the length of a snake (Perry's Appendix 268): compare the better-known frog who tried to be as big as a cow (Babrius *fab.* 28, Phaedrus *fab.* 1.24). The fly and the mule (Phaedrus 3.6): a fly perches on the pole of a wagon and urges the mule to go faster. The mule replies that it is the driver's whip and curb that controls his pace, not the fly's prattle.

The insect in Aesop's fables and Greek poetry 3

a fowler's attempts to snare the dove are thwarted when the ant bites him on the foot (Perry's Appendix 235).

This popular theme of the triumph of small over great[10] also occurs in a fable that is more famous and of considerable antiquity (Perry's Appendix 3): the eagle violates the asylum given by the dung-beetle to a hare and devours the hare. In revenge the beetle takes to destroying the eggs in the eagle's nest until the eagle, as the bird of Zeus, obtains permission to lay his eggs in the lap of the king of the gods. Not even here are they safe, however: the beetle flies up to Olympus and deposits dung on the god's lap, Zeus leaps up to brush it away, and the eggs roll from his lap and are broken. The tale was already well-known by the time of Aristophanes (died *c.* 385 B.C.)[11] who refers to it twice (*Wasps* 1446ff.; *Peace* 129ff.; cf. *Lysistrata* 695)[12] on the first occasion claiming that Aesop told it to the Delphians in order to persuade them not to violate the shrine at which he himself had taken refuge.[13] Here, however, the situation is rather more complex: an aetiological nature-myth, explaining why eagles lay their eggs at a time of the year when no beetles are around, seems originally to underlie the fable, and the very length and numerous stages of the narrative allow for differing

---

[10] A slightly less stereotyped instance (Perry's Appendix 259): the lion's depression that so noble an animal as himself should have a phobia about roosters is cured when he learns that the elephant, for all his size, must perpetually flap his ears if he is to prevent a gnat entering them and causing his death (see further on the versions of this fable Karadagli, *Fabel und Ainos* pp. 46ff.). Another variation (Perry's Appendix 564): a gnat challenges a bull to a contest of strength and, when a large crowd has gathered, tells the bull 'It's enough for me that you have treated me as an equal by turning up.'

[11] Meuli, *W.F. Otto Festschrift* p.72 = *Ges. Schr.* 2.738f. among others argues that the fable was used by the seventh-century iambic poet Semonides (on whose date and career see Lloyd-Jones, *Females of the Species* (1975) pp. 15ff.), a fragment of whose compositions depicted some character (Zeus?) as saying (of the dung-beetle): 'That insect flew past us which has the basest existence of all living creatures' (fr. 13 W). This looks like an adaption of a standard fable-closing formula: see Karadagli, *Fabel und Ainos* p.118f. Against Meuli's interpretation of the Semonidean fragment see M.L. West ap. *La Fable* p. 112.

[12] See further on the implications of these Aristophanic references to the story Karadagli, *Fabel und Ainos* p.18. Cf. H. van Thiel, *Antike und Abendland* 17 (1971) 113f. on the relationship between. Ar. *Lysistr.* 695 and the proverb (Zenob. cent. 2.53 (1.46 Leutsch-Schneidewin)).

[13] On the various accounts given in antiquity as to how Aesop came to offend the Delphians and why they wished to (and eventually did) kill him see Perry pp. xliiff.; cf. Karadagli, *Fabel und Ainos* p.19, A. Weichers, *Aesop in Delphi* (*Beitr. zur kl. Phil.* 2 (1960)) pp. 7ff.

morals to be drawn. Still, the most important (and probably the original) function of the tale was to stress, for the benefit of the down-trodden and oppressed, the overwhelming importance of justice in the matter of asylum, by showing how even the wretched and despised dung-beetle can triumph over the all-powerful eagle, the bird of Zeus, because backed by right.[14]

Another class of fable is what Perry (p.xxvi) terms 'the literary debate between two rivals, each of whom claims to be superior in some way, or more useful to man, than the other, praising himself and belittling his opponent'.[15] From the insect world this is exemplified by the dispute between the ant and the fly (Phaedrus *fab.* 4.25 = Perry's Appendix 521) or the butterfly and the wasp (Perrotti's Appendix to Phaedrus 31 = Perry p. 414f.). But the best-known instance is surely that of the grasshopper (or rather the cicada) and the ant (Babrius 140 = Perry's Appendix 373) closely similar to the first-mentioned example since in both the ant's habit of storing up grain for the winter is his source of pride. Very much the same point is made in the fable of the ant and the dung-beetle (Perry's Appendix 112). The reason for the fame of the version involving the cicada is presumably that that insect, with its summer associations (see below p. 115f.), is the very type of the thoughtless hedonist (see below p. 130).[16] In some fables the disputing insects receive judgment from a

---

[14] See Meuli, *W.F. Otto Festchrift* p.72 = *Ges. Schr.*2.738.; cf. Karadagli, *Fabel und Ainos* p.18. The theme of the victory of small over great can itself take an unexpected reversal at the end. A wasp repeatedly stings the head of a snake who kills himself and his tormentor by placing his head under a waggon's wheel (Perry's Appendix 216). A mosquito vanquishes a lion in combat by biting him on the hairless part of his snout but in the midst of his rejoicing becomes entangled in a spider's web and dies lamenting that he should perish at the hands of so insignificant a creature (Perry's Appendix 255; cf. Karadagli, *Fabel und Ainos* p.48f.).

[15] This type of fable also has Oriental analogies and precedents: see Perry p.xxvii n.1. See further on the motif of debate or strife Karadagli, *Fabel und Ainos* pp. 102ff. and p.104 n.1.

[16] The cicada features as the producer of mere song and nothing of utility in one or two fables (Perry's Appendix 397 and 299: on the latter see below p. 130 and cf. E.K. Borthwick, *CQ* 16 (1966) 111). The ant is looked at from a different viewpoint in another fable (Perry's Appendix 166) which explains that he was originally a farmer dissatisfied with the fruits of his own toil who stole the fruits of his neighbours. Zeus punished him by changing his form to that of an ant; not, however, his disposition, since he still goes around collecting the wheat and barley of others for his own use. For this sort of aetiological fable see Karadagli, *Fabel und Ainos* pp. 150ff. esp. p.152.

The insect in Aesop's fables and Greek poetry

1. Aesop converses with a fox on an Attic red-figure cup of the fifth century B.C. (Rome, Vatican Mus. Greg. 16552: ARV^2 916. 183); this artefact is important for the dating of various traditions about Aesop (cf. *La Fable (Entretiens Hardt* 30 (1984)) p.129); no ticks, however (cf. p.6), are visible on the fox.

supposedly impartial third party: thus in Phaedrus 3.13 (p. 278f. Perry) a wasp decides between bees and drones when the latter are mendaciously claiming the honeycombs of the former as their own, true to type (see below p. 62).

A more subtle and allusive comparison emerges from a further fable (Perry's Appendix 299) where a farmer refuses to abstain from cutting down an unproductive tree when birds and cicadas tell him they will sit in it and sing for his entertainment; on discovering a swarm of bees and honey inside, however, he does desist and treats the tree as something sacred.[17]

We may end this brief survey of the insect's rôle in fable with one final and famous example. Aesop's defence at Samos of a demagogue on trial for his life involved him in telling the story of the fox, caught in a chasm and pestered by ticks, who turns down the hedgehog's kind offer to pick them off on the grounds that they are largely sated and no longer suck much blood, but if removed will give place to a new hungry swarm that will suck him dry (Aristotle *Rhetoric* 1393b23ff. (p.116 Kassel), Plutarch, *Old Men in Politics* (*an seni sit gerenda res publica: moralia* 790C) = Perry's Appendix 427). The fable was long remembered[18] and was adapted, for instance, by the crafty Roman emperor Tiberius to justify his infrequent changes in the governorships of Roman provinces (see Josephus *Antiquities* 18.174f.). So flexible are the uses to which a fable may be put.[19]

In the specialised world of the fable, then, insects play an important and distinguished rôle. Nowhere else in Greek literature do they loom so (relatively) large and it is not hard to see why. Greek literature displays a strong sense of the proprieties due to the respective genres, and this was especially true of the elevated world of epic and tragedy. Peter Pindar's[20] *The Lousiad*, the first of whose four cantos began: 'The Louse I sing, who from some head unknown ... ' makes the point extremely well, for it is the very incongruity of epic dignity and scope lavished upon so insignificant a creature that makes us

---

[17] But just as the ant can be looked on in fables from several viewpoints, so a different aspect of bees and honey is stressed in a fable which tells how a shepherd who tried to take some of the latter soon gave up when surrounded and stung by the former (Perry's Appendix 400), and another which describes how the bees allow a thief to steal honeycombs from a beekeeper's shop but sting the owner (much to his expressed indignation) when he looks around for his stolen property (Perry's Appendix 72). Another fable again (Perry's Appendix 163) has it that when the bees asked Zeus to ensure that their stings would prove mortal to men who tried to steal their honey, he punished their malice by decreeing that they themselves should die after using their sting. For this sort of aetiological fable see Karadagli, *Fabel und Ainos* pp. 150ff. esp. p.156.

[18] On its original significance cf. Meuli, *W.F. Otto Festschrift* p.79 = *Ges. Schr.*2.745, Karadagli, *Fabel und Ainos* p.29f.

[19] On Tiberius' recasting of the fable, see further Karadagli, *Fabel und Ainos* p.31.

[20] This pseudonym concealed the identity of J. Walcot (1738-1819), and this particular poem was illustrated by the great Rowlandson. See J.R. Busvine, *Insects, Hygiene and History* (London 1976) p.77f. for a brief survey of the facts.

The insect in Aesop's fables and Greek poetry 7

smile at the parody.[21] The poems of Homer even exclude the fable as strictly conceived[22] from their scope (in contrast to the works of, say, Hesiod and Archilochus) because its popular (and perhaps populist) connotations would detract from the elevated and heroic world and style they are at pains to establish. Not that either *Iliad* or *Odyssey* is lacking in sensitive and sympathetic portrayals of the animal world. But these are confined, for the most part, to similes.

The epics of Homer contain several references to insects, but they too are confined – with one or two exceptions – to the similes. (It is instructive to compare and contrast the insect similes in Babylonian epic – on which see *Atra-Ḫasīs: The Babylonian Story of the Flood* ed. W.G. Lambert and A.R. Millard (Oxford 1969) p.163f.) The size of the Greek host at Troy is quite often conveyed by comparisons with the insect world: the assembled Achaeans are as numerous as flies near the farmer's milk in spring time (*Il.* 2.469ff.); the Greeks clustering around the body of Sarpedon evoke very much the same comparison (*Il.* 16.641ff.) though here one senses that the simile involves more than mere numbers, as it does at *Il.* 2.87ff. (the Greeks pouring forth to battle compared to bees swarming out of a hollow rock). The additional element of comparison is more explicit in *Il.* 12.167ff. where the Greeks defend their wall and ships against the Trojans as wasps or bees defend their home and young against attack.[23] *Il.* 16.259ff. is very similar in its description of Patroclus at the head of the Myrmidons, long starved of war, who pour out to battle like wrathful wasps teased and roused to action by irresponsible young boys (see p. 75f.). Somewhat less predictable similes employ the fly as a paradigm of persistent

---

[21] For the notion of an ancient hierarchy of animals with insects decidedly at the bottom, see below p. 20. We might further compare Gibbon's refusal (*Decline and Fall of the Roman Empire* 2, p. 422 and n.60 (ed. Bury)) to mention by name Julian the Apostate's lice (see p. 169).

[22] See K. Meuli, *Odyssee und Argonautika* (1921) p. 9f. = *Ges. Schr.* 2.599f. with the modification expressed in *W.F. Otto Festschrift* p.73f. = *Ges. Schr.* 2.739f.

[23] Literally 'against "hunters" ' (*thērētēres*). D.J.N. Lee, *The Similes of the Iliad and the Odyssey Compared* (1964) p.19 protests at 'the absurdity of the honey-seekers being referred to as "wild beast hunters" ', but it is hard to see why Homer should have had absolutely no sense of humour, and popular speech frequently (and humorously) applied the Greek for 'wild animal' (*thērion*) to the smallest creatures, including insects: see for instance, Headlam on Herodas 7.42, H. Petersmann ap. *Serta Indogermanica* (G. Neumann Festschrift (1982)) p. 261 n. 7.

endeavour (*Il.* 17.570ff: see below p. 155f.). Another simile has Athena ward Pandarus' arrow from Menelaus as a mother shoos a fly from her sleeping child (*Il.* 4.130ff.). Or again, in *Odyssey* 22.299 the poet compares the suitors who scatter in fear when Athena brandishes her aegis in support of the returned Odysseus to cattle set in frantic motion by the onset of the gadfly. In perhaps the most interesting of this class of similes (*Il.* 3.151ff.), the Trojan elders are compared to cicadas because like those insects they are to be heard chirrupping in soft, dry voices.[24]

We have claimed that the unelevated associations of insects would be at odds with the heroic atmosphere of these poems. The seeming exceptions prove this rule. Insects enter Homer's narrative very rarely,[25] as when Achilles expresses his fear that flies will invade the open wounds of Patroclus' corpse and there breed maggots (*Il.* 19.24ff.; cf. 24.414f.) and Odysseus returns home in disguise to find his hound Argus lying full of vermin on a dung-heap in front of the Palace (*Od.* 17.300). The same motive seems to govern the appearance of these details in both these particular places. The neglect of Odysseus' hound during his master's absence is a poignant symbol of the more general misuse of Odysseus' possessions by the suitors,[26] and the horrific detail of maggots in the wounds of the once great hero brings home the difference between life and death which is one of the

---

[24] The point of comparison has baffled some scholars (see, for instance, R. Böhme, *Jhb. d. deutsch. Arch. Inst.* 69 (1954) 51f. whose own explanation (see below p. 122 n. 89) seems far astray). A scholion ad loc. (1.385 Erbse) suggests an allusion to the legend of Tithonus: against this see below p. 126. The likeliest explanation seems that given above, following the terms of Leaf and Willcock in their commentaries on the passage (clearer than Kirk ad loc.). The word used of the cicada's voice by Homer (*leirioeis*) is rare and uncertain of meaning (see West's note on Hesiod's *Theogony* 41). Perhaps 'delicate, fine, thin' would be the best rendering. It also occurs in the Hesiodic line just referred to, where it is used of the Muses' voices. (For another epithet applied to both Muses and cicadas see below p. 117). A synonymous word is used of the cicada's sound in a second-century A.D. verse inscription (2027.10 Peek). The latest investigation of Homer's *leirioeis* (R.B. Egan, *Glotta* 63 (1985) 14ff.) associates it with flowering and honeydew (cf. p. 123) and renders it 'liquid, fluid, flowing'.

[25] On the use of the word 'dog-fly' as a term of abuse in two speeches from *Iliad* 21 see below p. 155f. It is sometimes assumed (e.g. M. Dickie, *HSCP* 82 (1978) 27; cf. *LSJ* s.v. and Leaf ad loc.) that *boubrōstis* in *Il.* 24.532 means 'gad-fly'; but this notion rests on an unlikely emendation in a scholion ad loc.: see Hopkinson on Callim. *Hymn to Demeter* 102 (p. 161f. and p. 162 n.1).

[26] Compare too *Od.* 21.395 where Odysseus fears that woodworm may have devoured his bow in his absence.

The insect in Aesop's fables and Greek poetry

2. Dog stung by a wasp (in the presence of a fly) on a carnelian scarab of the fifth century B.C. (Paris, Cabinet des Médailles): see G. Richter, *The Engraved Gems of the Greeks and the Etruscans* (1968) p.118, who rightly observes that 'there is no need to interpret the dog as ... Odysseus'.

great themes of the *Iliad*.[27]

Mention of vermin reminds us of one respect in which the absence of insects from the narrative of the *Iliad* is more significant than one might at first assume. 'I never saw a louse in the British Army before the First War; yet in the crowded dug-outs in France, before effective lousing became possible, I saw men of my Scottish division whose tartans could hardly be identified from the top part of their kilts, so encrusted was this with louse eggs.' So wrote a distinguished medical expert[28] of his

---

[27] See, for instance, Jasper Griffin, *Homer on Life and Death* (1980) passim. Dead hero and maggot produce a similar effect in the Epic of Gilgamesh (Penguin trans. p. 93).

[28] Sir William MacArthur (*CQ* 4(1954) 171) in refutation of D.L. Page's theories concerning the Athenian plague during the Peloponnesian War: see below p. 169.

experience in the First World War. In Aeschylus' *Agamemnon* the herald returning from the Trojan War has a similar tale to report as to how the drizzle and dews before Troy made the soldiers' garments[29] verminous (Aesch. *Ag.* 560-2). The tragedies of Aeschylus are rarely less elevated or heroic than the epics of Homer which were their frequent source (Aeschylus reportedly called his dramas dried slices of fish left over from the banquets of Homer (*Tr.G.F.* 3 T112A Radt)); but here, by means of a dignified though not altogether serious periphrasis,[30] one of the less sublime frets of campaigning is indicated: 'The worst of war is not its occasional dangers but its perpetual discomforts.'[31] Serious poetry could treat of the theme, then, but Homer preferred not to mention it, just as he omits many other features (e.g. the presence of seriously but not mortally wounded and mutilated warriors) that a strictly realistic treatment of the details of war would entail.

Most other references to insects in Greek tragedy again occur in similes. In his lost play *Phineus* (*Tr.G.F.* 4 F716 Radt) Sophocles mentioned *mastakes* (locusts: see below p. 146f.). Phineus, King in Thrace, was, according to legend, plagued by Harpies, foul half-human monsters equipped with wings, who polluted his food with their filth, rendering it inedible. It has therefore been suggested[32] that Sophocles compared these creatures to locusts, which similarly ruin the food of man. Aeschylus' reference to a locust (*okornos*: see below p. 147) in his

---

[29] Depending on the punctuation of this passage, the words may mean 'dews drizzled down upon us, to the constant ruin of our clothing, filling our hair with creatures' (so Lloyd-Jones in his translation of this play, and many other scholars: the hair is then literal and real) or 'making the hair (i.e. *wool*) of our garments full of creatures' (so, for instance, Fraenkel in his commentary ad loc. (Oxford 1950: vol. 2 p.283)). The former interpretation has recently been advocated by H. Petersmann ap. *Serta Indogermanica* (G. Neumann Festschrift (1982)) p. 261f. Our passage is linked with the popular belief (see below p. 21f.) that creatures can be spontaneously generated from moisture by H. Mac L. Currie, *Hermes* 96 (1968) 241f. and (independently) by Petersmann, pp. 259ff. (a link arbitrarily denied by A.J. Beattie, *CQ* 6 (1956) 28).

[30] See Fraenkel's commentary again: literally the phrase means 'making (our garments) full of beasts', the adjective *entheros* deriving from the nouns *thêr* or *thêrion* which are usually employed of large wild animals (see our remarks above p. 7 n. 23) and whose appearance here A.J. Beattie, *CQ* 6 (1956) 28 humourlessly found 'grotesque'.

[31] D.L. Page in the Introduction to his (and Denniston's) commentary on the play (Oxford 1957) p.xxxiii.

[32] By J.A. Hartung, *Sophokles Fragmente* (Leipzig 1851) ad loc.; Sittig, *RE* s.v. *Harpyien* (7² (1912)) 2427. 35ff.

The insect in Aesop's fables and Greek poetry

lost *Philoctetes* (*Tr.G.F.* 3 F256 Radt)) may also have been part of a simile, since we know that the play referred to a disease eating away the ulcerated foot of the hero. Also, a praying mantis seems to have been mentioned in Aeschylus' lost *Lycurgus* (play or trilogy): see Radt, *Tr.G.F.* 3 p. 234f.

A late mythographer (Apollodorus *epitome* 1.14f.) preserves a story wherein King Minos of Crete is trying to track down the famous inventor and craftsman Daedalus, builder of the labyrinth, who has escaped from his service. Minos ingeniously offers a prize to whoever succeeds in passing a thread through a particularly intricate shell. Daedalus betrays his presence by achieving the feat: he fastens the thread to an ant and bores a hole in the spiral shell so that the ant may pass through. The story seems to have been dealt with in Sophocles' tragedy *The Men of Camicus* (a reference to Daedalus' place of refuge). This play too is now lost but a fragment from it (*Tr.G.F.* 4 F324 Radt) clearly presupposes the stratagem of the ant: cf. Pearson, *Fragments of Sophocles* 2.3ff. Finally, a character in a lost play of Aeschylus remarked, 'I fear the stupid death of the moth that flies into the candle flame' (see below p. 190).

We turn now to consider insects in less elevated literary genres. A notorious fragment of the Ephesian poet Hipponax (flourished *c.* 540 B.C.) who was famous in antiquity for his scabrous verse, sordid realism and invective, describes in the first person the effects of an attempt to cure impotence (fr. 92 W): the victim (or rather beneficiary) has a leather penis inserted up his anus; this causes him to defecate; the smell attracts some dung-beetles who come 'more than fifty in number, whirring their wings' and fall on the feast.[33]

We cannot fail to be reminded of the most famous scene composed for a dung-beetle in Greek (or indeed any other nation's) drama: the opening of Aristophanes' comedy *Peace* (produced in 422/1 B.C.). Here the hero Trygaeus, despairing that the Peloponnesian War can ever be brought to a halt by normal means, flies up to Zeus' palace on the back of an enormous beetle. As K.J. Dover has observed[34] 'the choice of a

[33] For the details see M.L. West ad loc. (*Studies in Greek Elegy and Iambus* (1974) p.144f.).

[34] *Aristophanic Comedy* (London 1972) p.132 n.1. But it is hard to see why he should suppose (p.132) that Trygaeus has 'fattened up a dung-beetle to gigantic size'. The slave says at ll. 72ff. that his master brought home a huge dung-beetle that came from Mt. Etna, and we know that Etnean dung-beetles were said by comic poets to be particularly large: see below p. 87.

beetle rather than a bird is determined by (i) the comic extravagance of the idea, (ii) the opportunity so provided for jokes about excrement and (iii) the story of Zeus, the eagle and the dung-beetle which we mentioned above (p. 3).[35] The parody of Bellerophon's attempted flight up to Olympus on the back of the winged steed Pegasus[36] which underlies the whole passage is also funnier if the animal ridden is so absurdly undignified. It is pleasant that while Aristophanes is often indifferent to the fate of major (or seemingly major) characters in his plays, allowing them to disappear abruptly and without trace half-way through (Euelpides in the *Birds* is the most extreme instance), he is careful to tell us of the beetle's happy fate: like Pegasus he will carry the thunderbolts of Zeus (1.722) and, thanks to Ganymede, a steady supply of food (1.723f.) is assured.

Aristophanes in particular and Attic Comedy in general contain a much larger number of references to insects than the more elevated genres of Epic or Tragedy, and for obvious reasons. Old Comedy may well be often concerned with the transcendence of the rules and inhibitions that govern normal existence,[37] but it also embraced[38] with great gusto and occasional exaggeration the joys and anguish of everyday existence. We therefore encounter quite a few mentions of insects as a feature of everyday life, and the seamier sort of insect (bed-bugs, lice and so on) is particularly to the fore,[39] largely for

[35] Another fable tells how a presumptuous beetle emerges from his dung-heap and, seized with envy at the sight of an eagle soaring on high, tries to emulate it; but it soon becomes exhausted by the struggle with the strong breezes and falling to earth far from home longs in hunger for the old dung-heap (Perry's Appendix 650). We do not know at what time this fable came into being and whether Aristophanes can have been acquainted with it.

[36] And, more specifically, of Euripides' treatment of that tale in his largely lost tragedy *Bellerophon* (see below p. 164): on Aristophanes' parody of this play in the *Peace* see P. Rau, *Paratragodia* (*Zetemata* 45 (1967)) pp. 89ff.

[37] See, for instance, Dover, *Aristophanic Comedy* pp. 30ff.

[38] Cf. V. Ehrenberg, *The People of Aristophanes*² (1951) p.39: 'The conditions of Athenian life are described in comedy in two ways, now with intentional distortion *in deteriorem*, then again, ... simply as the reflection of reality.' On the difficulty of deciding which process is at work in a given passage see R.J. Hopper, *JHS* 73 (1953) 154.

[39] For a study of allusions to vermin in ancient Greek authors (largely humorous references, mainly from Attic Comedy) see S. Lilja, *Arctos* 10 (1976) 59ff. It is notable that of all the relevant plays Aristophanes' *Clouds* contains the largest number of references. This is presumably because of the close connection in the popular mind at that time between philosophers (the main target of that play's satire) and vermin and filth (see below p. 174).

The insect in Aesop's fables and Greek poetry

comic effect. We must not forget[40] the probable element of humorous exaggeration when trying to draw conclusions on such issues as the cleanliness or lousiness of the fifth-century Athenians.[41] A slightly different sort of consideration governed the inspiration behind Aristophanes' comedy the *Wasps* (see below p. 76).

Hellenistic literature[42] represents a deliberate reaction away from the spirit and values of what went before. In contrast to the sublime and heroic we find the homely and the intimate, in place of the elevated and sober we encounter the consciously mundane and the faux-naïf. Nowhere is this better exemplified than in what remains the best known and most popular Hellenistic genre, bucolic poetry and in particular the *Idylls* of Theocritus (*c*. 300-250 B.C.). This class of poetry embraces the life and loves of country-folk, their surroundings and the animals of the countryside. The latter, of course, include insects, but it is, in fact, surprising just how narrow a range are mentioned: apart from bees, cicadas and grasshoppers remarkably few. The reason for the frequency with which the three aforenamed insects feature is plain: the sweet singing of the cicadas and chirrupping of grasshoppers is a suitable point of comparison with the shepherds' songs and other musical contests that occupy so large a part of Theocritus' very partial and stylised[43] picture of country life, and bees were often represented as symbols of poetry, nurturers of poets and the like (see below p. 70f.).

The place of insects in the playful world of Hellenistic literature emerges perhaps more clearly from the epigrams collected within the so-called *Greek Anthology*.[44] It was a common device in this genre to compose epitaphs to commemorate the dead, and memorials for a dead pet jackdaw

---

[40] As so many scholars do (e.g. G. Morge ap. *History of Entomology* (ed. R.F. Smith *et al.*, *Annual Reviews Inc.* 1973) p.55 ('According to Aristophanes ... bugs were a veritable scourge in Athens').

[41] Cf. K.J. Dover, ap. *Fifty Years (and Twelve) of Classical Scholarship* p.129 on Aristophanes as a source for the sociologist. Cf. p. 12 n. 38 above.

[42] For a brief but penetrating characterisation of Hellenistic poetry see K.J. Dover's commentary on Theocritus (1971) pp. lxviiff. Cf. Lloyd-Jones, *Stud. It. Fil. Class.* 1 (1984) 52ff.

[43] See Dover ibid. p. lvif.

[44] For a list of the insects mentioned herein see N. Douglas, *Birds and Beasts of the Greek Anthology* (1928) p. 173.

or hound soon became popular (see Gow and Page, *HE* 2.90f.).[45] When within this sub-group we come across epitaphs for cicadas, grasshoppers and the like[46] we have no right at all to be surprised. 'Trivial subjects [are dealt with] in a dignified style' as Gow and Page comment on one such specimen. Note too their remark on a moving epigram by Antiphanes (*AP* 9.256 = *GP* 741ff.): 'Much care has been devoted to the narration of this trivial matter' (2.112). The spirit of Hellenistic poetry (or rather one important aspect of that spirit) is well seen in the mock-solemnity of these little poems, which, for all the care that has been put into them, are not above confusing (for literary effect) cicada and grasshopper, for instance (see p. 134 below).

Apollonius of Rhodes (born *c*. 295 B.C.) describes in his epic on the voyage of the Argonauts the descent to earth of Eros (3.275ff.); the god of love's mischievous state of mind is compared to a gadfly[47] that sets out to annoy grazing cattle, the fly that shepherds call the breese (see below p. 159f.). The same insect features in another of this epic's similes when the effect on Heracles of the news that his beloved Hylas has been lost is compared to the effect of a gadfly's sting on a bull (1.1265ff.). In both cases the popular comparison of the pangs of love to the bite of the gadfly (see below p. 164) underlies the comparison, and both are intensely unHomeric. A more conventionally epic simile is that at 4.1452ff. where the Argonauts milling around a spring of water that has miraculously opened up amid the parching desert are compared with ants round a hole or flies attracted by honey.[48] Finally, the women of Lemnos who come streaming out

---

[45] For a more detailed study of this literary genre (the mock epitaph for a dead pet, Catullus' lament for Lesbia's sparrow being perhaps the most famous) see the book by G. Herrlinger, *Totenklage um Tiere in der antiken Dichtung* (*mit einem anhang Byzantinischer, Mittellateinischer und Neuhochdeutscher Tierepikedien*) (Stuttgart 1930). He deals with insects on pp. 15f., 18f., 22ff., 27f., 34f. in particular.

[46] See, for instance, Anyte *AP* 7.190 = *HE* 742ff., Archias *AP* 7.213 = *GP* 3716ff., Argentarius *AP* 7.364 = *GP* 1407ff., Aristodicus *AP* 7.189 = *HE* 772ff. Mnasalces *AP* 7.192 and 194 = *HE* 2647ff. and 2651ff., Phaedimus *AP* 7.197 = *HE* 2931ff.

[47] The conception of Eros as a gadfly was not totally new in Apollonius' time: cf. Simonides 541.10 P where there is a reference to the mighty *oistros* of Aphrodite (see p. 164). Apollonius' description does not entail that 'Eros flew down to earth with the high-pitched note of a gadfly' (Dover's commentary on Theocritus p. lxix). See Vian's remarks ad loc. (2.120) and Lloyd-Jones, *Stud. It. Fil. Class*. 1 (1984) 69.

[48] For flies fatally attracted by honey see fable no. 80 in Perry's Appendix.

of their homes to surround the Argonauts when they are departing are compared to bees swarming forth from a rock to visit the flowers (1.879ff.). This recalls the simile at *Il.* 2.87ff. (see above p. 7). Likewise when Apollonius' elder contemporary Callimachus (fr.191.26ff. Pfeiffer) compares the Delphians who hang around the altar and carry off slices of sacrificed meat to flies swarming about a goatherd we are reminded of *Il.*2.469ff. (see p. 7).

There is another aspect of Hellenistic poetry that is highly relevant to our enquiry: the didactic genre. This versification of technical treatises, the poeticisation of seemingly intractable subject-matter, became an end in itself, a means of displaying the poet's virtuosity and learning. The drier the topic, the more resistant to poetical treatment it seemed, the more eagerly was it embraced. Vergil's *Georgics* are the most famous outcome of this attitude to literature, and one of the sources he drew upon, Nicander of Colophon (who probably lived in the late second century B.C.), was the author of two didactic works which still survive, the *Theriaca* and the *Alexipharmaca*.[49] The first of these deals with poisonous animals, the second with the antidotes to these creatures, and poisonous (or allegedly poisonous) spiders, scorpions and insects proper inevitably feature, though the latter are largely confined to the classes of bee, wasp and beetle.[50] The scientific value of these compositions is as small as is usually the case with works of didactic literature (where style and presentation rank above strict scientific accuracy), and what little they possess of genuine utility derives not from Nicander himself but his sources, in particular Apollodorus, who lived at the beginning of the third century B.C. and wrote a treatise on wild animals. 'In the polished poet himself we meet a characteristic type ... the man of letters transmuting the graceless raw material of science into accomplished verse or

---

[49] The best up-to-date account of these two rebarbative works is the commentary on them by A.S.F. Gow and A.F. Scholfield (*Nicander: The Poems and Poetical Fragments* (Cambridge 1953)) which deals well with such subsidiary problems as sources. A series of interesting articles by J. Scarborough, in *Pharmacy in History* 19 (1977) onwards, deals with various aspects of Nicander's toxicology: II.1 (21 (1979) 3ff.) specifically treats of spiders, scorpions, insects and myriapods. J.-M. Jacques' awaited study *Nicandre de Colophon: Contribution à l'étude des rapports entre la poésie et la science à l'époque hellénistique* will be fundamental.

[50] See Gow-Scholfield p.23.

16   Introduction

prose. So treated science quickly ceases to be an inquiry'.[51] It is, indeed, high time that we turned from this survey of non-technical literary illusions to insects[52] to that brief period in Greek history when science could claim to be an *inquiry* (*historia*, the very source of the English word 'history'). Writing specifically of the poets of the *Greek Anthology*, Norman Douglas said (*Birds and Beasts of the Greek Anthology* (1928) p.3): 'Not one of them can be called a poet-naturalist in the sense of some half-dozen English ones. Aristotle is modern, compared to the latest of them; indeed, he belongs to another world of thought.' Let us now try to consider just how accurate such a statement is.

Aristotle and the scientific study of insects

A recent monograph on Aristotle by a philosopher[53] concludes with a rather unexpected verdict: 'His greatest single achievement was surely his biology. By the work recorded in the *Researches*, the *Parts of Animals*, and the *Generation of Animals*,[54] he founded the science of biology, set it on a sure empirical and philosophical basis, and gave it the shape it would retain until the nineteenth century'. This is certainly a very striking tribute. Aristotle's works on natural history together comprise more than a fifth of his extant output (though of his total original *corpus* only a fifth in turn has come down to us intact). Nevertheless, it is surprising to find the philosopher placing even Aristotle's studies in logic second to his biology.

Surprising, but not uncharacteristic of the attitude of most scholars (be they professional biologists or classicists) towards Aristotle the zoologist ever since the academic rediscovery of this aspect of the man. The highly eulogistic tone of the vast majority of references has recently been analysed by Simon Byl (in his

---

[51] R. Parker, *Phronesis* 29 (1984) 186.
[52] This seems as good a place as any to remind the reader of the rôle played by insects in various Greek proverbs which may be thought to fall outside the scope of literature proper. On the frequent references to animals in such proverbs see C.S. Köhler, *Das Tierleben im Sprichwort der Griechen und Römer* (Leipzig 1881; reprinted Hildesheim 1967); cf. O. Crusius, *Märchenreminiszenen im antiken Sprichwort* (Versamml. Deutsch Philol. und Schulmänner (1889)).
[53] Jonathan Barnes, in the Past Masters series (Oxford 1982) p.87.
[54] On these titles see further below p. 26f.

Aristotle and the scientific study of insects

very important book *Recherches sur les grands traités biologiques d'Aristote: sources écrites et préjugés* (Brussels 1980) pp. viiff.), who shows the unrealistic extremes that this eulogy has sometimes reached and, in particular, the way in which it has denied or ignored the vast gap that separates modern biology from Aristotle's concept of the subject.[55] Instead of the pioneering scientific researcher and indefatigable observer of phenomena, whose activities cast so flattering a light of reflected glory upon his scientific heirs and upon the classicists who study him, Byl presents us with a largely convincing picture of Aristotle as a vastly talented encyclopaedist (cf. his p.xv). This unsentimentalised, unidealised Aristotle relies more than is usually allowed on earlier written sources even though he does not always name them explicitly (see pp. 3ff. of Byl's study). He is also influenced more than has hitherto been acknowledged by contemporary beliefs and prejudices: such *a priori* preconceptions as the superiority of male over female (cf. Byl pp. 304ff.), the importance of polarity (Byl pp. 210ff.), the hebdomadal rule whereby everything proceeds by sevens (Byl pp. 252ff.), the belief in spontaneous generation (see below p. 21f.), have clearly left their trace on his zoology. It is interesting to find an independent version of this picture in a recent work by two professional biologists: P.B. and J.S. Medawar, *Aristotle to Zoos: a philosophical dictionary of biology* (London 1984) pp. 26ff. Their view of 'the biological works of Aristotle' as 'a strange and generally speaking rather tiresome farrago of hearsay, imperfect observation, wishful thinking, and credulity amounting to downright gullibility' (p.28) is cruder than Byl's

[55] For a useful bibliography of studies of Aristotle as biologist see *Die Naturphilosophie des Aristoteles (Wege der Forschung* 225 (1975) ed. G.A. Seeck) pp. 413ff. and 416, to be supplemented by the lists in *Articles on Aristotle, 1. Science* ((Duckworth 1975) ed. J. Barnes, M. Schofield & R. Sorabji) p. 203f. and Peck's Loeb *Historia Animalium* 1 pp.xlff. Add to these such important recent contributions as G.E.R. Lloyd, *Magic, Reason and Experience* (Cambridge 1979) pp. 211ff. (on Aristotle and the development of empirical research); P. Pellegrin, *La Classification des animaux chez Aristote* (Paris 1982: cf. the review by J. Barnes, *CR* 33 (1983) 334f.); G.E.R. Lloyd, *Science, Folklore and Ideology* (Cambridge 1983) esp. pp. 14ff. on Aristotle's zoological taxonomy (for a review of the book see R. Parker, *Phronesis* 29 (1984) 174ff.). We should, perhaps, recall that 'the very notion of biology as the study of life and the living is comparatively modern. The ancients spoke not of biology but only of the study of animals and the study of plants' (D.M. Balme, *Journal of the Soc. for the Bibliography of Natural History* 5 (1970) 272). For a brief history of the word 'biology' in Modern Europe see C. Singer ap. *The Legacy of Greece* (Oxford 1921) p. 163 n.1.

painstakingly reconstructed picture, because more compressed, but it only slightly over-simplifies.[56] Nevertheless, in treating of an author for whom the golden mean was so important both philosophically and zoologically (for its intrusion into his biological thinking, see Byl pp. 238ff.) we should be particularly careful to ensure that the pendulum of reaction does not swing too far the other way.

What criteria should we use when judging Aristotle's achievement? If some scholars have underestimated the differences between Aristotelian and modern zoology, should we not, perhaps, avoid that juxtaposition altogether and turn to societies truly comparable in time, place, or conditions?[57] Perhaps that scientist has more perception who writes: 'To understand the origin and the development of entomology in antiquity, modern man must forget all he knows today of the anatomy, biology, ecology, or classification of insects, must ignore all the present equipment for their study, e.g. the optical applicances, and must think in terms of the conception of nature and the supernatural of that time'.[58] Aristotle is literally the first entomologist,[59] in as much as he is the first author to use the word *entomon*, which he defines (*HA* 487a33ff., 523b12ff.; cf. 531b20ff.) as referring to 'those creatures that have *entomai* (segments, sections, incisions) on their body': as Peck renders it in his Loeb translation of the relevant *loci*, '*insects* are creatures with *insections*'. But this generation of entomology out of etymology had unfortunate effects upon the very opening stages

---

[56] The frankness of the Medawars' estimate of Aristotle caused some flurry and consternation in the review and letter pages of the *TLS* in early 1984. Aristotle was not, of course, the only scientist ever to be affected by contemporary preconceptions and superstitions. The case of Newton rises at once to mind (for a brief account of how a form of the hebdomadal rule influences *his* colour theories see E. Ardener ap. *Social Anthropology and Language* (*ASA Monograph* 10 (1971)) pp. xx and lxxiv). And it is unfair, as past scholars have done (cf. Byl p. xvi) and as the Medawars still do (p.27), to blame Aristotle for the medieval scholasticism (on which see e.g. W.A. Wallace ap. *Science in the Middle Ages* (ed. D.C. Linberg (1978)) pp. 93ff.) whereby his ideas were elevated into a 'doctrinal tyranny' (to quote the Medawars) he can never have intended or even dreamed of.

[57] In this context the remarks of I. Harpaz ap. *History of Entomology* (ed. R.F. Smith *et al.*) pp. 21ff. on Middle Eastern entomology are highly instructive.

[58] Morge ap. *History of Entomology* p.37.

[59] For Aristotle treated specifically as entomologist see L. Bodson, *The Classical Outlook* Oct./Nov. (1983)3 with bibliography 5f.

Aristotle and the scientific study of insects 19

of Aristotle's attempts at classification, and produced what Byl (p. 325; cf. his remarks in *L'Antiquité classique* 45 (1976) 617) calls 'un obstacle épistémologique' that prevented a satisfactory resolution of the issue. For Aristotle's definition of insect notoriously includes a large range of creatures whose right to be so called modern science would stoutly resist (they include worms, spiders, scorpions and myriapods: for a full list, with references to the relevant Aristotelian passages, see Byl p. 325f.); also it can include a creature like the *ephêmeron* (see below p. 157) with allegedly fewer than six feet. And one can easily (like Byl) compare this classification unfavourably with the Linnaean classification that finally replaced it.[60] Linnaeus' selection of both segmentation into three regions (head, thorax, abdomen) and possession of three pairs of legs as his means of defining insects allowed easy separation of the class Insecta from the rest of the classes of the phylum Arthropoda (e.g. spiders, which have two segments – head (cephalothorax) and abdomen – and four pairs of legs). But it must be allowed that elsewhere (*HA* 531b26ff., a passage nowhere mentioned by Byl) Aristotle does state that a division into three parts (head, equivalent of chest and back, trunk with stomach) is common to all insects. And at *PA* 683b2f. he does at least recognise that all leaping insects have six feet (contrast ib. 682a37ff.: insects have many feet). For other criteria used by Aristotle to categorise insects see L. Bodson, *Classical Outlook* Oct./Nov. (1983) 3. For a modern definition that neatly excludes arthropods etc. see Howard Ensign Evans, *Life on a little-known Planet*² (1984) pp. 26ff.

J.B. Meyer, *Aristoteles Thierkunde: ein Beitrag zur Geschichte der Zoologie, Physiologie und alten Philosophie* (Berlin 1855) p.144, using as point of comparison the species identified in Bronn's *Allgemeine Zoologie* (1850) observed that Aristotle identified only 81 out of Bronn's 74,030 insects (compared with 160 out of 7,000 birds, 117 out of 8,000 fishes). The number of insects now available for comparison is nearer a million. G.E.R.

---

[60] Linnaeus' *Systema Naturae* (first edition 1735; tenth 1758). For a recent summary of Linnaeus' achievement see the various contributions to *Yearbook of the Swedish Linnaeus Soc. Commem. Vol.* (1978) especially S. Lindroth (p.10) for Aristotle's influence on Linnaeus, and P. Smit (pp. 118ff.) on the zoological dissertations of Linnaeus (pp. 124ff. deal with his entomology; cf. p. 125: 'More than anyone else L. contributed to the development of entomology', including the terms larva, pupa etc. (see p. 22 below)).

20 *Introduction*

Lloyd has claimed that 'value-judgments' (i.e. a general feeling that insects, being so much further down, in fact at the bottom of, a perceived hierarchy, in contrast to the heights represented by men and other warm-blooded animals, and constituting relatively less perfected creatures) will have played a part in this proportionately low level of identification, as well as the more obvious 'difficulties of observing very small creatures without optical aids'.[61] This raises an important issue of principle.

Many of Aristotle's errors in zoology, especially those pertaining to insects, have been explained away in terms of lack of instruments such as the microscope,[62] and it would be foolish to deny that such a lack may have caused some of the errors. Aristotle often explicitly complains that the smallness of insects hampers or excludes analysis of their internal structures and in particular of their modes of mating and reproduction (e.g. *HA* 625b11, *GA* 721a25 etc.). Now in *GA* 721a10ff. Aristotle makes a significant point about insect reproduction: he states that the males do not possess channels for semen and that generally speaking the male does not insert any part into the female, but the female inserts a part into the male from below (though the opposite has occasionally been observed). This general statement is specifically applied to flies. The peripheral implication that the male often mounts the female is correct, but over the major issue Aristotle is crucially astray: the male insect certainly *does* insert a part into the female, to whit the aedeagus or penis, though because the female's ovipositor (or egg-laying apparatus) is externally visible and often conspicuous and the aedeagus often concealed, the mistake is easily explained. The source of error is similarly clear at *GA* 721a21ff., where Aristotle states that in female insects the equivalent of the uterus is divided along the gut. In fact, ovaries lie on either side of the alimentary canal, and, connecting with the two ovaries, two oviducts ('the equivalent of the uterus') lie along the hind end of this canal. On dorsal or ventral view it can indeed seem as if the oviduct is divided along the gut.

On the other hand, there are several errors that are clearly not to be thus explained as due to the lack of optical instruments. As Byl points out (p.xxi), no such instruments were needed, for

[61] *Science, Folklore and Ideology* p.37.
[62] For bibliography see Byl. p.xxi n. 62.

Aristotle and the scientific study of insects 21

instance, to check the statement (*HA* 501b19f.) that men have a larger number of teeth than women. And (to cite a case more closely related to the world of insects) G.E.R. Lloyd (*PCPS* 10 (1964) p.68 n.2) has reminded us that 'when the dogma of spontaneous generation was challenged by Redi in the seventeenth century, the experiments he undertook to show that the worms found in decaying meat derive directly from the droppings of flies and not from the putrefaction of the meat itself, were not technically impossible in antiquity'. This brings us to the next item for consideration.

Spontaneous generation

The universal belief in spontaneous generation[63] continued until (and in some instances after) the decisive refutation by Louis Pasteur in 1864 of the notion that bacteria originated thus. The Italian scientists Francesco Redi (1626-1698) and Lazzaro Spallanzari (1729-1799) had already performed a like service as regards insects and maggots. It is often easy to see how the idea arose in the case of Aristotle's alleged instances, as with insects generated from decaying wood when the larvae actually live in such wood (below p. 96); or the larvae produced from snow (*HA* 552b8ff.) which has lain for a long time: this is said to turn red and generate hairy larvae of that colour; in reality the redness is caused by such algae as *Sphaerella nivalis* and the relevant insects are black.[64] Though he talks of lengthy investigations into the mating of insects, it is in this area (as conceived both

---

[63] On spontaneous generation in the writings of Aristotle and Theophrastus see the articles by W. Capelle, *Rh. Mus.* 98 (1955) 150ff. and D.M. Balme, *Phronesis* 7 (1962) 91ff. The latter (which nowhere mentions the former) provides a useful collection of direct quotations, but is more interested in tracing the development of the two philosophers' attitude to the phenomenon and in establishing a relative chronology of their references to it. See further Byl as cited above pp. 269ff. (with bibliography in p. 269 n.1). For general surveys of the issue see A. Vartanian ap. *Dictionary of the History of Ideas* (New York 1973/4) 4 s.v., J. Farley, *The Spontaneous Generation Controversy from Descartes to Oparin* (Baltimore 1977); cf. K.V. Thomas, *Man and the Natural World: changing attitudes in England 1500-1800* (1983) p. 87f. For its rôle in English literature from Elizabethan times on see P. Ansell Robin, *Animal Lore in English Literature* (London 1932) pp. 23ff.

[64] Horace Bénédict de Saussure (1740-1799), Swiss naturalist, first discovered the truth while investigating the Alps (see *Dictionary of Scientific Biography* s.v. (12.119ff.))

generally and specifically) that Aristotle perpetrates what modern research takes to be some of his most spectacular errors. In *GA* 715b2ff. and 721a2ff. he tackles this problem from slightly different angles[65] and distinguishes three classes of insect reproduction: (1) where they are sexually generated out of insects identical to themselves and in turn sexually generate identical creatures (this is the case with locusts, cicadas, spiders, wasps, ants); (2) where they are spontaneously generated from matter (e.g. rotting liquid or solid) and remain in a larval state as grubs; such insects in turn sexually generate larvae that do not develop beyond that stage (examples of this are fleas, flies and beetles);[66] (3) where they are spontaneously generated from matter and do not themselves produce offspring (e.g. gnats, mosquitoes). Implicit in all this is a thesis explicitly revealed at *GA* 758b6ff. that *all* insects originate as larvae. What modern investigation calls the actual egg of the insect was for Aristotle the pupa, any previous larval form being merely an earlier embryonic state; what we interpret as the egg deposited by the insect was for Aristotle only a motionless larva.[67]

Teleology

It is well known that Aristotle's zoology was teleological, i.e. pervaded by the notion that everything exists for a purpose: see Byl pp. 155ff. for an analysis of the faults caused by what he calls this 'finalisme anthropomorphique et intempérant'. He alleges two instances (p. 176f.) of cases where Aristotle's view of insects has been severely blurred by this particular prejudice, but again the facts are somewhat more complex than Byl allows. At *HA* 494b26ff. and *PA* 652b24ff. Aristotle claims that bloodless animals have no brain, whereas insects do indeed possess a brain; but according to Byl, since Aristotle believes them to be bloodless and to possess no heart (while really they have haemolymph and enjoy an open-heart system) any brain would be, by definition, without purpose, something his teleology will

[65] See Balme's note on the second passage in his translation of *Generation of Animals* Book 1 (Oxford 1972).

[66] Cf. Pliny *NH* 10.190. For analogies to his notion of generation from rotting matter see R. Riegler ap. Bächtold-Stäubli, *Handwörterbuch des deutschen Aberglaubens* 2.1631f.

[67] Note A. Platt, *CQ* 5 (1911) 255: 'Pupas ... are commonly called "eggs" to this day.'

Aristotle and the scientific study of insects 23

not allow. And at *de somn. et vig.* 456a11ff. and *de resp.* 471b19ff., Aristotle claims that insects do not breathe (which they do, by means of tracheae which open out into spiracles on the surface of their cuticle), a fact that Aristotle (quite apart from the difficulties caused by the lack of a microscope) would have found at odds with his teleology, since he takes the purpose of breathing to be to cool the animal heated by the action of the heart (*de resp.* 478a25ff.) and insects, apart from lacking blood and heart in the Aristotelian system (according to Byl), are also naturally cool.

Now Aristotle's view is not quite so monolithic as this implies, since as regards coolness he allows a group of exceptions in the form of longer-lived and usually hot insects, including the bee and cicada (*de resp.* 474b31ff; cf. *HA* 535b5 with Peck ad loc.: see below p. 120 n. 88). The attempt to allow for these exceptions admittedly leads him into error, as he explains that the insects in question are cooled by being divided at a point under the membrane which is therefore thinner. But at least some flexibility is evident. And further (as L. Bodson[68] points out) it may be somewhat misleading to state *tout court* that Aristotle thought insects bloodless and incapable of breathing. Aristotle certainly says they lack blood at *HA* 490b14f., *PA* 652b25f., *de resp.* 474b31ff.; but at *HA* 489a20ff. he confesses that every animal contains fluid: perhaps in the aforementioned passages he is thinking of red blood rather than, say, haemolymph. And the contexts of such passages as *HA* 487a31 and *de resp.* 475a29ff. make it clear that pulmonary (as opposed to the insect's type of) breathing is what Aristotle has in mind there (and presumably elsewhere) when denying that insects breathe. Byl's approach must be modified, therefore. Not so very drastically, though, since he might well retort that the automatic conception of breathing as pulmonary and blood as red exhibits that anthropocentricity which he elsewhere argues to be an inescapable feature of Aristotle's zoology (see p. x above and p. 61f. below).

Writing in *JHS* 75 (1955) 25, J.B.S. Haldane observed that Aristotle's 'explanations of biological facts are often faulty. His accounts of these facts fall into four classes. Some ... have been

---

[68] 'The beginnings of entomology in Ancient Greece', *Classical Outlook* Oct./Nov. (1983) 3.

confirmed and usually amplified.[69] Of some we can say, "The present-day representatives of the species which we believe that Aristotle was describing do not have the structure or behaviour which he stated. We believe that he was misinformed, or misinterpreted his observations"[70] ... Of other statements we can only say, "This has not yet been confirmed"; and it is a safe guess that some, at least, will be confirmed.[71] A fourth class, perhaps the most interesting of all, includes some statements about the physiology and behaviour of domestic animals ... If domestic animals do not behave in an Aristotelian manner to-day, there is at least a *prima facie* case that their physiology or instincts have altered.'

Much of this is reasonable enough, though little of it can be actually proved. The eventuality of Aristotle's reliance for many details upon the testimony of various experts rather than his own investigation has recently been stressed by F. Solmsen, *Hermes* 106 (1978) 467ff. and 107 (1979) 380ff. = *Kl. Schr.* 3.304ff. and 322ff.[72] Bee-keepers are explicitly cited as a source of information

---

[69] Haldane cites as an example of this class Aristotle's account of bees' 'dances'; see below p. 55f.

[70] Here Haldane gives the i ·tance of Aristotle's misinterpretation of pollen on bees as wax: see below p. 58.

[71] For some examples of statements in the *HA* originally greeted with scepticism or disbelief but later confirmed see e.g. G.E.R. Lloyd, *Aristotle: the growth and structure of his thought* (Cambridge 1968) p.80f.

[72] As Solmsen observes, this consideration may entail some modifying of the orthodoxy (see e.g. Byl pp. xxxviiif.) first propounded by D'Arcy W. Thompson (prefatory note to his Oxford translation of *HA* (1910); see too his lecture *Aristotle as a Biologist* (Oxford 1913) p. 12f. and his remarks in *The Legacy of Greece* (Oxford 1921) p. 144 ≃ *Die Naturphilosophie des Aristoteles (Wege der Forschung* 225 (1975)) p.10) 'that Aristotle's natural history studies were carried on ... in his middle age, between his two periods of residence in Athens' in view of the place names mentioned in *HA* and the areas where Aristotle is said to have lived from 347 to 335 (Troad, Lesbos, Macedon). As re-enforced by H.D.P. Lee's more detailed study of the place names (*CQ* 42 (1948) 61ff. ≃ *Die Naturphilosophie des Ar.* pp. 79ff.) this hypothesis has ousted Werner Jaeger's ambitious theory (*Aristoteles: Grundlegung einer Geschichte seiner Entwicklung* (Berlin 1923) p.352f. ≃ *Aristotle*[2] (Oxford 1948) p.329f.) of Aristotle's *philosophical* development during middle age, and set in its place the picture of 'a period ... in which the main features of his biological theories were probably first developed, and in which we should expect to find traces of the influence of these theories in his philosophy' (Lee p.65; cf. Lloyd, *Aristotle* p.68 etc.). But apart from the fact that the majority of Lee's allusions to the lagoon in Lesbos are of disputed authenticity (see p.27), we should remember (with Solmsen) that several pupils of Aristotle, not least Theophrastus, were natives of, or otherwise associated with, Lesbos.

Aristotle and the scientific study of insects 25

at *HA* 626b1ff., for instance, though given the problematic nature (to put it mildly) of many of the statements made in this context (see below p. 27) the citation is hardly reassuring. It is not open to us, however, to take refuge in the easy antinomy offered by C. Singer: 'We see Aristotle the naturalist at his greatest as a direct observer or when reasoning directly about the observations that he has made. When he disregards his own observations and begins to erect theories on the observations or the views of others, he becomes weaker and less comprehensible' (*Greek Biology and Greek Medicine* (Oxford 1922) p.54). This noble picture of the lonely scientist achieving his major discoveries in isolation from contemporary ideas must be dismissed, however popular it was once, as in fact the very reverse of the truth.[73] We must accustom ourselves to a picture of the father of zoology (and entomology) not so very different from more recent pictures of the father of history (Herodotus) in which intuitions and perceptions recognisable in modern terms jostle with preconceptions unfamiliar save under historical analysis.

Of Aristotle's treatment of the vascular system D'Arcy Thompson remarked: 'It is remarkable for its wealth of detail, for its great accuracy in many particulars, and for its extreme obscurity in others. It is so far true to nature that it is clear evidence of minute inquiry, but here and there so remote from fact as to suggest that things once seen had been half-forgotten, or that superstition was in conflict with the results of observation.'[74] The stress on superstition here is appropriate, as

[73] For instance one might ask whether Aristotle was automatically obliged to accept the views and observations of others, and of course we know that on occasions he did explicitly reject such views, including (cf.Byl p.xxiif.) the ideas of fishermen on hectocotylisation (*GA* 720b32f.), though he is still regularly accorded great glory for his supposed discovery of this process (see Byl p. xxiii n.74; cf. more recently J. Barnes, *Aristotle* (Oxford 1982) p.10f., who alludes, however, to *GA* sup. cit.). In this context we may note that the famous tradition preserved by Pliny *NH* 8.44 and others according to which Alexander the Great helped his alleged former tutor in gathering material for his work on zoology is rejected not only by Byl p.xii but also by such earlier scholars as Singer p.22f.: cf. A.-H. Chroust, *Classical Folia* 18 (1966) 26ff. ≃ *Aristotle* 1.125f.

[74] Compare the following more recent account (by R. Parker (*Phronesis* 29 (1984) 179, summarising the views of Lloyd, *Science, Folklore and Ideology*): 'Aristotle on male and female resembles Aristotle on man and the animals: binary presumptions (the series male – thick – pure – hot contrasts with female – thin – impure – cold), unobservable observations (men have more sutures on the skull than women), and unverifiable generalisations consort with accurate observations, some of them in conflict with the generalisations, and relevant arguments from empirical data.'

is the reminder that it and excessive respect for accepted beliefs can readily co-exist with painstaking observation, as in the case of Leonardo da Vinci (see e.g. K.D. Keele in the article on Leonardo in *Dictionary of Scientific Biography* 8 (New York 1973) where describing Leonardo's anatomy studies Keele says (p.204): 'L.'s mechanistic physiology did not take him far beyond Galen's views on urology ... In a number of cases L. repeated Galen's mistakes in substituting animal for human parts'; cf. M. Clagett ib. pp.227 and 230 on Leonardo's mechanics).

Researches and investigations into animals

Let us now turn aside, for a moment, to consider the individual works of Aristotle the zoologist. First and foremost, the *Historia Animalium*: the two most useful English translations are that by D'Arcy W. Thompson for the *Oxford Translation of Aristotle* (published 1910)[75] and that by A.L. Peck for the Loeb series (vol. 1 1965; vol. 2 1970). The former's merits are generously summarised by the latter (vol. 1 p.xl): 'Thompson combined the knowledge of an expert and original zoologist with the training of a classical scholar, and his work is an outstanding achievement in both respects. He offers a number of conjectures for the text, in addition to generous annotations'. The translation is indeed a work of great and characteristic elegance; but it must be said that the conjectures are the least satisfactory part and the annotations refer to works that often had an archaic charm about them even at the start of this century: they are now badly out of date. Besides, Thompson provided (consonantly with the scheme of the series) no more than a very brief (albeit influential)[76] prefatory note. These defects are largely remedied by Peck who supplies a copious and useful general introduction including a very valuable bibliography of students and studies of Aristotle's zoology.

An irritating area of complication is that concerning the authenticity of certain parts of the *HA*, both short passages and whole books. For a brief summary of views on this question see

---

[75] Recently republished (1984) as part of the *Revised Oxford Translation* (edited by J. Barnes) Princeton (Bollingen Series LXX1.2 vol. 1 pp. 774ff.) without Thompson's invaluable footnotes but with the addition of a translation of the tenth (spurious) book by Barnes.

[76] See above p.24 n. 72.

Aristotle and the scientific study of insects

Peck vol. 1 pp. liiiff. What particularly concerns us here is the doubt that has been cast on Book 9, which contains much information on wasps and bees. The criteria used in deciding the authorship of that portion in particular and other areas in general are supposed inconsistencies and incompetences. Unfortunately these criteria run the risk of circular argument,[77] since they presuppose that Aristotle was a zoologist who was never guilty of inconsistency and whose ideas would never seem incompetent to the modern mind. As Byl observes (p.xxiii with bibliography in nn. 75-6), certain scholars have used the hypothesis of alterations or interpolations in order to preserve their picture of an ideal Aristotle untainted by error. Nevertheless the possibility of interpolation is not totally excluded merely by some scholars' misuse of it. We generally try to remind the reader of the possibility in our discussions below when it is relevant. For the theory that the author (or at least source) of *HA* 9 was Aristotle's pupil Theophrastus (on whom see below p. 28f.) see e.g. U. Dierauer, *Tier und Mensch im Denken der Antike* (Amsterdam 1977) pp. 162ff. esp. p. 166 n.19. On Book 9's unAristotelian status see further Bühler's edition of Zenobius 4.181, 253, 315.

As regards the other works of Aristotle,[78] his *Generation of Animals* is excellently translated and annotated by A.L. Peck, again in the Loeb series (1953) as is his *Parts of Animals* (1955). The first book of each work has also been translated with important notes by D.M. Balme (Oxford 1972). Among other specimens of Aristotle's massive output, his little monograph *de respiratione* (*On Breathing*) in particular will be mentioned from time to time below. A work wrongly attributed to Aristotle, *On*

---

[77] Cf. Parker, *Phronesis* 29 (1984) 181: 'It is almost impossible to rescue argument here [viz. in 'problems of authenticity'] from a vicious circle, since the case against the suspected books rests in part (and rightly) on the naïvety of beliefs displayed there'.

[78] On the relative chronology of the three principal Aristotelian works of zoology (*HA, PA, GA* in that order) see Byl p. xlf. The *peri Zôiôn* (*On Animals*) of Aristophanes of Byzantium (c. 257-180 B.C.), a work preserved in excerpt by various Byzantine miscellanies, seems to epitomise a lost Aristotelian work in four books with the same (or similar) title. On this work and its influence upon Aelian and the late lexicon known as the Suda see E.L. de Stefani, *Stud. It. Fil. Class.* 12 (1904) 421ff., I. Düring, 'Notes on the History of the Transmission of Aristotle's Writings', *Acta Univ. Gotob.* 56 (1950) 55ff., P. Frazer, *Ptolemaic Alexandria* (Oxford 1972) 1.460f. There is an edition by S.P. Lambros, *Suppl. Aristotelicum* 11 (1885); cf. W. Slater, *Aristophanis Byzantii Fragmenta* (1986) p. 141f.

Marvels Heard, is an anecdotal collection of old wives' tales and the like concerning various animals including insects. Nothing could better underline the true achievement of Aristotle than a comparison of this farrago of tittle-tattle with his genuine works. And this leads us back to our main theme.

Aristotle as zoologist will continue to fascinate scientists and classical scholars, not least as regards the correct principles of scientific inquiry. The conclusion of his remarks on the reproduction of bees in *GA* 760b27ff. has often been quoted:

> This, then, appears to be the method of reproduction of bees, according to theory, together with the apparent facts. But the facts have not been satisfactorily ascertained, and if ever they are, then credence must be given to observation rather than to theory, and to theory only in so far as it agrees with what is observed.[79]

But perhaps the best way to grasp the scale of Aristotle's achievement is to compare him with his successors. 'Most of the extant Greek and Latin texts that tackle different aspects of the subject of animals after him revert to the anecdotal', as G.E.R. Lloyd has rightly observed,[80] ' – a trend especially pronounced in such writers as Pliny and Aelian. ... They often preferred to devote more attention to the strange and the marvellous than to emulate Aristotle's careful and detailed investigations of "noble" and "ignoble" creatures alike.' Let us turn to consider some of these individuals.

In fact we do not have to travel far in time or place to encounter Theophrastus, Aristotle's pupil and successor as the head of the Lyceum. In those portions of his work which most directly interest us he reveals himself as the first serious botanist and in this rôle one of his concerns was, of course, the protection of plants and crops from damage by insects. This naturally led

---

[79] This passage seems to have fired the minds of several scientists. It is quoted, for instance, in the preface to Sir William Harvey's *Exercitationes de generatione animalium* (1650/1) ≏ *Anatomical Exercitations concerning the generation of living creatures* (tr. M. Llewelyn (?) 1653). Cf. G. Keynes, *The Life of William Harvey* (Oxford 1966) pp. 332ff. and 336f.

[80] *Science, Folklore and Ideology* p. 56f. See too J. Richmond, *Chapters on Greek Fish-Lore* (*Hermes Einzelschrift* 28 (1973)) p. 47f. on 'the fate that overtook Greek zoological science after Aristotle'. In particular 'the establishment of great libraries and the taste for paradox led to compilation of second-hand accounts, and a reluctance to distinguish between the probable and the incredible'. Cf. U. Dierauer, *Tier und Mensch im Denken der Antike* (Amsterdam 1977) pp. 106 and 170.

Aristotle and the scientific study of insects 29

him to a study of the geographic distribution of insects, their patterns of migration and other related issues. It is not surprising, therefore, that M.H. Hatch should have devoted a study to 'Theophrastus of Eresus as an economic entomologist' (*Journal of the New York Entomological Society* 46 (1938) 223ff.), though this transpires to be merely a list and translation of the relevant Theophrastean passages with the gratuitous suggestion appended that Theophrastus 'may well have been the "research assistant" in some of [Aristotle's zoological] studies [see above p. 24 n. 72] and have shared the fate of many another research assistant – that of doing much of the work and receiving none of the credit' (p. 223). In fact 'Theophrastus' contribution to entomology, while rightly recognised as second in importance only to Aristotle's, still awaits extensive examination' (L. Bodson, *Classical Outlook* Oct./Nov. (1983) 4). [G. Wöhrle, *Theophrasts Methode in seinem Botanischen Schriften* (Amsterdam 1985) appeared too late for us to consult it.]

For a succinct exposition of post-Aristotelian biology, C. Singer's various studies are still well worth consulting. Thus on Pliny (A.D.23-79) his verdict is eminently just:[81] 'Though a Latin [he] owes almost everything of value in his encyclopaedia to Greek writings. In his *Natural History* we have a collection of current views on the nature, origin and uses of plants and animals such as we might expect from an intelligent, industrious and honest member of the landed class who was devoid of critical or special scientific skill. Scientifically the work is contemptible, but it demands mention in any study of the legacy of Greece, since it was, for centuries, a main conduit of the ancient teaching and observations on natural history.' Cf. H. Leitner, *Zoologische Terminologie bei Älteren Plinius* (Hildesheim 1972).

There is a very handy Loeb text and translation of Aelian's second- to third-century A.D. monograph *de natura animalium*

---

[81] This particular version comes from *The Legacy of Greece* p.185. See too his remarks in *A History of Biology to about the year 1900* (London 1959) pp. 58ff. and in *A Short History of Scientific Ideas* (Oxford 1959) p. 106f. These works also contain useful summaries of the achievement of Theophrastus and will tell the reader what he needs to know about Dioscorides (first century A.D.) and Galen (second century A.D.), two Greek medical writers mentioned from time to time in our text. For a more up-to-date evaluation of the latter see G.E.R. Lloyd ap. *The Legacy of Greece* (ed. M. Finley Oxford 1981) pp. 293ff. The same scholar's *Science, Folklore and Ideology* well traces the varying fate of the spirit of scientific enquiry after Aristotle.

(*On the Characteristics of Animals*) by A.F. Scholfield in three volumes (1958-9). His Introduction to the first volume conveys everything that most people will need to know about the author in question and his work and sources. Note in particular Scholfield's verdict (p.xiii) that 'we are of course prepared to encounter much that modern science rejects, but the general tone with its search after the picturesque, the startling, even the miraculous, would justify us in ranking Aelian with the Paradoxographers rather than with the sober exponents of Natural History. Mythology, mariners' yarns, vulgar superstitions, the ascertained facts of nature – all serve to adorn a tale and, on occasion, to point a moral ... the folly and selfishness of man are contrasted with the untaught virtues of the animal world' – including insects.

Finally we cannot conclude our survey of written sources without a brief mention of Plutarch, whose writings often preserve interesting fragments of animal lore, sometimes relating to insects. This is especially true of his work *On the Intelligence of Animals* (*de sollertia animalium*) for a brief introduction to which see D.A. Russell, *Plutarch* (1972) p.13f.[82]

Insects in Greek art

Long before any of the literary references to insects mentioned in this book, seals, gems and other artefacts of Minoan Crete were depicting bees, butterflies and other insects. For a recent survey of Bronze Age Minoan seals showing butterflies and dragonflies see J.G. Younger, *Kadmos* 22 (1983) 127f. Note too the famous gold pendant from Mallia in Crete (2000-1700 B.C.).[83] Animals were often portrayed in Greek art of the ancient world in general (for a pleasant illustrated introduction to the subject see *Das Tier in der Antike* (Zurich 1974)). Because of their relative

---

[82] There is often close similarity in details between Aelian's *NA* and this particular work of Plutarch's, and the fact has naturally led to speculation as to the relationship between the two, the dependence either of one on the other or of both on a now lost source. For a full treatment of the issue see Richmond, *Chapters on Greek Fish-Lore* pp. 5ff. and 50ff. who concludes (p.21) that Aelian drew on Plutarch's source (a zoological compendium).

[83] Our Fig. 12 on p. 61. There has been a lively controversy as to the actual identity of the two insects that make up this artefact (bees or wasps?). See E. Crane, *The Archaeology of Beekeeping* (1983) p. 229f. for a brief survey of recent attempts to identify the creatures. Cf. Willetts, *Selected Papers* 1.288ff.

 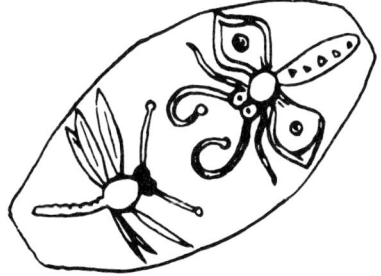

3. Butterfly and dragonfly on Aegean seals from Knossos, c. 1500 B.C.: see J.G. Younger, *Kadmos* 22 (1983) 128.

smallness and supposed insignificance (see above p. 20) insects figure less commonly than other creatures one might mention, but a study of their manifestations in art is still rewarding.

Sculpture

In view of their minuscule size one would hardly expect many plastic renderings of these creatures. But the very element of challenge involved seems to have had a stimulating effect. The great artist Phidias (born c. 490 B.C.) is reported to have fashioned a bee, a cicada and fly (for the literary references to this see J. Overbeck, *Die antiken Schriftquellen zur Geschichte der bildenden Künste bei den Griechen* (Leipzig 1868) p.140),[84] and the sculptors Callicrates and Myrmecides[85] were much admired for their small works which apparently included ants and a chariot drawn by a fly (references collected in Overbeck p. 422f.).

Turning to extant works, a number of plastic representations of cicadas are to hand in e.g. R.A. Higgins, *Catalogue of Terracottas in the British Museum* 1 (1954) nos. 694-5 (p. 184) and 707 (p.187). Most splendid is the terracotta cicada sitting on the omphalos of a fifth-century *phiale* in Boston (*ARV*² 772: our Fig. 26).

[84] 'It is possible that Phidias amused himself with such minutiae, but the passage [Julian the Apostate *epist.* 8] reads like one of those many trite ecphrastic epigrams in the *Anthologia Palatina* [see below p. 161],' says P. Jacobsthal, *Greek Pins* (Oxford 1956) p. 76.

[85] 'Toreuts of unknown date, more likely archaic (Lippold, *RE* 10.1640, 16.1105) than Hellenistic (Brunn, *Geschichte des griechischen Künstler* 2.405ff.)' according to Jacobsthal as cited in previous note.

Introduction
Vase paintings

Morin-Jean, *Le Dessin des animaux en Grèce d'après les vases peints* (Paris 1911) has a mere three references to insects in his Index, the last of which runs (p. 246) 'les insectes notamment les ont laissés quelque peu indifférent'. This is a rather misleading inference to draw when one considers the relative popularity of insects in other types of art. The fact is that insects are the wrong size and shape for very effective representation on Greek vases, as a glance at a black-figure cup from the Louvre (our Fig. 31) where the locust is all but invisible will confirm. None the less they do feature effectively from time to time: in particular bees frequently serve (especially on Cretan vases) as a decorative motif: see Jacobsthal, *Greek Pins* pp. 73ff, and various types of insect serve as shield devices on Greek vases (see, for instance,

4. Flying insect as a shield device on an Attic black-figure cup by the Amasis Painter, *c.* 560-525 B.C. (Paris, Louvre F75: *CVA* Louvre 9 pl. 81.10 = *ABV* 156.81): D. von Bothmer, *The Amasis Painter and his World* (1985) no.57 (p. 211f.). On the insect's identity see *CVA* ad loc. (p.68): 'la guêpe (ou frelon, mais ce n'est pas une abeille)'.

Insects in Greek art

5. Insect under the handle of an Attic red-figure cylix by the Nicosthenes Painter, c. 510-500 B.C. (Los Angeles County Museum of Art (William Randolph Hearst Collection) 50.8.15: *CVA Los Angeles* 1 p.41 = ARV^2 125.11); perhaps a grasshopper, as suggested by P.M. Packard and P.A. Clements in *CVA* ad loc.

C.T. Seltman, *Athens, its History and Coinage before the Persian Invasion* (Cambridge 1924) pp. 24ff.) See our frontispiece and Fig. 4. Insects also crop up from time to time under the handles of vases (see Fig. 5).

It seems worth stressing here that it is the unsurprising rule for insects to be represented far larger than life and reality require in many depictions of them from the ancient world. And this is especially true of vase-paintings (see e.g. Fig. 13).

Jewellery

In ancient Greece, as in modern times, insects figured on jewellery and adornments of various sorts. For a fine, sympathetic survey see Jacobsthal, pp.73ff. We have already mentioned one of the most famous instances, the Mallia pendant

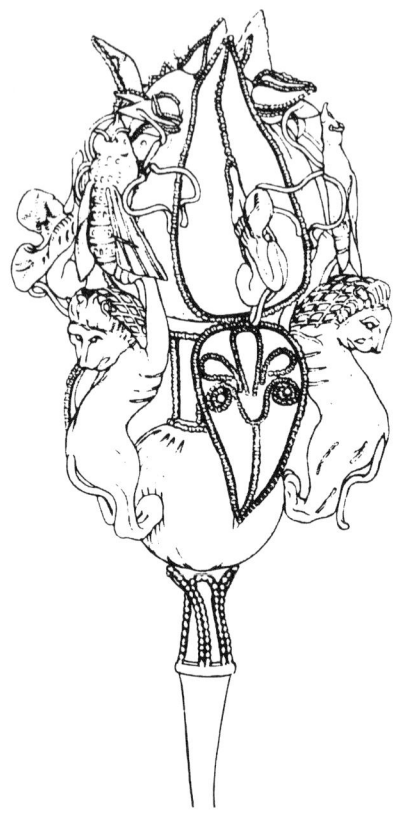

6. 'Sphinx pin' from the Peloponnese, fifth century B.C. (Boston Museum of Fine Arts 96.7.7: from Jacobsthal, *Greek Pins* (Oxford (1956) fig. 276).

(above p. 30). Two other familiar examples are constituted by a pair of fifth-century Peloponnesian gold pins now in the Boston Museum of Fine Arts (96.7.7 and 718). On these see Jacobsthal pp. 65ff. with figs 274-9 and H. Hoffmann and P.F. Davidson, *Greek Gold: jewelry from the age of Alexander* (Boston 1966) pp. 181ff. with figs 69a-70c. The first and earlier (the so-called 'Sphinx pin') shows four bees sucking from as many flowers with as many lions rampant beneath the bees and three sphinxes couchant upon three covering leaves. The second (the so-called 'Capital pin') has four lions similarly placed beneath four bees

Insects in Greek art

creeping up between as many roses. On both, the insects' 'bodies have the horizontal striations characteristic of bees and always rendered in Greek art. The veins of the bee-wings in the Sphinx pin are drawn in vertical straight lines. The veins of the bee-wings in the Capital pin are truer to nature' (Jacobsthal p.73).

Coins, gems and finger rings

It is in this area of visual depiction that insects really come into their own. The relative smallness of the artefacts involved[86] was doubtless the main inspiration behind their relatively frequent depiction. In the case of coins local and national considerations also play a part (e.g. cicadas on Athenian tetradrachms: see below p. 125). Well-illustrated introductions to the relevant fields of study may be found in G.K. Jenkins, *Ancient Greek Coins* (1972) and John Boardman, *Greek Gems and Finger Rings: early Bronze Age to Late Classical* (1970). Among all the different ranges of artefact these represent insects most sympathetically and accurately.

Illustrated manuscripts

MSS of such writers on nature as Nicander (see above p. 15) or Dioscorides (see above p. 29 n. 81) were sometimes appropriately illustrated, and these illustrations sometimes include insects. See Z. Kádár, *Survivals of Greek Zoological Illuminations in Byzantine Manuscripts* (Budapest 1978) for a study of these.

Fantasy played a large part in ancient art, let us not forget, and one aspect that concerns us involves the ingenious combination of different animals, or of man and animal, to form that imaginary mixture that the Germans call 'Mischwese'. (For a study of the general practice see G. Hafner, *Wiener Jahreshefte* 32 (1940) 25ff.) Sometimes the animal involved is an insect, and

---

[86] Which can sometimes have a misleading effect. See, for instance, the lapidary comment of J. Boardman in his review of a study of ancient gems (*JRS* 48 (1958) 201): 'a mouse; no elephant has such a tail'.

so we find, for instance, man and cicada, or man and grasshopper combined, and the resulting creature engaged in normal human activity.

Another related phenomenon, dealt with by Hedwig Kenner in his book *Das Phänomen des verkehrten Welt in der griechisch-römischen Antike* (Klagenfurt 1970) pp. 17ff., involves the parodying of normal human activities by replacing human beings with animals, including insects. Confining ourselves to instances involving the latter we may cite the notable wall-painting at Herculaneum which shows a grasshopper being drawn along in a chariot by a parrot. Indeed, many of the scenes which concern us involve chariots, constituting a sort of parody of the notion of a triumphal entry (see Kenner pp. 25ff.). A wall-painting at the city of Vesuvius shows a butterfly being similarly drawn by a griffin. And there is a large number of similar scenes to be found on various seals and rings (Kenner p. 26 suggests an apotropaic purpose[87] in the depiction of insects on these): for further instances from the first century B.C. and onwards see M.-L. Vollenweider, *Deliciae Leonis: Antike geschnittene Steine und Ringe aus einer Privatsammlung* [Leo Merz] (Mainz 1984) p. 210f.

---

[87] See A. Delatte and Ph. Derchain, *Les Intailles Magiques Gréco-Égyptiennes* (Paris 1964) pp. 162ff. (scarab beetle), p. 182 (bee) and p. 278 (bee or butterfly as soul) for this view of insects.

Glossary

1. ANT (myrmêx/formica)

Etymology: see Gil Fernández p.23f., Chantraine s.v. (3.723). The existence of a number of variant forms of the word (*bormax, burmax, hormix* are attested by Hesychius s. vv. (1.335, 354, 2.776 Latte)) suggests a number of Indo-European forms (*moru̯o-, *u̯ormo-, *mormo-) with the last supplying the most familiar Latin and Greek versions. An allegedly Doric formation (*myrmêdôn*) supplied by Hesychius s.v. (2.686 Latte) is easily

7. Ant on a ringstone, first century B.C. (Ashmolean Museum 1890. 257): Boardman-Vollenweider, *Engraved Gems and Finger Rings in the Ashmolean Museum, Oxford. I: Greek and Etruscan* (1978) no.339.

explained on analogy with *anthrêdôn* (see below p. 79), *tenthrêdôn* (below p. 82) etc. (cf. Latin *formido*), but may, as Latte suggests ad loc., be an invention to explain the name Myrmedon (see below p. 42). For the second part of the word compare *sphêx* (below p. 75), *skôlêx* (below p. 102).

Some have, some lack, wings (says Aristotle HA 523b20, PA 643b2 (→Pliny NH 11.110). Aristotle HA 606a6 (→ Pliny NH 11.110) claims the winged variety is absent from Sicily. (Aristotle's word for this winged variety is often said to be the compound *hippomyrmêx* ('horse-ant' *LSJ* s.v.), but as Gil Fernández shows (p. 55f.; so too Thompson ad loc. and others) the MSS evidence (and Hesychius s.v. *hippês* (2.370 Latte)) suggests *hippês myrmêx* ('horseman ant'): for the formation cf. *sphêx ichneumôn* ('ichneumon wasp': see below p. 80f.).

Their civilised and orderly way of life

This won the admiration and praise of numerous ancient authors. It has also, of course, been studied more recently (e.g. M.V. Brian, *Social Insects: ecology and behavioural biology* (1983), K. Dumpert, *Das Sozialleben der Ameisen* (1978) ≃ *The Social Biology of Ants* (1981)). Aristotle (*HA* 488a10) ranks them with man as a 'political' (or, as we should say, social) animal[1] (like the bee and the wasp) and adds (*HA* 622b20ff.) that they are the most industrious of all living creatures (together with the bee, the wasp and the hornet).[2] Plutarch's monograph (see above p. 30) *On the Intelligence of Animals* (*moralia* 967D-968B) has an eloquent chapter on the affection, courage, temperance and sheer hard work displayed by ants. Those that bear no burden considerably give way to those that do (a detail also recorded by Aelian *NA* 2.25), for instance, and they gnaw through or dismember objects that are difficult to carry in order to make easier loads for several. The twists and turns of the tunnels within the anthill also evoke Plutarch's admiration, as they do Aelian's (*NA* 6.43) who mentions them in the same breath as the Cretan labyrinths and explains that their very tortuousness is meant to foil enemies. The excavated soil (Aelian continues) is set as a barrier against rain around the mouth leading into the

---

[1] But note that Thompson (*CQ* 39 (1945) 55) suggested *anthrênê* (see below p. 79) for *anthrôpos* here: cf. *HA* 531b23, 622b20.

[2] Plato *Phaedo* 82b compares the social life of ants, bees and wasps.

1. Ant

tunnel, and partition walls separate cells of different purposes. He ingeniously identifies three types: the 'men's quarters', the 'women's quarters' (for pregnant ants to give birth in) and a final treasury for the seeds they have collected. Plutarch, by contrast, distinguishes common dwelling-place; storehouse for provisions; and a place for the dying.[3] We must, of course, be on our guard against the excessive anthropomorphicism to which such writers were prone (see above p. 30), but many of these details are confirmed by modern research. Thus, even Plutarch's final statement may not be a total fantasy: 'Towards corpses [social insects] are especially fastidious. Social wasps, bees, and some ants drag their dead from the nest and abandon them. Other ants may eat their dead, consign them to refuse heaps, or pile them in deserted nest chambers or galleries' (R.W. and J.R. Matthews, *Insect Behaviour* (1978) p.213). Cf. Dumpert p.206 (on an Australian species of ant): 'The waste from the colony, formed from pupal cocoons, dead nest mates and the inedible remains of prey, are collected in the least safe and at the same time least habitable side passages, 3-20 cm under the surface.' As for the rest of the description in Plutarch and Aelian, this same Australian species forms nests with passages 'leading into the ground almost vertically and widening out into a brood chamber at its base' (Dumpert p. 205), while a harvester ant of the Sahel area (in North Africa) nests in two parts, 'the upper section ... which dried out completely in the summer, served as a corn store whilst the deeper section ... was used as accommodation for the colony' (ib. p. 207f.).

Aelian has two main accounts of the ants' activities above ground (*NA* 2.25, 6.43; Pliny *NH* 11.108ff. has a basically similar description; Aristotle *HA* 622b24ff. is much briefer). The biggest lead the way like generals, while the others follow in single file or two (or sometimes three) abreast. When the crops are reached, it

---

[3] Here as elsewhere (see above p.30 n.82), Plutarch and Aelian agree on most details: the one divergency concerns the third chamber, used for dying ants according to Plutarch, for pregnant ones according to Aelian. There is an ingenious explanation of this disagreement in Richmond, *Chapters on Greek Fish-Lore* p.12f. who interprets it in the light of his regular hypothesis of a common source, here misinterpreted by Plutarch. But the explanation is self-confessedly speculative, and *pace* O. Keller, *Die Antike Tierwelt* 2.418 approved by Richmond p.14 n.5, Aelian's statement is not necessarily the more accurate. Aelian has one detail not in Plutarch (the excavated soil as barrier): perhaps they diverged elsewhere over what to reproduce from their source.

is the leaders who crawl up the stalks, bite through the stems or stalks of the ripe ears of corn and throw these ears down to the remainder stationed at the foot of the stalks, who cut off the chaff and peel off the protective capsules from the wheat. Thus laden they return home, bore through the middle of each grain and fill the pits in their store-chamber. What falls out as a result of the second of these actions is eaten by the ant; the remainder, being rendered infertile, does not put out fresh shoots if and when it comes into contact with rain. This precaution is also commented on by Plutarch *moralia* 968A and Pliny *NH* 11.109; cf. *Geoponica* 15.1.26. Saint Basil in the ninth of his *Homilies on the Hexameron* 83B (p.494 Giet) takes over this detail and adapts it to a new and Christian purpose. Pliny observes that ants carry burdens which far exceed their own bodily size, some in their mouths, larger ones with hind feet and shoulders. Most of these details are reasonable and accurate, and in keeping with the findings of modern research. On ants as eaters of seeds (an important source of protein and sugar) see J.H. Sudd, *An Introduction to the Behaviour of Ants* (London 1967) pp. 107ff. (cf. Brian pp. 26ff.) and on food-traffic among workers the same scholar's remarks pp. 114ff.

Aristotle assures us that their mode of operating is always easily visible since they continue it during nights lit by a full moon (*HA* 622b27; similarly Aelian *NA* 4.43, with an indignant outburst at mankind's contrasting addiction to festivals, Pliny *NH* 11.109 etc.). At the new moon, however, they rest according to Aelian (*NA* 1.22) and Pliny (*NH* 2.109, 18.292). Hesiod (*Works and Days* 778) mentions the ant as working at noon time on a day near full moon. This sensitivity to the stages of the moon is a counterpart to the sensitivity to coming weather mentioned below (p. 43).

Aelian (*NA* 6.43) observes how the ants' economical way of life is maintained without any Ischomachus (pompous propounder of a system of domestic economy for humans in Xenophon's *Oeconomicus*) to teach them. In his and Plutarch's accounts (quoted above) of the ants' activities the comparison with human society is at least implicit.

Aelian *NA* 16.15 has an account of the burrows of Indian ants not conspicuously different from his description (quoted above p. 39) of European ants, save we are told that they avoid floods by building high on rising ground.

Treatment of the dead

Aelian has several remarks on this (*NA* 5.49: they carry away the dead and cleanse the nests; 6.43: they bury dead relations in capsules of wheat as humans bury theirs in coffins; similarly Pliny *NH* 11.110: they are the only creatures beside man that bury their dead). The basic picture is correct (see above p.39), though the capsules of wheat seem whimsical. Incidentally there are several epitaphs for ants in the *Greek Anthology*: see Gow-Page, *Hellenistic Epigrams* 2.79.

Communication

A fragment of Cleanthes of Assos (fr. 515 Von Arnim (*Stoicorum Veterum Fragmenta* 1.116)) mentioned by both Plutarch (967E) and Aelian (*NA* 6.50) relates as a matter of personal autopsy how some ants brought a dead ant to an anthill and handed it over to the inhabitants after receiving a grub or worm as if it were a ransom for the corpse. This exchange was allegedly preceded by two or three seeming consultations or conversations between the two respective parties. Pliny too (*NH* 11.110) pictures ants busily questioning and conversing with each other. Communication during exchange of food among ants has been much studied recently: see, for instance, Dumpert pp. 105ff. Mouth-to-mouth contact is used to stimulate regurgitation of food on the part of the food carrier, for example, and note this description (quoted by Dumpert p. 106) of the activity of the species *Formica sanguinea* as captured on high frequency film: 'The ant requesting food first rapidly runs its antennae in a trilling motion over a nest mate, which thereupon usually turns towards the requesting ant. The animals then stand face to face, the requesting ant giving the "initial signal" for the giving of food by rapidly beating with its small forelegs, simultaneously feeling the head of the ant giving the food all over with its antennae.' Such action could well be construed as questioning and converse. Cleanthes' anecdote, of course, has usually been dismissed as 'ganz phantastisch' (Keller, *Antike Tierwelt* 2.418), but note that ants very occasionally exchange solid food in the form of so-called 'trophic eggs' (ant eggs incapable of development), which exchange is preceded by communication similar to that described above (see Dumpert p.103).

Other writers who compare and contrast the societies of man and the ant include Dio Chrysostom (c. A.D. 40-120) *orat.* 40.32 and 40f., 48.16 (ants helpful and not quarrelsome, unlike humans) and Aelian (*NA* 4.43: men, unlike ants, have all sorts of festivals or holidays). Lucian parodies such an analogy in his *Icaromenippus* (19 (1.301 Macleod)). From a slightly different angle, Aristophanes (*Thesmophoriazusae* 100 = Agathon *Tr.G.F.* 1.39.T21) and Pherecrates fr. 145.20ff. (1.188K) comically compare the musical novelties introduced by the poets Agathon and Timotheus to the intricate windings of the ants' tunnels (cf. E.K. Borthwick, *Hermes* 96 (1968) 59f.). This reminds us of the legend of Daedalus and the shell-threading ant mentioned above (p. 11). And so we turn to the rôle of the ant in legend.

Legend, folk-tale and fable

The legend that Zeus transformed ants into men for Aeacus on the island of Aegina ([Hesiod] fr. 205MW; Schol. *Il.* 1.180 (1.60 Erbse): for a brief list of other sources see Frazer on Apollodorus 3.12.6 (2 p.53 n.5); for a fuller list and discussion see J. Schmidt in *RE* 16^1 (1935) s.v. *Myrmex* (5) (1106) and s.v. *Myrmidones* (1109.44ff.)) The motif may have been drawn upon by the comic poet Pherecrates in his lost play *Ant-men*: see K.J. Dover, *JHS* 86 (1966) p.41 and n.4.

The reverse process occurs in a fable quoted above (p. 4 n.16) wherein we are told that the ant was once a man devoted to agriculture whom Zeus punished by transformation because he stole the fruits of his neighbours. For folk-tale analogies to both parts of the story from various regions of the world see J.R. Klíma ap. *Enzyklopädie des Märchens* s.v. *Ameise* (1.448), Stith Thompson, *Motif-Index of Folk-Literature*[2] D 182.2, N 453. For other references to the ant in fable see above p. 4. Some, like the immortal tale of the ant and the cicada, presuppose that the creature lays up stores for the winter (cf. Vergil *Aeneid* 4.403: (*formicae*) *hiemis memores*, Proverbs 6:8f. where the ant 'provideth her meat in the summer, and gathereth her food in the harvest').[4] This is certainly not true of North European ants; but Mediterranean ants and those of other regions with a hot, dry

---

[4] For other such references see T.H. Gaster ad loc. (*Myth, Legend and Custom in the Old Testament* (1969) p.802).

1. Ant

season can accurately be described as harvesting ants (see e.g. Sudd, *Introduction to the Behaviour of Ants* pp. 107ff., Dumpert pp. 247ff.), though recent research on American harvester ants (W.P. and E.E. Mackay, *Sociobiology* 9 (1984) 31ff.) suggests such activity is mainly a protection against predatory enemies since the seeds are not, in fact, utilised during the winter when foraging is impossible.

Zeus' habit of transforming himself into various entities (especially animals) to facilitate the consummation of an intrigue with a mortal woman is familiar in the case of bull, swan and the like. Less familiar is the story that he became an ant in Thessaly and begot the significantly named Myrmidon on Eurymedusa (for the tale's sources see Cook, *Zeus* 1 p. 532f. n.12).

In folk-tales and the like ants are credited with powers of revealing the future. King Midas, when a child, had grains of corn placed on his lips by ants while he slept, as a prediction of the vast wealth that was to be his (the authorities for this tale are listed in A.S. Pease's note on Cicero *de divinatione* 1.78 (p.228)). They are likewise weather prophets (if they carry their eggs[5] up from the ant-hill to the high ground it is a sign of rain; if they carry them down it is a sign of good weather: [Theophrastus] *de signis* 22, Aratus *Phaenomena* 956, Vergil *Georgics* 1.379f., Pliny *NH* 18.364). Artemidorus' work on dreams (*Oneirocritica* 3.6 (p.206 Pack)) says that if farmers dream of ants a good harvest is portended, though winged ants presage disaster. Ants feature in omens foretelling an individual's death at Plutarch *Life of Cimon* 18.4, Suetonius *Life of Tiberius* 72.2 (the emperor's pet snake eaten alive by ants: a scene brilliantly evoked in Robert Graves' *I Claudius* p.365) and *Life of Nero* 46.1 (the emperor dreams he is covered by flying ants).

Proverbially, the ant features as a type of wisdom and foresight (see West on Hesiod *Works and Days* 778) like Milton's 'parsimonious emmet, provident of future' (*Paradise Lost* 7.485);

---

[5] Plutarch (*On the Intelligence of Animals (moralia* 967F)) says some would read êia ('provisions') for ôia ('eggs') in the passage of Aratus cited below and detect a reference to stored *grain* which the ants see growing mildewed from the damp and wish to dry in the sun, and this process is certainly conceivable; but the confusion of sunny with rainy weather implied rings oddly. For comparable tales see P.J. Marriot, *Red Sky at Night Shepherd's Delight: weather lore of the English countryside* (1981) p. 189f. observing that worker ants often move eggs or larvae in nest chambers due to change of temperature; E. Stemplinger ap. Bächtold-Stäubli, *Handwörterbuch des deutschen Aberglaubens* 1.362 (German); A. Hauser, *Bauernregeln* (Zurich 1973) pp. 96ff. (Swiss).

of ceaseless activity (see August Otto, *Sprichwörter d. Römer* pp. 690ff.); of vast numbers (Gow on Theocritus *Id.* 15.45 (2.280)) and of great wealth (Gow on Theocritus *Id.* 17.107 (2.342f.) and Boardman-Vollenweider, *Engraved Gems and Finger Rings in the Ashmolean Museum, Oxford. I: Greek and Etruscan* (1978) p.99). Also of smallness and insignificance: 'No path even for an ant' (see R. Strömberg, *Greek Proverbs* (Göteborg 1954) p. 77); the saying 'Even an ant has venom'[6] (see Archilochus fr. 23.16 W (cf. S.R. Slings, *ZPE* 45 (1982) 69f.), L. Cohn, *Philol. Suppl.* 6 (1882) = *Corp. Paroem. Graec.* Suppl. (IV) p.244 (283)) the equivalent of our 'Even the worm will turn'. The notion of a venomous ant recurs in the picture of a snake that has eaten ants and beetles and is thus filled with poison. This may be found in e.g. a scholion on *Il.* 22.94 (5.288 Erbse), Eustathius *Il.* 1259.41 etc. For a modern account of the employment and the constitution of ants' venom see Brian pp. 52ff. On the proverb 'Woe to the ant that flies' cf. R. Strömberg, *Greek Proverbs* (Göteborg 1954) p. 43. On the proverb 'He who spits on an ant-hill will have swollen lips' (a real mystery) see ib. p. 34.

Miscellanea

Ants are a source of food for bears (says Pliny *NH* 10.198, 419). 'The smallest animals quarrel as much as the largest' he also claims (*NH* 10.206) and among his evidence cites the fact that a tree infested by ants is hollowed out by caterpillars.

Aelian *NA* 10.42 reports the idea that there is a deadly species of ant (as of wasp) known as Laertes (in Greek legend the name given to the father of Odysseus). Philip *AP* 9.438 = *GP* 2987ff. has an amusing account of ants sailing in straw-husks (*not* bridges of straw as often supposed: see Gow-Page ad loc. (2.359)) across the water set in protection around honey-pots. *Myrmêx* was the name of a type of boxing-thong: see M. Poliakoff, *Studies in the Terminology of the Greek Combat Sports* (*Beitr. zur kl. Phil.* 146 (1982)) pp. 54ff.

Aelian *NA* 17.42 tells us that in Babylonia there occur ants whose generative organs face backwards in the opposite direction to those of all other ants. Herodotus 3.102ff. describes (on

---

[6] For the equivalent proverb in English ('the fly has spleen, the ant gall') see Tilley, *Dictionary of Proverbs* (above p.2 n.7) F 393.

1. Ant

Persian authority) gold-guarding creatures in the Bactrian desert which are the shape of Greek ants but the size of something between a fox and a dog. They throw up sand which contains gold in the course of making their homes in burrows. Later authors add various details and the actual idea can be paralleled from ancient India and China's Mongolian region (with its stories of 'red ants as huge as elephants and wasps as big as gourds'). On the whole fascinating topic see J.D.P. Bolton, *Aristeas of Proconnesus* (Oxford 1962) pp. 66f., 80ff. and subject-index s.v. 'ants, gold-guarding and monstrous', J.W. Sedlar, *India and the Greeks* (1980) pp. 12f and 255f. G. Jennison, *Animals for Show and Pleasure in Ancient Rome* (Manchester 1937) pp. 190ff. argues that these are real creatures, to be identified with the Indian pangolin or scaly ant-eater (an ambiguous animal whose resistance to easy classification has recently interested anthropologists: see R. Parker, *Phronesis* 29 (1984) 175f.) but like e.g. Thompson, *CR* 52 (1938) 77 we are unconvinced.

Some late Greek authors (Agatharchides (second century B.C.) quoted by Photius *Bibl.* 455^a (7.174 Henry) and Artemidorus (first century B.C.) quoted by Strabo 16.774.15) identified these creatures with the lion, and this was the ultimate inspiration for the compound *myrmêko-leôn* ('ant-lion') which seems to have been coined by the translator into Greek of Job 4:11 as a way of relieving the monotony induced by that passage's numerous references to lions ('The roaring of the lion, and the voice of the fierce lion, and the teeth of the young lions, are broken. The old lion perisheth for lack of prey, and the stout lion's whelps are scattered abroad', to quote the Authorised Version). The original Hebrew merely has 'lion' pure and simple. Various Church Fathers and late commentators on this passage (transcribed by Gil Fernández p. 57f.) were understandably baffled by this 'ant-lion' and explained it (not very helpfully) in terms of a real ant, a real lion, or a mixture of both. Thence it became incorporated into medieval lore and bestiaries and finally became a serious zoological term for a genuine insect that preys on ants (*Myrmeleontidae*: see e.g. Imms, *Textbook of Entomology*^{3} p.502). For a full account of this mythical 'ant-lion' and a clear distinction between it and *Myrmeleontidae* see Mia I. Gerhardt, *Vivarium* 3 (1965) 1ff. For a similarly composite creature see G. Silliti, *Tragelaphos: storia di una metafora e di un problema* (1984).

For the *myrmêkeion*, an insect that mimics the ant, see Nicander *Ther.* 747 and Gow-Scholfield ad loc., J. Scarborough, *Pharmacy in History* 21 (1979) 13.

2. BED BUG (koris/Cimex lectularius)

Much interesting information about this creature in varying times and climes is assembled by J.F.D.Shrewsbury, *The Plague of the Philistines* (London 1964) pp. 146ff., and Busvine, *Insects, Hygiene and History* (1976) pp. 33ff., 63ff., 171ff., 183ff. etc. On this aspect of vermin in ancient Greece see S. Lilja, *Arctos* 10 (1976) 59ff. It is often mentioned as a feature of everyday life in Aristophanic comedies (e.g. *Clouds* 634, cf. 742; *Plutus* 541; see above p. 12 n.38) and its existence even in the Underworld is taken for granted (*Frogs* 115). Its name, which derives from the verb *keirô* (meaning 'bite, cut'),[7] allows Aristophanes a number of puns involving those other ancient enemies of Athens, the Corinthians[8] (*Clouds* 710, *Frogs* 443), and Parmenio *AP* 9.113 = *GP* 2598f. an untranslatable[9] series of plays upon words. The *Greek Anthology* has relatively little to say of the creature, but it is referred to as a *koitês thêrion*, 'a wild beast [cf. above p. 7 n.23] of the bed' in Meleager *AP* 5 184.6 = *HE* 4375 and pedantic grammarians are called 'bed-bugs who live off eloquent authors' in Antiphanes *AP* 11.322.6 = *GP* 776 (cf. below p. 111).

Aristotle too has very little in the way of remarks on the insect: at *HA* 556b25ff. fleas, bugs and lice are listed as animals that arise by means of spontaneous generation, the bug being generated from the moisture of living animals (see above p. 21f.).

Existing before the invention of DDT (or cleanliness), the

[7] Further influence from the verb *kerannunai* ('to be full, sated', cf. below n.9) is suggested by Sturtevant (*Class. Phil.* 7 (1912) 240).

[8] The joke may have a basis in euphemistic slang on the popular level: H. Hatzfield, *Leitfaden der vergleichenden Bedeutungslehre* (Munich 1927) p. 147 pointed out that embarrassment at having lice and other vermin is often covered by resort to such euphemisms (e.g. British soldiers in the First World War referred to their lice as 'Scots grey' (cf. above p. 9f). See further F. Déchelette, *L'Argot des poilus* (1918), E. Partridge, *A Dictionary of Slang and Unconventional English*[8] (ed. P. Beale) s.v. 'Scotch (occ. Scots) Greys', and on the general principle of euphemism in slang Partridge's *Slang Today and Yesterday* (London 1950) Index s.v.

[9] 'The fleas fed on me till full, but I had my own fill fully flicking off the fleas' is the (entomologically loose) rendering by Gow and Page (1.293).

3. Bee/wasp

ancients were fairly helpless against the onslaught of the creature. For alleged remedies cf. W. Theiler, *RE* Suppl. 14 (1974) 823.20ff. The notion that the feet of hare or stag hung around the feet of a bed will prevent infestation by bugs is implausibly attributed to the sixth-century philosopher Democritus by the *Geoponica* (cf. Diels-Kranz, *Vorsokratiker* 2.215 (fr. 8)). For bed-bugs used medically in antiquity see Busvine pp. 177ff. (cf. Theiler, 824.22ff.). The Acts of John 60-1 (from the New Testament Apocrypha) has the apostle miraculously banish the bugs from a bed in the inn where he is staying.

3. BEE/WASP

Bee (melissa/apis)

Etymology: there is an unusually large range of wildly different names for this insect throughout the world, as becomes clear merely if we glance at the English, Greek and Latin names just cited. See further Darling Buck, *Selected Synonyms* s.v. Bee, Gil Fernández p.151 n.51 etc. One group of names derives from the insect's connection with honey, and it is here that the Greek word belongs, *meli* being Greek for honey. There is admittedly some uncertainty as to the origin of the second part of the word (see Gil Fernández p. 152f.).

So much material exists concerning this creature's rôle in ancient Greece that the present section must be brutally selective: a whole book could be written on the bee in antiquity. Indeed a number of general surveys of this insect have been written, in which the ancient Greek bee looms large. We would draw attention in particular to Hilda Ransome's delightful *The Sacred Bee in Ancient Times and Folklore* (London 1937) and H. Malcolm Fraser, *Beekeeping in Antiquity*[2] (London 1951) whose assessment of the literary evidence is supplemented by E. Crane, *Archaeology of Beekeeping*, which treats its chosen topic from a mainly archaeological (i.e. non-literary) viewpoint. Much recent scientific research is encapsulated in Charles D. Michener's *The Social Behaviour of the Bee: a comparative study* (Harvard 1974). On the religious and ritual use of honey see Ransome pp. 119ff., L. Bodson, *Hiera Zôia: contribution à l'étude de la place de l'animal dans la religion grecque ancienne* (Brussels 1978) pp. 22ff. On the bee in folklore see K. Ranke and J.R. Klíma ap.

Enzyklopädie des Märchens s.v. Biene (2.296ff.).

Ancient writers on bees

There are fifty or so references to the bee in the *Greek Anthology*: on some of them see Douglas, *Birds and Beasts of the Greek Anthology* pp. 180ff. Nicander's *Melissurgica* (a now lost work on bee-keeping: see Gow-Scholfield, *Nicander* p.215) must be mentioned here, as, of course, must Vergil's Fourth Georgic (on whose accuracy and lack of it see Byl, *Ludus Magistralis* 16/17 (1968) 9ff.). But easily the fullest treatment of bees and their ways to have come down from antiquity is that preserved in the works of Aristotle, and in particular the *Historia Animalium* (see Fraser pp. 13ff.) Readers of the relevant passages, however, often report a paradoxical reaction: 'Aristotle's account of bees is remarkable for its extent. He has given more attention to these than to any other group of insects. Yet ... although his account contains many accurate and striking observations, it also contains numerous errors and is obviously largely drawn from hearsay and from secondhand accounts' (C. Singer ap. *Studies in the History and Method of Science* 2 (Oxford 1921) p.50).

The question of authenticity (see above p. 27) must, of course, be borne in mind. Apart from this, the best, most recent and most detailed analysis of Aristotle's treatment of bees is that by Byl, in *Recherches sur les grands traités biologiques d'Aristote* pp. 340ff. He takes as his starting point the very remarkable fact that Aristotle devotes to the creature more space not merely, as Singer says, than to any other insect, but than to any other animal bar man, and that surely is extraordinary. One may at first choose to explain this in terms of dispassionate and objective scientific interest, and to detect an argument against the notion (see p. 20 above) of a hierarchical prejudice against insects in general. However, closer investigation of what Aristotle actually says of bees tells in favour of Byl's thesis that here too Aristotle was not completely immune to the popular beliefs and attitudes of his own time, and that a pre-scientific attitude to bees has left its stamp upon him. For not only does the sheer scope of his treatment seem determined by such extra-scientific factors as the religious and ritual significance of bees and honey (below p. 64), but he appears to reflect common ideas as to the holiness of the bee (see below p. 69) with his

3. Bee/wasp

highly unscientific statement (*GA* 761b) as to its element of the divine (he says the same of man (see Byl p. 304f.); cf. his remarks on the bee's intelligence (*PA* 648a5ff., 650b24ff., *Met.* 980b23)). Similarly his failure to avoid the common mistake over the sex of the queen bee (below p. 62f.) and his gross (if not grotesque) over-estimation of the life-span of the domestic bee (below p. 62) suggest a firmly idealising or conventional approach. On the other hand Byl rather exaggerates the anthropocentricity of Aristotle's account (see below p. 60); but he is prepared to admit (pp. 350ff.) that 'certaines affirmations témoignent d'une observation minutieuse et admirable et elles sont corroborées par la science la plus récente.' (In fact he could have been even more cautious (p. 353) concerning the possibility that Aristotle anticipated von Frisch's discovery of 'the dance of the bees': see below p. 55f.). For the existence of such careful observation cheek by jowl with prejudice and presupposition in the zoological works of Aristotle see above p. 25f. and n.74.

How Aristotle came to know (or think he knew) so much about bees was obviously a moot point from early on in some quarters, since the Arab writer al-Damīrī Kamāl al-Dīn (died A.D.1405) among others preserves in his encyclopedia of animals (Hayāt al-hayawān: ed. Bulag (1868) vol. 2.404) a tradition that, wishing to investigate the production of honey, Aristotle made a glass observation hive, only to be thwarted by the bees, who, indignant at his prying, smeared the inside of the glass with clay. Unfortunately al-Damīrī is not very specific as to the source of this tale.[10]

More recently Fraser (p.17) has decided from internal evidence that 'Aristotle must have seen the interior of a hive' and suggests that Aristotle was acquainted with a (top-bar) wicker-hive similar to those described by Sir George Wheeler in seventeenth-century Attica (*A Journey into Greece* (London 1682) p.412). The Greek beekeeper N.J. Nicolaidis (in a book

---

[10] Inaccurately referred to by Ransome p.80f. We owe our more scholarly citation to Professor W. Madelung. For further information on al-Damīrī and his zoological lexicon see the works cited by F.E. Peters, *Aristotle and the Arabs* (New York 1968), p.133 n. 133. The nature of the tale rather reminds one of the tradition that Aristotle committed suicide out of frustration that he could not solve the problem of the ebb and flow of the Euripus (see A.-H. Chroust, *Modern Schoolman* 44 (1967) 177ff. ≃ *Aristotle* 1.177ff. on this and similar stories of thwarted philosophers and wise men).

50   Greek Insects

published (in modern Greek) in Athens (1959)) has come to a similar conclusion. On such hives and on the question of whether it is likely that they existed in antiquity see now the full discussion by Crane pp. 196ff.

On other ancient references to bees and bee-keeping in antiquity see Fraser pp. 22ff. (pseudo-Aristotle), 70ff. (Pliny), 80ff. (Theophrastus), 82ff. (Aelian), and 90ff. (*Geoponica*).

Wild bees

[Note that the Greek phrase *agrios melissa* though literally translatable as 'wild bee' refers, in fact, to the wasp: see Gil Fernández p.160. On a very wild-sounding 'bee' mentioned by Clitarchus see below p. 82f.]

8. Wild bee on a gem from a private Swiss collection [Leo Merz], second or first century B.C.: see M.-L. Vollenweider, *Deliciae Leonis: Antike geschnittene Steine und Ringe aus einer Privatsammlung* (Mainz 1984) no.108 (p.72).

3. Bee/wasp

Homeric similes such as *Iliad* 2.87ff. and 12.167ff. (see above p. 7) reveal an awareness that clefts in rock or stone form the natural abode of bees: compare the Biblical phrase 'honey out of the rock' (Deuteronomy 32:13, Psalms 81:16). Strabo 2.72.14 mentions Hyrcanian bees (see below p. 83) nesting among trees, and in rocks. In the absence of such a rock a hollow tree-trunk would serve as well. Hesiod *Works and Days* 233 has a vision of the Golden Age when the top of the oak yielded acorns, the middle bees (for other references in Greek literature to bees nesting in hollow trees see West on Hesiod *Theogony* 594, for honey flowing from hollow oaks in the Golden Age his note on *Works and Days* 233). Samson's experience with the bees swarming and making honey in the dead lion (Judges 14:8) presupposes that animal carcasses provide a further source of accommodation (we recall how the Amathusians cut off the head of Onesilaus and hung it over their gateway: being already hollow a swarm of bees entered and filled it with honeycomb according to a grisly tale recorded by Herodotus 5.114). Bees usually shun carrion (cf. below p. 65f.), but Fraser (p. 12) observes[11] that if the lion's carcass were dry it might be used by swarms. Wild bees often feature in descriptions of a beautiful countryside, in simile or vignette in Greek literature: see, for instance, *Iliad* 2.87ff. (see above p. 7), Euripides *Hippolytus* 76f. (see below p. 70), Theocritus *Id.* 7.80ff. and *Id.* 22.40ff., Apollonius of Rhodes *Argonautica* 1.879ff., Nonnus 5.243ff., Longus *Daphnis and Chloe* 1.9.1. Especially interesting and charming is an anonymous lyric in Anacreontic metre from the first century A.D. or earlier (Powell, *Collectanea Alexandrina* p.185f. no. 7) which describes the activity of bees in a mountain glade. For some useful comments cf. J.U. Powell, *New Chapters in the History of Greek Literature, First Series* (1921) p. 56f. and *Second Series* (1929) p. 62f. Text and translation also in Page, *Greek Literary Papyri* pp. 410ff. As Powell observes, the description seems to be a mixture of personal observation and literary convention, and the use of an adjective signifying 'stingless' is not literally accurate; but 'any one accustomed to watch [wild bees] at work would soon find out that they were practically quite inoffensive, and were distinguishable by this from the irritable hive-bee'. They are called *askepês* (lit. 'uncovered', i.e. without benefit of hive), and much of what is

---

[11] Cf. A.E. Shipley, *Journ. Phil.* 34 (1918) 98ff.

said of them would be consistent with an identification (reported by Powell) with *Chalicodoma sicula* ('perhaps the most abundant and conspicuous of all Mediterranean Megachilidae'). For some reservations here see above p. ix.

Domesticated bees

Legend attributed this invaluable invention to the hero Aristaeus (see below p. 67f.). In actual fact the earliest extant mention[12] of domesticated bees occurs in a simile from Hesiod's *Theogony*, where the female sex is compared to drones (594ff.; cf. *Works and Days* 304, where Hesiod's idle brother is at the receiving end of a comparable simile). Homer does not have any analogous passage, though it would be rash to infer from this absence that he was ignorant of the practice or to draw any conclusions as to the date of its introduction into Greece.[13] Various terracotta horizontal hives have been discovered in archeological excavations (see Crane pp. 45ff.), the most numerous in Athens (from c.400 B.C. onwards), and, not surprisingly, many were found in the vicinity of Mount Hymettus, famed in antiquity as the source of the best Attic honey (see Nisbet-Hubbard on Horace *Odes* 2.6.14 for relevant references).

Instructive as to the widespread popularity of beekeeping in Attica of the sixth century B.C. is one of Solon's laws (Plutarch *Life of Solon* 23 = F 62 Ruschenbusch)[14] which enjoins that an individual wishing to raise a stock of bees must place them 300 feet from those raised by anyone else.

Sting

A sting is present only in most females (cf. Michener p.212).

---

[12] For Hesiod's likeliest date cf. M.L. West, *Hesiod's Theogony* (Oxford 1966) pp. 40ff.

[13] Olck (*RE* 3 s.v. Bienenzucht (1899) 450) suggests that artificial hives are presupposed by *Odyssey* 13.103ff. where bees use two-handled jars within the cave of the Nymphs as a place to store honey, but this is a rash deduction, since bees (like several other insects) are prepared to take over man-made objects as nests when suitable.

[14] An edition of the laws of Solon as fragmentarily preserved (*Historia Einzelschrift* 9 (1966)).

3. Bee/wasp

Aristotle *HA* 553b5ff. was aware that drones do not possess a sting. According to *HA* 626a18ff. (Pliny *NH* 11.60; cf. Vergil *Georgics* 4.237 etc.) a bee dies when it stings because it cannot extract the sting without also extracting its intestines; once the sting is lost the animal must die. A sentence which Thompson ad loc. suspected of being interpolated adds that the bee will recover if the victim presses the sting out, and this is certainly true of *A.cerana* which is capable of working free the sting and flying away. See further below p. 63.

Bees' distinctive buzz

Aristotle recognised that the noise began and ceased when the bee began and ceased to fly (*HA* 537b8f.→Pliny *NH* 11.266) and acknowledged that the opening and closing of the wings produced a special sound (*HA* 535b10: this has been confirmed by modern research: see e.g. Michener p.132: when a bee makes a buzzing run it produces a series of short buzzes with its wings at the usual flight frequency of 180 to 250 cycles per second) but was misled into complex ideas concerning the bee's internal *pneuma*

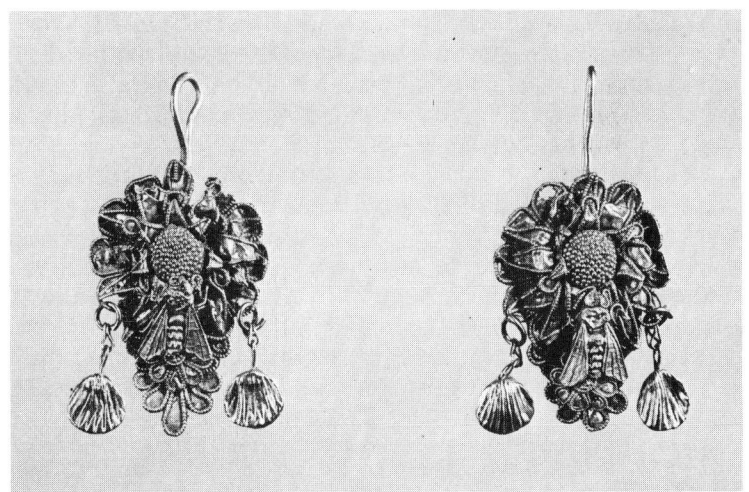

9. Gold earring (in the shape of a bee on a flower) from Ephesus, mid-fifth century B.C. (Hamburg Museum für Kunst und Gewerbe 1957, 54a and b, St. 78/9).

whose vibration against the membrane of the *hypozôma* (see p. 120 n.88) he supposed to be the source of the buzz. See *HA* 535b6ff. with Peck's note ad loc. (2 p.74f.n.c); cf. above p.23.

Bee's wings are membraneous, says Aristotle (*HA* 490a6) and do not grow again if plucked off any more than the sting grows again once removed (*HA* 519a27ff.).

Communication and perception

It is uncertain, according to *HA* 627a18f. whether bees can hear or not; later authors present a bafflingly wide variety of traditions to the effect that bees are frightened (Varro *de re rustica* 3.16, Columella 9.8.12, Lucan 9.288f.), or pleased (Pliny *NH* 11.20, *Geoponica* 15.3) indeed positively attracted (Aelian *NA* 5.13) by cymbals clashed, or distressed (Vergil *Georgics* 4.49f.) by the effect of echo. Aristotle preserves the claim of some (*HA* 627a15ff.) that bees can be mustered into the hive by rattling crockery or stones.[15] Among modern scholars who considered the problem must be counted the eighteenth-century naturalist Gilbert White (*Natural History of Selbourne,* letter 38 to Daines Barrington: 'It does not appear from experiment that bees are in any way capable of being affected by sounds: for I have often tried my own with a large speaking-trumpet held close to their hives, and with such an exertion of voice as would have hailed a ship at a distance of a mile, and still these insects pursued their various employments undisturbed, and without showing the least sensibility or resentment'). This scepticism was frowned on ad loc. by E.T. Bennett, White's nineteenth-century editor, but is confirmed by the latest research (cf. e.g. Michener p. 19: 'Bees do not appear to respond to airborne sound, but only to vibrations in the substrate and surfaces being touched').

In contrast, ancient authors are united in their agreement that bees perceived (and disliked) strong smells: so Aristotle *HA*

---

[15] 'Even bees could be communicated with, for, when they swarmed, their owners would whistle, clap their hands, ring bells and tinkle basins and kettles. This was an ancient practice, going back to Roman times, but still universally observed in eighteenth-century England' (Thomas, *Man and the Natural World* p. 96, who argues that the purpose was originally legal (to establish the bee owner's right to follow the bees onto another's land) but that 'by early modern times the noise was widely regarded by country people as a means of addressing the bees themselves'). For ancient references to collecting swarms by making a din see Frazer on Ovid *Fasti* 3.741 (3.136f.).

3. Bee/wasp 55

534b18, fr. 358 Rose; Aelian *NA* 1.58, 5.11, Plutarch *Natural Questions* (see below p. 70), *Geoponica* 15.2.9. Pliny *NH* 11.61 says they attack strongly perfumed persons, Columella *de re rustica* 9.14 that they are disturbed by those who reek of wine, Vergil that they shun foul odours, especially that of crabs roasting on the fire (*Georgics* 4.47ff.), phenomena which antiquity found it easy to connect with the bees' temperate life style (see below p. 69f.). Modern research has certainly confirmed the idea of sensitivity to smell by various experiments (for a brief summary see Brian, *Social Insects* p. 55f., Michener p.18. The antennae are the relevant areas of perception, sensitive to atmosphere humidity, temperature, pheromones, etc.).

Bees could allegedly foretell the weather (compare the similarly prophetic powers attributed to the ant: above p. 43) or at least the coming rain: Aristotle *HA* 627b10, Pliny *NH* 11.20, Aelian *NA* 1.11, Vergil *Georgics* 4.191 etc. Pausanias 9.40.1f. relates how bees aided the Boeotians when they were in search of a remedy against drought: the Delphic Oracle bade them consult the oracle of Trophonius at Lebadea and a swarm of bees helped them locate it. For bees as an omen in Roman and later Greek writers see Bühler's edition of Zenobius 4.254f. Some analogous ideas in E. Hoffmann-Krayer ap. *Bächtold-Stäubli, Handwörterbuch des deutschen Aberglaubens* 1.1229ff. (German), A. Hauser, *Bauernregeln* (Zurich 1973) pp. 95f., 384f. (Swiss).

Dance of the bees

In a series of publications[16] the Austrian scientist Karl von Frisch showed that when scout bees discover a rich source of nectar they return to their hive with a full load of pollen or nectar and communicate the location of the find, its compass-bearing vis-à-vis the sun, and its distance from the hive, by the famous waggle (or figure-of-eight) dance. In this the angle of the dance relative to the vertical face of the combs is determined by the sun's position relative to the food. Several scholars have claimed that this phenomenon was already described by Aristotle in his *Historia Animalium* (see e.g. the optimistic remarks of J.B.S.

---

[16] Most notably *The Dancing Bees* (London 1954) and *The Dance Language and Orientation of Bees* (1967). For a handy summary of the findings of these books see W.H. Thorpe ap. *Non-Verbal Communication* (ed. R.A. Hinde, Cambridge 1972) pp. 132ff. Cf. A.M. Wenner ap. *Advances in the Study of Communication and Effect* vol. 1 (London and New York 1974) pp. 133ff.

Haldane in *JHS* 75 (1955) 24f.). However, a close investigation of the relevant passage (624b) shows the matter to be considerably more complex (see in particular G.B. Whitfield, *CR* 8 (1958) 14f.). In the first place the authorship of this section of *Historia Animalium* has been disputed (see above p. 27). Then again, the significance of some key words is far from plain. We are told that when the bees return to the hive they *aposeiontai*: the natural translation of this verb would be 'shake themselves free' and that is how most translators have taken it (see Whitfield p.15). 'They waggle themselves' is a possible rendering, since the corresponding noun *aposeisis* can be used of lascivious dances (so Pollux 4.100 (1.230 Bethe) in a list of other such dances), but the possibility that the bees are to be envisaged as shaking off their load still remains, and the most that can be claimed,[17] as Whitfield says, is that 'the actual movements on which von Frisch relies were noticed by the author' of the passage just considered. That author's interpretation of the movements is another matter.

Food

(a) *Honey*. Bees collect this important product from flowers in the form of nectar[18] (more accurately, therefore, the anonymous poet of *Collectanea Alexandrina* p. 185 (see above p. 51) 'they gather the sweet honey-flowing nectar' than Aristotle's account cited below). Many ancient authors, however, erroneously supposed it to originate in honey dew. Thus Aristotle, for instance (*HA* 553b29ff. → Pliny *NH* 11.30), states that honey (dew) falls from the skies (Pliny adds speculation as to whether it constitutes the heaven's sweat, the stars' saliva or the atmosphere's purgation: on the whole concept cf. W.H. Roscher, *Nektar und Ambrosia* (1883) and S. Byl, *Ludus Magistralis* 16/17 (1968) 15f.; for parallel notions (manna etc.) see T.H. Gaster, *Myth, Legend and Custom in the Old Testament* p. 242f.; compare Vergil's picture of honey shaken from the leaves of trees

---

[17] The sequel to the verb *aposeiontai* in *HA* 624b is that three or four bees busy themselves about the returning bees. There follows the erroneous detail about the collecting of wax considered below (p. 58).

[18] For an interesting historical sketch of the scientific discovery of nectar and nectaries and its relation to views on flowers and insects see J. Lorch, *Isis* 69 (1978) 514ff. (p. 524f. on Aristotle's failure to understand the process fully).

3. Bee/wasp 57

10. Bee on a coin (reverse) from Hybla (British Museum: wrongly identified as from *Megara* in *Brit. Mus. Cat. of Greek Coins.* p.96 no.1). Hybla, a town on the southern slopes of Mount Etna in Sicily, was famous for its honey (see e.g. Vergil, *Eclogue* 1.54, 7.37, Strabo, 6.267.2; A. Otto, *Die Sprichwörter und Sprichwörtlichen Redensarten der Römer* p.168).

(*Georgics* 1.131; cf. *Eclogues* 4.30 and West on Hesiod *Works and Days* 233)). Aristotle proceeds to describe (*HA* 554a11ff.) the bees' collection of honey from flowers (see further the remarks of Aelian *NA* 5.42), but other authors supposed that bees gathered it from the upper air, visiting flowers only for wax. Scientifically speaking, honeydew is an excretion from plant-sucking bugs which usually lands on leaves, whence it is collected by ants and wasps as well as bees. It is particularly useful to insects at times when open flowers are not available. Compare the probable origins (see below p. 123) of the delusion that cicadas live off dew.

Further opportunity for confusion is offered by Milton's

reference to 'the bee with honied thigh' (*Il Penseroso* 142), like its model Vergil's *crura thymo plenae* (*Georgics* 4.181). Honey is not carried in the hairy 'pollen-basket' on the hind-legs but in the honey stomach or crop, a vastly extendable sac, whence it is regurgitated. Aristotle's reference to bees collecting juices with their tongue-like organ and later vomiting the honey into the cells (*HA* 554a14ff.) is correct. In the same passage he states that it is wax and bee-bread that the bee carries on its leg.

(b) *Pollen and wax*. Pollen is collected from flowers, wax is produced by the bees themselves from epidermal glands on their abdomens, a process not visible (hardly surprisingly) to the unaided eyes of Antiquity. *HA* 554a14ff. we have already considered; more problematic is *HA* 624a34ff., towards the end of which (624b) a substance is mentioned in terms of a load collected from returning bees and used to build combs. Wax is certainly used for this purpose (cf. Brian, *Social Insects* p. 109), but this has just as certainly been confused with pollen because a little earlier on the passage described how bees scramble up the stalks of flowers and gather beeswax with their front legs. Furthermore this description is followed by an account of how the wax thus gathered is wiped off on to the middle legs and thence to the hind legs. This may pass as a fairly accurate picture of how movements of the hind legs help remove wax scales from their position between the abdominal sclerites where they originate. For a modern detailed description of this see Michener p.62 with fig. The wax thus freed is manipulated by the bee into the material of the dump and later cut off to be used for building purposes.

(c) *Water*. The water-carrying of the bees is referred to by Aristotle (*HA* 625b19) and Aelian (*NA* 1.10, 5.11; a reference to it may also underlie the corrupt 5.42 = Nicander fr. 93 Schneider: cf. the remarks of Gil Fernández p. 174f. n.2) and is brilliantly transformed into an elaborate poetic image by Callimachus, *Hymn to Apollo* 110 (see F. Williams' note ad loc.).

Modern scientific research (cf. Michener p. 203f.) has clarified the functions of this process: water is necessary (i) for the adaptation of honey towards the feeding of the young: that is, it is used to dilute honey in the preparation of fodder for the brood; (ii) for cooling the hive when the outside air becomes sufficiently

3. Bee/wasp

hot (*c.* 34° centigrade). The water is placed in drops within the cells or exposed in films by the proboscis movement of workers for easier evaporation. Bees' drinking of water is mentioned by Vergil *Georgics* 4.54: they do not drink on the wing, of course! The amusing notion that bees ballast themselves with stones (Aristotle *HA* 626b24ff., Aelian *NA* 5.13, Plutarch *de sollert. anim.* (*moralia* 967B),[19] Vergil *Georgics* 4.194) is, one must sadly confess, quite wrong. (Compare the analogous idea that storks swallow stones for the same reason: see Thompson, *Glossary of Greek Birds* p.72.) It is often suggested that the objects mistaken for small stones were, in fact, dead larvae or pupae or refuse being carried away from the hives. Material for nest-building might be an alternative explanation (cf. Byl p.348 n.45: Aristotle has confounded domestic and mason bee).

Home-management

Semonides' bee-woman (7.83ff.W), the only good wife made by Zeus, may owe something of her good reputation to her chastity (see below p. 70), but most of it will relate to her house-management (economy). In Xenophon's treatise on this subject, *Oeconomicus* 7.32ff., Ischomachus tells his wife ('that paradigm of the "dear little wifey" ')[20] that her rôle about the house is analogous to the queen bee's (see p. 62). Many authors stress the bee's industry, as for instance Aristotle *HA* 622b20ff., 627a19ff., Aelian *NA* 5.12, Pliny *NH* 11.12.

Social organisation

Semonides' bee-woman (fr. 7.83ff.W) is the first in a long line of images (like our 'busy as a bee') illustrating this aspect of the

---

[19] Plutarch and Aelian give almost identical accounts, save that Plutarch says that bees resort to this strategem in order to round windy promontories, Aelian that they do it when surprised by windy weather. This slight discrepancy is explained by Richmond, *Chapters on Greek Fish-Lore* p. 15f. with the supposition that Plutarch has misunderstood in a common source (see above p. 30 n.82) a statement which he represents by the reference to *akrôtêriois* (promontories) and Aelian more accurately reproduces by alluding to *akrois tois posi* (the bees hold the stones *with the tips of their feet*).

[20] To quote F.D. Harvey, *Échos du monde classique/Classical Views* 3 (1984) 68, an interesting study of this woman: cf. D. Nails, ib. 4 (1985) 97ff. On the bee-woman cf. L. Schear, ib. 3 (1984) 46ff.

60   *Greek Insects*

11. Bee on a didrachm (obverse) from Ephesus, *c.* 420-400 B.C.: see
    Brit. Mus. Cat. of Greek Coins: Ionia (1892) p.518.

bee's existence. The bees became, like the ants (see above p. 38), a prototype for human society, a point of view which achieves its most memorable (and complex) treatment in Vergil's *Fourth Georgic* (see the remarks of Jasper Griffin, *Greece and Rome* 26 (1979) 62f. = *Latin Poets and Roman Life* p.165 and n.9). Origen *contra Celsum* 4.81, writing in the third century A.D., takes over from such writers this general social picture (not without adding a mistake of his own: see H. Chadwick, *Journal of Theol. Studies* 48 (1947) p. 37 n.2). In England 'the ancient parallel between human society and the beehive was never more popular than in the Stuart period, when numerous published treatises on bee-keeping gave as much attention to the insects' political virtues as to their practical utility' (K.V. Thomas, *Man and the Natural World* p.62f. with examples). And more recently J. Michelet was of the view that 'the beehive is the veritable Athens of the insect world' (*L'Insecte*[5] (Paris 1863) p.329). We might also cite such titles as Michener's *The Social Behaviour of the Bees*, though, as Michener himself reminds us (p.38), 'only the

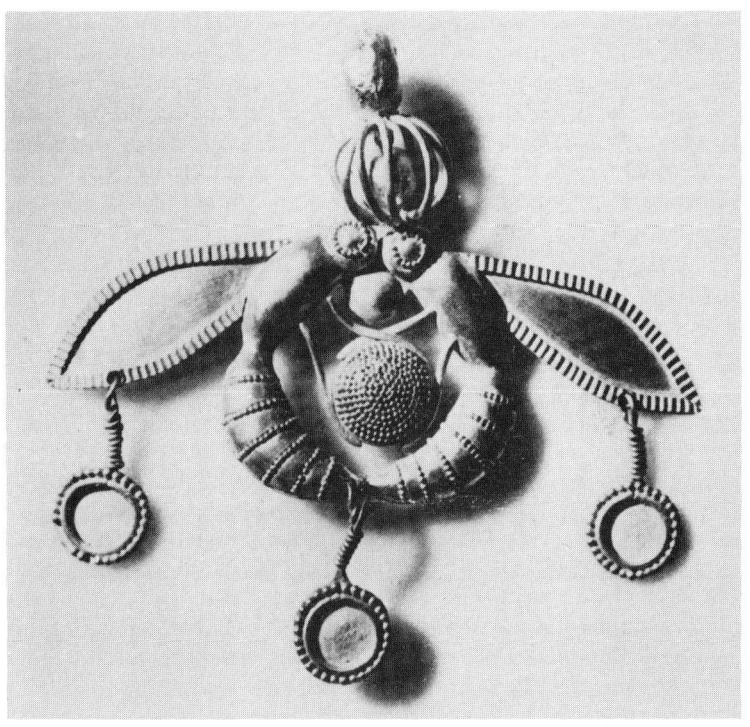

12. Bees or wasps on Mallia pendant from Mallia, Chrysolakkos, *c.* seventeenth century B.C. (Crete, Heraklion Museum).

highly eusocial bees remain permanently at that level. Nearly all other forms change during their life cycles, usually from solitary to some social pattern'.

HA 625b17f. and 627a20 stresses the division of labour (with different bees carrying water (see above p. 58f.) or flower-produce; smoothing and ranging the combs; making wax and honey (see above pp. 56ff.); engaged in out-of-door work). This is a fairly accurate picture, though as Byl observes (p. 346) Aristotle does not know (how could he?) that the same bee does different tasks at different stages of development (on this and all other details of division of labour see Michener pp. 119ff.). More obviously and inaccurately anthropomorphic is the notion (*HA* 626b10 → Pliny *NH* 11.21, Vergil *Georgics* 4.178ff.) that elderly bees stay at home and do less work. This idealising and humanising tendency reaches its extreme with the statement (*HA* 554b6f. → Pliny *NH* 11.69; cf. Vergil *Georgics* 4.206) that the bee usually lives for six years, exceptionally for seven[21] (and a very well-managed swarm can last for nine or ten years). In fact, the average summer life-span of a worker is six *weeks* (!) and the most spectacular recorded winter longevity, extending to most of the following summer, can only boast a maximum of 400 days (details and graph in Michener p. 359).

The Greeks were acquainted with the worker/drone distinction[22] and incorporated it into their metaphors (for the drone metaphor in general see above pp. 5 and 52 and J. Taillardat, *Les Images d'Aristophane*² (Paris 1965) p. 243. For its employment at Plato *Republic* 552C - 573A (a striking passage) see D. Tarrant, *CQ* 40 (1946) 33f.). Even more interesting is the issue of the 'king' (= queen).

The king (= queen)

It is notorious that Greek and Roman writers mistook the sex, as did most others too, the truth only emerging thanks to the Dutch microscopist Jan Swammerdam in 1637-8.[23] T. Hudson-Williams in *CR* 49 (1935) 2ff. usefully assembles the relevant passages from ancient literature. He shows that though the vast majority of writers concur in speaking of 'king bee'; and though Xenophon's *Oeconomicus* is suspect since its references to a 'queen bee' (7.17, 32, 38f.: literally 'female leader of the bees') occur in the context of a comparison with a wife in the home (see above p. 59 and cf. Semonides 7.83ff.W), Aristotle, nevertheless, quotes 'some' as calling the bees' 'rulers' (or 'leaders') 'mothers', 'on the grounds that they bear the bees' (*HA* 553a29) and two passages of the second-century A.D. writer Arrian *(Indike* 8.11; *Epictetus' Discourses* 3.22.99) are most naturally to be

---

[21] Seven years also mentioned in *de resp.* 475a4f.; cf. *Length and Brevity of Life* 466a4ff., 467a4f. (less specific remarks on the bee's longevity).

[22] By analogy Aristotle *HA* 628b1ff. → Pliny *NH* 11.74 describes male *wasps* as 'drones' and contrasts them with 'workers'.

[23] 'His work was not published until 1740 and then only in Dutch and Latin. His findings were disseminated by René Antoine Ferchault de Réaumur in 1741 and in an English translation of Gilles Augustin Bazin, *The Natural History of the Bees* (1744). When John Thorley upheld the new view in 1744, he had to defend it against the opinions of some 'modern writers'; *Melissélogia* or, *The Female Monarchy* (1744), 75' (Thomas, *Man and the Natural World* p. 62 note).

3. Bee/wasp

interpreted as calling the ruling bee *basilissa* the queen. Still, these are isolated passages, and it is hard not to feel that anti-female prejudice[24] has played its part in determining even the views of Aristotle (cf. Byl pp. 304ff. for *prima facie* instances of this prejudice in his zoological works). Byl (p. 342) would similarly explain Aristotle's erroneous statement (*HA* 553b14ff.) that each hive has several[25] 'leaders'[26] and that hives fail either from shortage of leaders or superfluity thereof (leading to factions) as due to an excessively anthropomorphic conception of bees (see above p. 61f.) here tinged with a characteristic leaning to oligarchy. Aristotle does, however, stress that his alleged sufficiency of 'leaders' is required not to avoid anarchy but to generate the bees.

Aristotle was aware (*HA* 626a20ff.) that the queen bee does not use her sting on a human being (cf. Aelian *NA* 1.60: the creature has no sting or does not employ it: a moralising explanation is characteristically appended to the latter alternative: it would be wrong for one who rules and directs so many to do an injury). It is in fact the case that the queen bee's sting has fewer and shorter barbs in comparison with worker bees (the ratio is 2-5:8-11) and is not employed except against rival queens (cf. A. Dietz ap. *Social Insects* 3 (1982: ed. H.R. Hermann) p. 344).

Diseases and infestations of the hive

A list of these is given by Aristotle (*HA* 605b12, 625a6, 626b16ff.; → Pliny *NH* 11.63ff.) most of which can be identified (cf. Singer ap. *Studies in the History and Method of Science* 2 (p.55f.), Thompson ad loc.).

(a) The *klêros* (*HA* 625a6, 626b16). A growth of little worms on the floor of the bee hive; when these develop, a kind of cobweb

---

[24] Compare the Arabic incredulity over the sex of this creature recorded by H. Ingrams, *Arabia and the Isles* (London 1924) p. 174f. ('It is the leader ... and whoever heard of a woman leading an army like that?') For debate over the alleged 'sexism' of Aristotle's biology in general see further M.C. Horowitz, *Journ. Hist. Biol.* 9 (1976) 183ff. and J. Morsink, ib. 12 (1979) 83ff.

[25] Normally there is only one queen to a hive, as first demonstrated by the Frenchman mentioned above (in n. 23) in the year 1740.

[26] The self-same term is used of the *wasps'* queens by Aristotle (*HA* 554b22) but another passage of the *HA* (628b1 → Pliny *NH* 11.73) states that these 'leaders' are also known as 'mothers', which constitutes a correct identification of the sex.

spreads over the whole hive so that the combs decay.

Generally identified as *Trichodes (Clerus) apiarius*, a red and blue beetle which destroys the larvae of the honey bee. But mould is likely to develop on a honeycomb that has been destroyed, no matter what the cause of destruction. On the cobweb see below under (b) and (c).

(b) The *pyraustês* (*HA* 605b11; cf. Aelian *NA* 1.58, below p. 109). A moth (attracted by lighted candles) which engenders insects covered with fine down. It is not stung by bees and can only be removed from the hive by means of fumigation. Galleriidae (esp. *Galleria mellonella* or *cereana* – the familiar 'wax-moth') inhabit and consume hives. The cobweb mentioned under (a) may have been confused with the cocoon of this species.

(c) The *terêdôn* ('borer') (*HA* 605b12). A caterpillar engendered in hives: again the bee does not attack it. Most probably larvae of species of the Galleriidae. Since some of these spin their cocoons into a mass there may be some confusion between this and the cobweb of (a), the fine down of (b).

(d) Lassitude that attacks the bees and produces a malodorous hive (*HA* 626b18). The famous *foul brood* produced by spore-bearing organisms.

Bees conceived as souls

Cf. K. Ranke and J.R. Klíma ap. *Enzyklopädie des Märchens* s.v. Biene (2.305), Stith Thompson, *Motif-Index of Folk-Literature*[2] E734.2, Ransome, Index s.v. 'Bee-souls'. A widespread belief in winged and insect souls (see below pp. 99ff.), was in the case of bees doubtless encouraged by their sudden appearance out of cleft, or (seemingly) carcass (cf. above p. 51). Note too the use of honey in ritual at tombs (cf. Ransome pp. 119ff.; Bodson, *Hiera Zôia* p. 23 n. 95). The neo-Platonic scholar Porphyrius' treatise *The Cave of the Nymphs in the Odyssey* 18[27] (composed in the third century A.D.) interpreted *Odyssey* 13.106

---

[27] For up-to-date text and translation see *Seminar Classics* 609 (State Univ. of New York at Buffalo) *Arethusa* Monographs 1 (1969) p.18.

3. Bee/wasp 65

with its reference to nymphs (see below p. 69) and bees (see above p. 52 n. 13) as alluding to bee souls, and quoted Sophocles *Tr.G.F.* 4 F879 ('The swarm of the dead hums and rises upwards': cf. 'the swarm' of the dead in Aeschylus *Psychagogoi* (*Tr.G.F.* 3 F273A8 Radt)). On this and other relevant passages from Porphyrius cf. Cook, *JHS* 15 (1895) 16f. The reference to a bee in Euripides *Hippolytus* 76 (see below p. 70) is taken as an allegorical allusion to the soul by a scholion (2.14 Schwartz); see also commentators (cf. M. de G. Verrall, *CR* 24 (1910) 44ff.) on Vergil *Aeneid* 6.706ff., which compares the souls of the dead in the Underworld destined to return to life with bees swarming on a summer's day. Various gold or bronze bees found probably or definitely in graves have been identified as tomb decorations intended to symbolise the surviving soul: cf. Cook pp. 1 and 19f. and B.C. Dietrich, *The Origins of Greek Religion* (1974) pp.119ff. on the evidence from Crete and from a south-west Anatolian neolithic burial site whose finds often remind us of what we can infer of Minoan cultic practice. See too the gem mentioned below p. 68f. The picture of the soul leaving the body in the form of bees is an important element in the popular belief considered next.

Bougonia

One of the most interesting notions about bees entertained in antiquity was that they could be generated from the carcass of an ox (*bougonia* means 'birth from an ox'). The most famous treatment of this process occurs at the end of Vergil's *Fourth Georgic* in connection with the story of Aristaeus, the alleged inventor of the practice. For other accounts see Cook, *JHS* 15 (1895) 9f. and A.E. Shipley, *Journ. Phil.* 34 (1918) 100ff., Gow, *CR* 58 (1944) 14f.; cf. Ransome pp. 112ff. In general, an ox was to be beaten to death with clubs (care being taken not to break its skin) and left in a specially constructed building with its orifices plugged and thyme spread about. It is usually supposed that the notion of bees thus generated was Egyptian in origin, spreading to the Greek world in Hellenistic times (whence its absence from Aristotle's works) and arose, like the connection of bees with animal carcasses (cf. Cook p. 18), from a confusion between bee larvae and blow-fly maggots, and between bees and drone-flies which frequent rotting matter (unlike bees, which shun carrion,

66 *Greek Insects*

as Aristotle was aware (*HA* 625b21)). This explanation is due to C.K. Osten-Sacken, *On the Oxen-born bees of the Ancients (Bugonia) and their relation to Eristalis tenax, a two-winged insect* (Heidelberg 1894).[28] Perhaps the phenomenon should not be studied (as it all too often is) in isolation from analogous beliefs such as the generation of beetles from asses' carcasses (see below p. 84f.) and of wasps from horses' (see below p. 77f.). Cf. Servius' note on Vergil *Aeneid* 1.435 (2.207 ed. Harv.): bees from oxen, drones from horses, hornets from mules, wasps from asses. For examples and discussion of similar ideas on the creation of new life from the dead cf. Fraser, *Ptolemaic Alexandria* (Oxford 1972) 1.779, 2.1087.

Myth and legend

For a full account of 'the bee in Greek mythology' see Cook, *JHS* 15 (1895) 1ff.; cf. Ransome pp. 91ff. We give a selection here. According to Columella *de re rustica* 9.2.4, quoting Nicander fr. 94 Schneider, bees were first born in Crete in the time of Saturn. Legend, indeed, frequently associates the insect with this island (Cook p. 2f.).[29] Thus bees are variously connected with Zeus' birth in the Dictaean cave on Crete. (They helped birds feed the infant Zeus in some accounts: see Cook p.3, Ransome p. 93f., R.F. Willetts, *Cretan Cults and Festivals* (1962) pp. 216ff.) Boeus, as preserved by Antonius Liberalis *Metam.* 19, told how four men, having clad themselves in bronze armour as protection against the bees whose honey they meant to steal, found the bronze splitting and falling from their limbs when they caught sight of the cradle and swaddling clothes of Zeus. As a punishment he turned them into birds. A black-figure amphora from Vulci (British Museum B177 : *CVA* 3 III He (datable *c.* 550)) shows the naked intruders stripped of their armour and beset by the bees. (The legend's origins are ingeniously explained

---

[28] See Gil Fernández p.199 and n.5 for other works by this author on the topic and for a list of some scholars who have been convinced. The most sceptical view of Osten-Sacken's theory is that of Fraser pp. 10ff. who objects, for instance, that 'the practical bee-keeper would soon discover that the oxen-born "bees" produced no honey' (p.11). For a brief biography of Baron Karl Robert Romanovich Osten-Sacken see Howard Ensign Evans, *Life on a little-known Planet*[2] (1984) p. 55.

[29] Cf. Jacobsthal, *Greek Pins* p.73: 'The Cretans were fond of bees and their vases swarmed with them.'

3. Bee/wasp

13. Naked men being stung by bees on a black-figure amphora from Vulci, c. 550 B.C. (British Museum B177: *CVA* 3 III He).

by Cook and Willetts as cited above, though the latter (p.216) need not have invoked the bees' dance (see p. 55f. above)). Antonius Liberalis 13 citing Nicander tells the tale of Meliteus son of Zeus, who was reared on nourishment supplied by bees and finally founded a town in Phthia called Melite. (Coins of Melitaea in Phthiotis showing Zeus' head on obverse, a bee on the reverse side probably refer to this legend as Cook p.4 n.21 supposed). Note too Didymus (fr. 14 Schmidt (p.220f.): cf. Cook p.3) on Melisseus King of Crete and his daughter Melissa; and Melissaeus as an epithet of Zeus (Hesychius s.v. (2.644 Latte)). Apart from Zeus and Meliteus, numerous deities and heroes in Greek legend are recorded as having been nurtured on honey or by bees in infancy: they include Dionysus (cf. Apollonius of Rhodes 4.1129ff.) and Iamus (Pindar *Ol.* 6.45ff.).[30] Aristaeus, the alleged inventor both of bee-keeping and of *bougonia* (see above p. 65f.) must be mentioned here of course: for details on him see

---

[30] For world-wide examples of the mythical motif of honey as food for new-born babies see Gaster, *Myth, Legend and Custom in the Old Testament* pp.319, 753f.

68   *Greek Insects*

Cook pp. 10f. and 15f., A.S. Pease's note on Cicero *de natura deorum* 3.45 (2.1065f.), K. Thraede, *Reallexicon für Antike und Christentum* 5.1197. Bees also feature in the 'curiously complex myth' (in Hyginus *fab.* 136) of Polyidus and his restoration to life of Minos' son Glaucus who had fallen into a honey-jar while playing (cf. Cook, *Zeus* 1. p.469 n.7): 'The bees which were kept from entering the wine-bin by the owl apparently symbolise the soul of the deceased endeavouring to regain the body within – an omen which was likely to direct Polyidus' attention to the jars in the bin' (quotations from Cook p.11. For a study of the legend as a whole see A.W. Persson, *The Religion of Greece in Prehistoric Times* (1942) pp.9ff. and Willetts as cited above on p. 66). Several scholars have detected an illustration of some part (or some form) of this myth in a scarab which shows a figure bending over a jar out of which emerges a much smaller figure with a bee

14. Late Etruscan gem (now lost: drawing from Cook, *Zeus* 1. p.469 fig.325) which probably depicted Polyidus resurrecting Glaucus, with bee-soul hovering above the latter: P. Zazoff, *Etruskische Skarabäen* (Mainz-am-Rhein 1968) no.515 (p.155); cf. id., *Die Antiken Gemmen* (Munich 1983) p.16f. and n.47.

3. Bee/wasp

flying over his head. But since the details are not identical there is some uncertainty as to whether it may not represent Hermes summoning forth a soul (see below p. 104, Persson (as cited above) p.19, P. Zazoff, *Archäologische Anzeiger* (1965) 54) or merely adapt that schema to the story of Polyidus. Mnaseas of Patara tells of Peloponnesian nymphs called *melissai* who made mortals abandon cannibalism, wear clothes and use honey. Charon of Lampsacus (*F.Gr.Hist.* 262 F 12) told how a tree nymph agreed to lie with the mortal Rhoecus as a reward on the condition that he sleep with no other woman. A bee was to summon him to her, but when the bee arrived while Rhoecus was playing draughts he spoke to it impatiently and was punished by the nymph (for details and variants see Jacoby ad loc. (pp. 20ff.)). This brings us to bees' association with chastity.

Holiness, purity, chastity

According to Aristotle (*GA* 761a5) 'wasps possess no element of the divine, *unlike the race of bees*'; the notion of bees as divine recurs in, for instance, Vergil *Georgics* 4.219ff., Petronius *Satyricon* 56.6. Pindar fr. 123.10f. Snell calls them 'holy' (fr. 158), Xenophon *Oeconomicus* 7.32 (see above p. 59) says the queen bee carries out the tasks ordained by god. Antiphilus *AP* 9.404.7 = *GP* 1049 calls bees 'pure creatures'. Aristotle (*HA* 535a3, 596b15ff. → Pliny *NH* 11.72) notes their fastidious voiding of excrement far from home and their avoidance of anything unclean: this is elaborated by Callimachus *Hymn to Apollo* 109ff. (see F. Williams ad loc.). A swarm of bees nesting and making honey in a tree renders that tree sacred according to the voice of fable (Perry's Appendix 299: see above p. 5f.). For the notion that such bees gave rise to the ancient idea of bee-nymphs (by analogy with tree-nymphs) see Cook, *JHS* 15 (1895) 15ff. and 19. For some ingenious speculation as to the connection between bees as nymphs in the zoological (see below p. 74) and mythical senses and bees conceived as souls (see above p. 64f.) see Gil Fernández p. 210f; cf. M. Detienne, *QUCC* 12 (1971) 16f. Bees were associated with oracles in Greece and Rome (see S. Scheinberg, *HSCP* 83 (1979) 20): for instance, the second of Apollo's oracles at Delphi was allegedly built by birds and bees out of feathers and wax (Pindar fr. 52, i. 60ff. Snell, Pausanias 10.5.5ff: cf. C. Sourvinou-Inwood, *CQ* 29 (1979) 238ff.).

Priestesses of various female divinities were known as 'bees': on the 'bees' of Demeter see Cook, pp. 14ff., Bodson, *Hiera Zôia* pp. 26ff. and F. Williams on l.110 of Callimachus' *Hymn to Apollo*; on those of Artemis see Cook p. 12f., Bodson pp. 38ff., and R. Fleischer, *Artemis von Ephesos* (Leiden 1973) p. 99f. On the sooth-saying bee-maidens of the *Homeric Hymn to Hermes* see S. Scheinberg, *HSCP* 83 (1979) 1ff., Sourvinou-Inwood, *CQ* 29 (1979) 240ff. The Pythia at Delphi was known as 'the Delphic bee' (Pindar *Pythian* 4.60: see Sourvinou-Inwood p.240).

The chaste Hippolytus in the tragedy by Euripides named after him, offers the similarly chaste hunting-goddess Artemis a garland culled from a virgin meadow through which the spring-time bee passes (l.76). The bee's chastity (partly a product of antiquity's ignorance as to this insect's mode of reproduction) is commented on by Aristotle *HA* 533a11f., 596b15f. and among other authors by, for instance, Vergil *Georgics* 4.197ff. and the author (see above p. 51) of the poem printed in *Collectanea Alexandrina* p.185f., where they are described as 'averse to love'. Bees therefore are irritable towards men who have had intercourse with women, according to Plutarch *Conjugal Precepts* 44 (*moralia* 144D; cf. Columella 9.14.3, *Geoponica* 15.2.15) and punish adultery according to the Latin translation which is all that survives of Plutarch's *Natural Questions* (5.399 Bernardakis = 11.218ff. in the Loeb text) and interprets Theocritus *Id.* 1.106f. in this light. Compare Charon of Lampsacus cited above (p. 69), and cf. M. Detienne, *QUCC* 12 (1971) 7ff., *Les Jardins d'Adonis* (1972) pp. 154ff. ≃ pp. 79ff. (Engl. transl.).[31]

Bees and their connection with poets and poetry

This topic has been made the subject of a monograph by J.H.Waszink, *Biene und Honig als Symbol des Dichters und der Dichtung in der griechisch-römischen Antike* (Rheinisch-Westfälische Akademie der Wissenschaften, Vorträge G 196

---

[31] Compare and contrast the notion that bees do not sting the pure at heart, reported from the Yemen (G.W. Bury, *The Land of Uz* (London 1911) p. 312). Similarly in India there are superstitions concerning the need for abstention from intercourse before taking a bee's nest or its honey (see J.H. Hutton, *The Angami Nagas* (London 1921) p.236 and *The Sema Nagas* (London 1921) p. 72). See further Ransome pp. 174, 236, 285; cf. Thomas, *Man and the Natural World* p.98 n.48, Frazer, *Totemism and Monogamy* 2.411, E. Hoffmann-Krayer, ap. Bächtold-Staübli, *Handwörterbuch des deutschen Aberglaubens* 1.1251.

3. Bee/wasp

(Opladen 1974)). We select some interesting examples.

Poets (especially Pindar) frequently referred to themselves or their poems as 'honey-voiced' or the like (see S. Scheinberg, *HSCP* 83 (1979) 23), and it is not surprising to find poets comparing themselves to bees: so, for instance, Bacchylides *Odes* 10.10, Lucretius *de rerum natura* 3.11, Horace *Odes* 4.2.27ff. Poets compare other poets to bees as well: Aristophanes *Birds* 748ff. (on Phrynichus) is one such, fairly early, example of this; the image may derive from Phrynichus himself (so Fraenkel, *Beob. zu Aristoph.* (1962) p. 209, Lloyd-Jones, *Estudios sobre la Tragedia Griega* (1966) p. 31 n.27); later both Leonidas of Tarentum *AP* 7.13.1f. = *HE* 2563f. and Christodorus *AP* 2.110 refer thus to the poetess Erinna, and Christodorus *AP* 2.69 to Sappho. Sophocles is called a bee by several late writers (see *Tr.G.F.* 4 T 1.88f. with Radt's note ad loc. and T 109-12). See

15. Bees as decorative device on an early Orientalising Cretan hydria (from *Annual of the British School at Athens* 12 (1905/6) p.30, fig.5).

further Waszink and Scheinberg as cited. Similarly, several famous individuals (poets among them) are said to have been nurtured by bees[32] (see A.S. Pease's note on Cicero *de divinatione* 1.78 (p. 228); cf. Cook, *JHS* 15 (1895) 8, Lefkowitz, *Lives of the Greek Poets* p.59 n.12) including Pindar and Plato. Sophocles' tomb is described as frequented by bees in Erucius *AP* 7.36 = *GP* 2262ff. On Plato *Ion* 533Eff. (a famous passage involving poets and bees) see Scheinberg p.25f.

Like the cicadas, therefore, (see below p. 122) bees were connected with the Muses: Aelian (*NA* 5.13) writes of their 'love of song and love of the Muses'; Varro, indeed, calls them the birds of the Muses (*de re rustica* 3.16), and Philostratus has it that the Muses took on the shape of bees when guiding the Athenians to Ionia (*Imagines* 2.8.6; cf. Himerius *Orat.* 59.1 (p.218 Colonna)). They sent bees to feed their favourite the Sicilian herdsman Comatas when he was imprisoned in a wooden chest for two months as punishment for sacrificing his master's goats to the Muses (Theocritus *Id.* 7.78ff., *Syrinx* 3). In this general context we should note a gem showing a woman-headed insect and a lyre; both bee and cicada have been suggested in attempts to specify the non-human section of this composite creature (see Ransome p. 103). For an excellent survey of the rôle of the bee in Greek (especially Cretan) art see Jacobsthal, *Greek Pins* pp. 73ff. For the bee on Greek coins see J. Nivaille, *Cercle d'Études Numismatiques* Bulletin 15.4 (Oct./Dec. 1978) 61ff. and 16.1 (Jan./March 1979) 1ff.

Bembix/bombyx

Listed with *pemphrêdôn* (see below p. 81) as a stinging insect by Epiphanius *Panarion haer.* 41.3 (2.93 Holl), *bembix* is mentioned in the company of the bee (*melissa*) and given the epithet 'mountain-dweller' at Nicander *Ther.* 806 and is also named at id. *Alex.* 183 in similar company and with similar epithet. The scholion on the latter passage (p. 88f. Geymonat), mentioning a variant form *bembis*, identifies it as a wasp-like bee sometimes called *bombyx*; the scholion on the former passage (p.286 Crugnola) says it is black and has a wasp-like sting. *Bombyx* is further known to Pliny *NH* 11.75 as a large

[32] Compare the folk-tale motif of gods and heroes thus reared (see above p. 67).

3. Bee/wasp

Assyrian species of bee or wasp. Hesychius s.v. *bombykes* (1.333 Latte) compares it to the wasp. The attempts at onomatopoeic rendering of the characteristic buzz of the bee are unmistakable (cf. Gil Fernández pp. 131ff., Chantraine s.v. *bombos* (1.184) etc.) but hardly help towards a specific identification. Gow and Scholfield on Nicander *Ther.* think it the same as *bombylios* (see below).

Bombykion[33]

Diminutive form of the preceding. Aristotle *HA* 555a13ff. uses it of mason-bees in the context of a description of various types of comb. This bee makes a pointed nest of clay smeared with spittle in which it lays white larvae in a black membrane. As Thompson observes ad loc., these details fit the *Chalicodoma muraria* except for the pointed (rather than round) nest, in which respect (though in no other) the solitary wasp *Eumenes coarctata* is recalled. A very general use of the word to cover bees, flies, the *kônôps* (see below p. 165) and whatever buzzes is alleged by a scholion on Aristophanes *Clouds* 157 (*Schol. Aristoph.* I.III.2 p.32 Koster).

Bombylios[34]

Aristophanes *Wasps* 107 and Aristotle *HA* 623b12 mention this, the latter stating that it is the largest bee of all (a bumble bee?). Another onomatopoeic word.

Siren (seirên)[35]

Mentioned as a solitary insect that resembles bee or wasp in form at Aristotle *HA* 623b12ff. (cf. fr. 359 Rose) in a list of all insects that construct a honeycomb. To be more precise, Aristotle distinguishes a smaller dun-coloured and a larger black and speckled variety. Solitary wasps (*Eumenes, Synagris*) have been suggested by D'Arcy Thompson, following earlier scholars. Thompson remarks that 'we seem to have *seirênes* for *kêphênes*'

---

[33] Also used of a cocoon (see *LSJ* s.v.).
[34] Also used of a cocoon (see *LSJ* s.v.).
[35] The form *seirêdôn* occurs in a scholion on Homer's *Iliad* 24.253 (5.566 Erbse) and in Ausonius *Id.* 11.20 (Latin): compare such forms as *anthrêdôn* (cf. *anthrênê/tenthrêdôn*) cited below p. 79.

(= drones: see above p. 62) sirens, 'workers' and 'moulders' (see below p. 77); a (corrupt) reference to *kêphênes* follows); cf. Pliny *NH* 11.48f.: *cetera turba cum formam capere coepit, nymphae vocantur, ut fuci seirenes aut cephenes.* Hesychius s.v. *seirên* glosses the word as sometimes referring to bee or bee's house and some type of bird, Suda s.v. *seirên* (4.346 Adler) derives its information from Aristotle while adding the proverb that 'siren announces friend, bee (*melissa*) stranger'. For other references to this proverb see Zenobius *cent.* 32 (4.252) and Bühler ad loc. (p.253f.) who gathers together other allusions and scholars' attempts at explaining the proverb and identifying the insect.

The question of the appropriateness of 'siren' as a name for a bee or wasp is considered by Gil Fernández pp. 215ff., who points out that the correspondence may extend beyond such superficialities as wings. Sirens in Greek mythology were associated with poetry, music and song, but were also variously connected with the dead and their spirits (see e.g. J. Pollard, *Seers, Shrines and Sirens* (1965) pp. 137ff., D.L. Page, *Folktales in Homer's Odyssey* pp. 86ff. (with notes)). The same can be said of bees (see p. 64f. above). Compare, in particular, the ideas that

16. Wasp on a rock crystal scaraboid of the fifth century B.C. (Leningrad, Hermitage Museum 583): Boardman, *Greek Gems* (1970) no.505.

3. Bee/wasp

souls could be conceived as taking the forms both of sirens (cf. Page p. 128 n. 38) and bees (see p. 64f. above).

Wasp (sphêx/vespa)

Etymology: very uncertain. See the detailed discussion in Gil Fernández pp. 29ff. who approves the notion of an original Indo-European *u̯opsâ (whence Latin *vespa*, English *wasp*) which became Greek *hopsê* and then (by metathesis and on analogy with *myrmex* (see above p. 37) on the one hand and *psên* (see below p. 81f.) on the other) *(ho)sphêx*. Cf. Chantraine s.v. (4.1077) for arguments against this approach and for a further survey of attempted explanations.

We place wasps here partly for structural reasons (see above p. xi), but also because Greek literature often associates them with bees (e.g. *Iliad* 12.167ff., where the Greeks on the defensive are compared to wasps or bees protecting their young; Aristotle *HA* 622b20 (both types of insect industrious)) and sometimes confuses them (e.g. Aristophanes *Wasps* 1116 and *Lysistrata* 475 (in the first passage[36] wasps are said to produce honey), Philostratus Iun. *Imag.* 13.3 (bees associated with a wasp's comb)), or is at least indifferent to the distinction.[37]

Irascibility

The main feature that fixed itself in the consciousness of antiquity was the wasp's ferocity and readiness to sting when angered.[38] These characteristics are already presupposed by a memorable simile in Homer's *Iliad* (16.259ff.) where 'the Myrmidons are compared with wasps which make their nests on the roadside, and which the children often irritate to such an extent, that if an unsuspecting passer-by happens to go near and rouse them, they fall on him and sting him' (the paraphrase comes from J. Th. Kakridis, *Hermes* 88 (1960) 250ff. ≃ *Homer*

---

[36] MacDowell's note ad loc. emphasises that we should not necessarily infer that Aristophanes thought these insects identical: 'He was more interested in composing a striking metaphor than in observing entomological precision'.

[37] For wasps regarded as degenerate forms of bees, see Plutarch *On Having Many Friends* 7 (*moral.* 96B), Lucian, *Charon* 15 (2.15 Macleod); Tertullian *adv. Marc.* 4.5.3 (2.270 Evans).

[38] It is perhaps surprising that Aesop's fables have so little to say of this aspect of the wasp; but see above p. 4 n. 14.

Revisited (Lund 1971) pp. 138ff. who aptly explains the simile's details and defends its integrity against earlier ill-considered criticism). The same idea is inherent in later metaphors which represent the aggressive poet as a wasp (so Callimachus fr. 380.2 Pf. and Gaetulicus in *AP* 7.71 = *FGE* 197ff. of Archilochus; Philip of Thessaly *AP* 7.405.4 = *GP* 2864 and Leonidas of Tarentum *AP* 7.408.2 = *HE* 2326 of Hipponax; cf. Antisthenes fr. 139 Caizzi of the surly cynic philosopher Diogenes). Alexander Pope was called 'the wild wasp of Twickenham'.

This line of thought receives its fullest and most effective manifestation in Aristophanes' comedy the *Wasps* (produced 422 B.C.), so called after its chorus of elderly Athenian jurors who display their waspish nature when roused, especially in their treatment of enemies and miscreants (see esp. ll. 222ff.; 404ff., esp. 420 and 430; 1101ff.; on all these passages see D. MacDowell's commentary (Oxford 1971) ad locc. and his summary p.11. See further G.M. Sifakis, *Parabasis and Animal Choruses* (London 1971) p.128 n.15, Taillardat, *Les Images d' Aristophane*² p.210f. for this aspect of the wasp in this play and Greek thought in general). Like many modern tongues, ancient Greek had the saying 'stir up a wasp's nest' meaning 'bring trouble on oneself': see Pausanias Atticistes, s.v. (Erbse, *Untersuchungen zu den Attizistischen Lexika* (1950) p.210 and Erbse ad loc.), Pearson on Sophocles *Tr.G.F.* 4 F 778 Radt (3.28).

Nuisance value

This reputation for anger and belligerence was not altogether undeserved. It was known in antiquity that wasps will attack bees (Aristotle *HA* 626a8, Pliny *NH* 11.61, Aelian *NA* 1.58, 5.11, Quint. Smyrn. 11.146ff. etc.) and flies ([Callisthenes] 2.16.2 (p.85 Kroll)). Even worse could happen: Aelian *NA* 11.28 reports how whole human populations were driven from their place of habitation by swarms of the brutes; compare Philo *de praemiis et poenis* 96 on certain passages in the Old Testament which he interprets in a similar way. Fruits such as grapes were also liable to attack by wasps (cf. Pliny *NH* 15.67, *Geoponica* 4.10; for sprinkling with oil (supposedly fatal to wasps) as an alleged remedy see Sextus Empiricus *Pyrrh.* 1.55).

Nicander *Ther.* 811ff. has a list of remedies for the stings and bites of these and other creatures. Other remedies are mentioned

3. Bee/wasp

by (among others) Pliny, especially in *NH* 23 (cf. 43, 198 etc.); for a full list see W. Richter in *RE* Suppl. 15 (1978) 907.

Achilles Tatius 2.7.2 mentions Egyptian incantations meant to still the pain from stings of wasps and bees. Aristotle (*HA* 627b → Pliny *NH* 11.73f.) ranks the stings of the 'wild wasp' (*agrios sphêx*, see below p. 79) as particularly painful; he claims that the 'leaders' (see above p. 63 n. 24) probably do possess stings but do not use them (cf. Aelian *NA* 5.16: the wasps' king stingless and docile), but that the male wasps (see above p. 62 n. 22) have no sting and all wasps shed stings in winter (the last two details are quite erroneous).

Aristotle further says that wasps (and bees) have their sting inside (*HA* 532a15f., *PA* 683a8). According to Aelian *NA* 5.15f. wasps obtain their poisonous sting by drawing up the venom from dead vipers. The same writer assures us (*NA* 9.15; cf. Pliny *NH* 11.28) that if a wasp happens to have tasted a viper's flesh its sting becomes fiercer. This cannot fail to remind us of the statement in [Aristotle] *Marvels Heard* 8(844b): wasps on the island of Naxos eat adders and therefore sting worse than those snakes.

Social life (cf. above p. 59f.)

On the growth and construction of a wasps' colony from an original small nest of four cells see Aristotle *HA* 627 → Pliny *NH* 11.71ff. Wasps' combs are described by Aristotle (*HA* 554b25ff. simplified by Pliny *NH* 11.71ff.) as located in holes or (when they have a 'leader' (see above p. 63 n. 24) – a strange distinction) below ground; hexagonal, of bark-like, netted material. The brood is placed within it and one finds them in the respective cells at different stages of development (larval, pupal, or developed enough to fly), for the leaders do not produce their offspring all at one time. The emerging adult must break through the sealed cell (cf. *HA* 551a29ff.).

Reproduction

It was widely believed that wasps breed in horses' carcasses: see Aelian *NA* 1.28 (naively adding that the swiftest animal has winged offspring), Pliny *NH* 11.70, Archelaus (the various sources are collected in Page, *FGE* p.22), Nicander *Ther.* 740: see Gow-Scholfield on the latter passage for other authors who quote

17. Flying wasp (above reclining half-nude woman who pets a heron) on a chalcedony scaraboid (*Brit. Mus. Cat.* 531); for the insect's shape and identification, see frontispiece caption.

Nicander for the idea. Compare pp. 66 above and 84f. below. More scientifically, Aristotle *GA* 761a2ff. allows that unlike the bee (see above p. 70) they reproduce sexually, though he expresses bafflement (*HA* 551a29ff., *GA* 759a1ff.) as to how the larvae receive the food which their excrement presupposes. He was ignorant, then, as to their feeding by workers.

Miscellanea

Foxes' stratagem for raiding wasps' nests after disposing of inhabitants by means of their bushy tails (Aelian *NA* 4.39).

Wasps to be caught by luring them with smelt, sprat, minnow or sardine as bait in cage (Aelian *NA* 1.58); to be smoked out if troublesome (Euripides *Cyclops* 475; Aristophanes *Wasps* 457, Lycophron 181f.).

Swarms of wasps in autumn portend the onset of winter storms ([Theophrastus] *de sign.* 47, Aratus *Phaenomena* 1064ff.). Of wasps themselves only the leader (see above p. 63 n. 26) survives the winter (Aristotle *HA* 628a3ff. →Pliny *NH* 11.73 correctly: various types of wasp hibernate in hollows and holes).

An interesting vase-painting that depicts a wasp is illustrated and discussed by H.P. Laubscher, *Archäologische Anzeiger* (1966) 488ff.

Agrios and *hêmerôteros* ('fierce' and 'gentle') are distinguishing epithets applied to differing types of *sphêx* in *HA* 627b22ff. 'Fierce' probably identifies the *hornet* (this type of wasp is characterised as rarer, bigger, darker and fiercer and connected with hills and hollow trees) as e.g. Thompson ad loc. supposes. 'Hornet' is still sometimes seen as a rendering of the word *anthrênê* also used by Aristotle. But *sphêx* is not always distinguished from *anthrênê* by this author (though see e.g. *HA* 554b22ff.) or most others, and a closer examination of the word will reveal further arguments against the rendering.

Anthrênê/anthrêdôn[39]

For the two forms cf. *tenthrênê/tenthrêdôn* (see below p. 82). Hesychius s.v. *anthrêdôn* (1.178 Latte) actually glosses that word with *tenthrêdôn* (cf. below p. 82) The word's etymology is a complex question – see the detailed discussion by Gil Fernández pp. 73ff. hazarding a derivation from the root that expresses such concepts as point (→ sting) whence such words as *antherix* ('beard or ear of corn'), *athêr* ('barb of a weapon'). For the ending cf. *tenthrêdôn, pemphrêdôn*. A full description in Aristotle *HA* 628b tells us that they differ from bees by virtue of not culling from flowers but rather subsisting by and large on animal food. They therefore hover about dung, chase big flies there until they catch them, then cut off their heads and fly off with the rest of the carcasses. D'Arcy W. Thompson (ap. *The Legacy of Greece* p.152 ≏ *Die Naturphilosophie des Aristoteles* p. 17f.) compared the similar remarks made by Henri Fabre (*Souvenirs entomologiques* (Paris 1.241)) on a large wasp of South Europe which captures big 'taons' or horse-flies: 'pour donner le coup de grâce à leur Taons mal sacrifiés, et se débattant encore entre les pattes du ravisseur, j'ai vu des Bembex mâchonner la tête et le thorax des victimes.' In his note on the relevant passage of Aristotle

---

[39] The form *anthêdôn* preserved in lexiocographers s.v. (Hesychius (1.177 Latte), Et.Gud. (1.146 de Stefani: see his note ad loc. for other such references)) who gloss it as bee (cf. p.75), Aelian *NA* 15.1 (who mentions it in the company of the bee and the wasp), and other writers, is probably (see Gil Fernández pp. 73ff.) a mere variant, prompted by the popular etymological derivation from *anthê* and *edein* ('to eat flowers') mentioned in some of the aforesaid lexica.

(n.2) Thompson observes that one would indeed normally identify Aristotle's insect with this *Bembex rostrata* which buries its gad-fly victims in sandy soil, save that such an animal is solitary, whereas Aristotle proceeds to equip his *anthrênai* with larger 'leaders' (on the analogy of 'bee-kings') and describes their underground nests. He has, Thompson concludes, confused *Bembex* with a similar common species (unless he is describing a now lost species).

At *HA* 554b23ff. Aristotle distinguishes *anthrênai's* practice in making combs for their brood from that of wasps: *anthrênai* make theirs high up, and they are much neater than those of the wasps. In the cells, near the brood, is a drop of honey. The eggs and grubs cling to the side wall, the larvae emerge in autumn. The detail as to neatness of nest led Thompson ad loc. to identify the creature with *Polistes*. Certainly *anthrênê* here seems to mean something different to what it does in the first passage cited.

Dellis-ithos

Explained by Hesychus s.v. *dellithes* (1.416 Latte) as 'wasps or like a bee'.[40] Gil Fernández p.73 would ultimately derive the name from *belonê* or *obelos* (dialect form *odelos*) meaning 'dart, point'. Cf. G.P. Shipp, *Modern Greek Evidence for the Ancient Greek Vocabulary* (1979) p.209 for the survival of the word *dellis* in some Southern European dialects.

Ichneumon wasp

Mentioned by Aristotle *HA* 552b26ff. and *HA* 609a5(→ Pliny *NH* 10. 204, 11. 72). The real ichneumon was an Egyptian quadruped (cf. Lloyd's note on Herodotus 2.67 (2.302)) which, according to Aelian *NA* 10.47, being both male and female, compelled its vanquished enemy to bear its offspring. It is not, then, hard to see why the name should be applied to wasps which, in Aristotle's account, kill spiders and carry off their corpses to a wall or other place equipped with a hole: for they smear the hole with mud and produce grubs inside, and (though Aristotle does

---

[40] The latter definition recurs in the grammarian Herodian (see Lentz's Index to *Grammatici Graeci* III.II s.v. *dellis* (p. 1020)) who also says it means a small wasp.

3. Bee/wasp

not specifically state this) it is clear that they lay their eggs in the bodies of the spiders. The solitary wasps of the families Pompilidae and Sphecidae so provision their nests with insects or spiders in whose living bodies they lay their eggs. The *Pelopaeus* (*Sceliphron*) *spirifex*, from Southern Europe, behaves in a way very similar to that described by Aristotle, as D'Arcy Thompson observes in his note ad loc., and is particularly fond of building nests in human habitations.

Kentrinês

A type of *psên* (see below p. 81f.) which is as lazy as the drone and kills the *psênes* entering the figs, thus bringing about its own death according to Theophrastus *HP* 2.8.2 → Pliny *NH* 17.255.

The name is derived from *kentron* ('sting'): cf. Strömberg p.9. At Aelian *NA* 9.11 (cf. 1.55, 6.51) the MSS display some confusion, with *kentritês* appearing by mistake. On the form see further G. Redard, *Les noms grecs en -TÊS/-TIS* (Paris 1949) p.9.

Pemphrêdôn

Mentioned in the company of the *ioulos*[41] (millipede?), the wasp and the *skolopendra* at Nicander *Ther.* 812 where it is given the epithet 'small' and at id. *Alex.* 183 (together with assorted bees and wasps). The scholion on the latter passage (p. 88 Geymonat) says that it is a wasp-like creature, larger than ant, smaller than bee, which is black and white in colour and nests in hollow oaks. Some sort of tree wasp seems indicated, especially since Epiphanius mentions it as a stinging insect (cf. above p. 72).

If we can accept the hypothesis (cf. Gil Fernández p.129, Chantraine s.v. (3.880)) of an original **per-phrê-dôn*, the name could be explained as an example of 'expressive reduplication' (see below p. 114), meant to convey the insect's repeated buzz.

Psên

Etymology: see Gil Fernández p. 117. Connections have been sought with such Greek verbs as *psan*, *psêkhein* within the

---

[41] On which creature see J. Scarborough, *Pharmacy in History* 21 (1979) 18, *Class. Phil.* 75 (1980) 138ff.

sphere of meaning 'rub down', but the word remains a mystery. Herodotus 1.193.4-5, in the context of a description of Babylonian agriculture, has cause to describe the culture of date-palms which he compares with the culture of fig-trees in Greece. Unfortunately this comparison leads him into erroneously stating that the gall-wasp is involved in the pollination of date-palms: he alleges that the fruit of those palms which the Greeks call male are tied to the fruit-bearing palms so that the gall-wasp will enter the fruit and ripen it. In fact, date palms are pollinated by wind: it is the fig-tree in whose pollination the wasp is involved. The facts are lucidly summarised by Laura Georgi, *Class. Phil.* 77 (1982) 224ff.

The insect's pollination of the fig-tree, hinted at by Aristotle (*HA* 557b25ff.), is described by Theophrastus (*HP* 2.8.1ff.; cf. *CP* 2.9, 3.18): 'gall-insects' come out of the wild figs hanging there, eat the tops of the cultivated figs and thus make them swell. Figs thus treated are red, parti-coloured and stout; untreated are pale and sickly. The passage contains two erroneous statements: (1) that these insects are engendered from the seeds, the proof alleged being that when they emerge no seeds remain in the fruit and in the process of emerging a leg or wing is generally left behind; (2) that with both fig and date the 'male' aids the 'female' (i.e. the fruit-bearing tree) but while the fig exhibits a union of the two sexes, the palm effects its result differently.

On the creature's emergence from its larval stage's husk see Aristotle *HA* 557b26ff. → Pliny *NH* 11.117: cf. 15.80.

Tenthrênê/tenthrêdôn

For the two forms cf. *anthrênê/anthrêdôn* (above p. 79). Nicander *Alex.* 547 has *tenthrênê* which he uses prima facie as a synonym for a bee. Aristotle *HA* 629a31 has the second form used of a species of wasp or bee similar to the *anthrênê* but speckled.[42] Hesychius s.v. *tenthrêdôn* uses the word of a wild bee. Consistently with the etymologising of *pemphrêdôn* above, Gil Fernández p.129 postulates an original *ter-thrê-dôn* to convey the buzzing drone of the creature.

The rhetorical writer Demetrius (*de elocutione* 304) quotes Clitarchus, a third-century historian of Alexander the Great,

---

[42] Cf. Dioscorides *de nat. med.* 5. 109.4 (3.81 Wellmann).

4. Beetle/cockchafer

18. Two-winged beetle on a carnelian scarab (Vienna, Kunsthistorische Museum 207): E. Zwierlein-Diehl, *Die Antiken Gemmen des Kunsthistorischen Museums in Wien* 1 (Munich 1973) no.9 (p.34).

(*F.Gr.Hist* 137 T10 = F14) as having described a type of *tenthrêdôn* found in Hyrcania by the Caspian Sea. According to Demetrius this creature, similar to the bee and given to roaming mountains and flying into hollow oaks, received from Clitarchus an exaggerated treatment more appropriate to a wild bull or the Erymanthian boar (Hyrcanian *tigers* were notoriously savage (cf. Shakespeare's *Henry VI Part 3* 1.4.155, *Hamlet* 2.2.446, *Macbeth* 3.4.101, all deriving from Vergil *Aen.* 4.367)). Diodorus Siculus 17.75.7 in a passage deriving from Clitarchus has a description of a honey-producing creature smaller than the bee which he calls the *anthrêdôn* (cf. p. 79). See L. Pearson, *The Lost Histories of Alexander the Great* (1960) p. 220.

4. BEETLE/COCKCHAFER
Kantharos/mêlolonthê

Ancient writers are not particularly careful to distinguish these, and the two relevant Greek words can be used to gloss each other (see e.g. scholia on Aristophanes *Clouds* 763 (*Schol. Ar.* 1.III.1 p.

159 and 1.III.2 p. 114 Koster)).

Dung beetle (kantharos/Scarabaeus pilularius)

The ancient etymology[43] which derives the word from *kanthôn* ('ass') has been dismissed with contempt by several modern scholars but is taken seriously (at least as a pejorative or humorous usage) by so good a scholar as Strömberg p. 10f. who points to the ancient belief that beetles were produced from asses (see below p. 84f.).[44] Gil Fernández pp. 226ff. surveys the various other explanations advanced and ends (p. 227) by approving Strömberg's. An alternative ancient etymology brought in the word *thoros* (= semen). According to both Plutarch *Isis and Osiris* 74 (*moralia* 381A) and Aelian *NA* 10.15, the creature has no female and pours its semen into a heap of dung which it then rolls up and keeps warm. After twenty-eight days the young emerge. (Hence the wearing of scarabs engraved on their finger rings by Egyptian warriors as a sign of masculine valour, say Aelian at the end of his account and Plutarch *Isis and Osiris* 10 (*moralia* 355A): see J. Gwyn Griffiths' note on the latter passage (p. 289) for the real (religious) significance of such emblems). The *Suda* s.v. *kantharos* (3.25 Adler) also has this explanation of the word.[45] The error presumably arose from this beetle's habit of laying eggs in the ball of dung.

Reproduction

The notion (cf. above) that beetles are produced from the bodies of asses (so, for instance, Pliny *NH* 11.70, Origen *contra Celsum* 4.57 and 59) that are decaying (Plutarch *Life of Agis and Cleomenes* 29.3) has parallels (see above p. 77f.). Compare the fable of the wolf and the beetle which is no. 659 in Perry's Appendix ('While a wolf was sleeping in a cave, a beetle crawled into his hind end, and he woke up in no little pain. After he had rolled around on the ground for a long while the beetle came out by the way he had entered') and the beetle's alleged preference

---

[43] So e.g. the *Suda* s.v. *kantharos* (3.25f. Adler), scholion on Aristophanes *Peace* 82 (*Schol. Ar.* II.II p. 23 Holwerda), Origen *contra Celsum* 4.57 and 59.

[44] *Onos* ('ass') was the name for a type of winged *trôxallis* according to Dioscorides (see above p. 29 n. 81) which provides a parallel of sorts.

[45] The lack of a female sex and the injection of semen recur in Clement of Alexandria *Strom.* 5.4 (2.339f. Stählin). Stählin's note ad loc. lists other late writers who have these details.

4. Beetle/cockchafer

for asses' dung (cf. *Suda* s.v. *kantharos* (3.25 Adler)).

Aristotle (*HA* 552a17ff. → Pliny *NH* 11.98) describes how it rolls dung into a ball, hides away therein during winter, and produces its larvae in it (cf. Aelian *NA* 10.15). Henri Fabre was the first to show (in the work mentioned above p. x) the accuracy of this observation for several species of dung beetle though not for *Scarabaeus sacer*. D'Arcy-Thompson ad loc. detected a reference to the female's protection of her offspring to maturity (a characteristic of *Copris* species).

How to kill a beetle

[Aristotle] *Marvels Heard* 147 (845b), Aelian *NA* 1.38, 6.46, Theophrastus *CP* 6.5.1; Aelian *NA* 4.18 and Pliny *NH* 11.279 say that perfumes or roses kill beetles; Clement of Alexandria *Paed.* 2.8 (1.197 Stählin) says that oil of roses will work too. [Aristotle] *Marvels Heard* 120 (184a) → Pliny *NH* 11.99 tells of a place in Thracian Chalcidice near Olynthus called *Cantharolethrus* ('beetle-slayer') which, though no bigger than a threshing floor, causes those beetles that enter it to fly round and round compulsively until they perish of hunger. (The tale recurs in Plutarch *Quiet of Mind* 15 (*moral.* 473E), Strabo 7 fr.30, Antigonus of Carystus *mirab.* 14 (p. 4 Keller)).

The first of these modes of killing obviously presupposes an antipathy of opposites (similar to that revealed in the notion (cf. Thompson, *Greek Birds* p.84) that the carrion-loving vulture is repelled by the scent of myrrh, or Yeats' poetic fancy ('*Coole Park and Ballylee, 1931*') of a swan 'So arrogantly pure, a child might think It can be murdered with a spot of ink'). Related but less extreme is the idea that dung beetles hate (Plutarch *moral.* 710E, 1058A, 1096A, Artemidorus *Oneirocr.* 2.22(p. 139f. Pack), Sextus Empiricus *Pyrrh* 1.55) or are harmed (Theophrastus *de odoribus* 4) by sweet smells, and will reject honey, even if it is poured before them (Dio Chrysostom *orat.* 32.98). Hence the proverb (cf. R. Strömberg, *Greek Proverbs* (Göteborg 1954) p. 20)) 'a beetle will produce honey sooner than you will produce anything good'. For the adoption of the idea in English literature see P. Ansell Robin, *Animal Lore in English Literature* (London 1932) p. 113f. The question of their diet is best considered in detail in connection with our next item.

Etnean dung-beetle (Aitnaios kantharos)

The beetle on which Trygaeus flies to Olympus in Aristophanes' *Peace* is identified as this by one of Trygaeus' slaves at 1.73. The scholion on this passage (*Schol. Ar.* II.2 p.20 Holwerda) is our main source of ancient information on this insect. It quotes various ancient writers, either comic poets or authors of satyr plays:

Epicharmus' *Heracles* (fr. 76 Kaibel): 'The leader of the Pygmies <leapt from the chariot drawn by one> of those large dung-beetles which they say Etna rears.'

Aeschylus' satyr play *Sisyphus the Stone-roller* (*Tr.G.F.* 3 F233 Radt): 'It is an Etnean dung-beetle toiling violently.'

Sophocles' satyr play *Daedalus* (*Tr.G.F.* 4 F162 Radt): 'Well, he certainly isn't a beetle, not even an Etnean one.'

Plato Comicus fr. 37 (1.610 K) in *Feasts (Heortai)*: 'How big Mt. Etna is said to be you can judge from the fact that the saying goes there are beetles there no smaller than a man.' (The word used here for 'beetle' is *kantharis* (see below p. 92)).

Sophocles' satyr play *The Trackers* (*Ichneutae*: *Tr.G.F.* 4 F 314.307 Radt) also mentions a horned Etnean beetle.[46] Note besides the tetradrachm from Etna now in Brussels (Collection de Hirsch 269 [our Fig. 19]: full description in Jenkins, *Ancient Greek Coins* p. 147) and dating c. 470/465 which shows on one side a head of Silenus with a beetle below it: the inscription runs *AITNAION*. For an excellent survey and analysis of the literary evidence see Fraenkel, *Beobachtungen zu Aristophanes* (Rome 1962) pp. 53ff. who clears away the misconceptions of earlier scholars, reminds us that Aeschylus is known to have visited Sicily and Etna,[47] and reaches the unavoidable conclusion that whatever the real size of the beetles that scrambled about the crags of Mt. Etna, mainland Greeks, from the first third of the

---

[46] And the phrase is proverbial according to lexicographers (e.g. Hesychius s.v. (4.408 Latte)): cf. Köhler p. 99.

[47] See Aesch. *Tr.G.F.* 3 TK 88ff. Radt, C.J. Herington, *JHS* 87 (1967) 74ff. esp. 82ff.

4. Beetle/cockchafer

19. Beetle and head of Silenus on a Sicilian tetradrachm (obverse), c. 470/465 B.C. (Brussels: Collection de Hirsch 269).

fifth century onwards, could refer to the vast size and dimensions of these insects as an established and familiar idea. He also cites the above-mentioned coin as evidence not, of course, for the insect's relative size, but for its status as an instantly recognisable symbol of Etna at the relevant time: Jenkins states that 'it seems likely that this outstanding coin was minted towards the end of the period of Hieron's Etna', and confirms that 'the beetle stands for the typical local fauna of Mt. Etna'. The other side of the coin shows Zeus Aetnaeus enthroned, and his bird, the eagle, perched on a pine-tree: Head, *Historia Numorum* (1911) p.132 had already recognised this latter as a local symbol and remarked that vines too grew prolifically in the vicinity of Etna (hence the head of Silenus). The beetle thus fits perfectly.

Fraenkel explicitly resigned the question whether such insects really existed 'to the entomologist'. Entomology can at least resolve one issue raised by Aristophanes' play.

G. Halffter and E.G. Matthews, *The Natural History of Dung Beetles of the Subfamily Scarabaeinae (Coleoptera, Scarabeidae)* in *Folio Entomologica Mexicana* 12/14 (1966) have much useful information on the creature. Coprophagy (the consumption of dung) is indeed the fundamental feature of their biology and in Mediterranean towns several varieties exhibit a preference for human excrement (p.17) because 'the degree of plasticity of the excrement food ... is a very important factor affecting behaviour toward it'[48] and human excrement 'is generally more pasty' (p.93). Aristophanes' jokes about the beetle eating only carefully prepared excrement that has been rubbed and kneaded into shape (ll. 4ff., 27f.), even the claim that it prefers excrement from boys who have been buggered because it will be better moulded (l.10f.; compare the joke about Zeus' bed-fellow Ganymede in l. 724) are not, then, so totally fantastic. Likewise the numerous remarks when Trygaeus has mounted his 'steed' as to its scenting dung on the ground: for these insects 'olefaction is the dominant sense' with visual and auditory stimuli very little, if at all, developed (Halffter and Matthews p.87) and 'food-search behaviour ... is carried out on the wing, as a rule' (p.88; cf. p.91) with antennae the principal organs of chemoreception over long distances.

The slaves' account of the beetle's eating habits, however, is problematical, not least because in reality the dung is made into a ball, rolled overground and buried intact: it is only consumed (or made into a nest) underground. Yet we receive from the two slaves a most vivid and vigorous account of how the beetle 'snatches up the kneaded dung, turns it round with its two feet and then wolfs it down' (ll. 6ff.), and later of how it 'bows its head like a wrestler, moving its molars from side to side and swinging round its head and both hands like rope-makers plaiting ropes for ships' (ll. 34ff.). Much of this is comic fantasy, of course, and the interchangeability of feet and hands in the two passages hardly encourages us to look for close zoological accuracy (compare Dover's note on Aristophanes' *Clouds* 145). Those scholars who consider the matter at all[49] have explained

---

[48] 'Moist and soft' dung is mentioned as desirable for a beetle in an Aesopic fable (Perry's Appendix no. 84).

[49] So, for instance, B.B. Rodgers in his commentary ad loc. (London 1867), followed by Platnauer in his commentary (Oxford 1964) p. 67; cf. Sommerstein's recent commentary (1985) p. 136.

4. Beetle/cockchafer

ll. 6ff. as referring to the use of the hindmost pair of legs to roll the dung-ball back to the beetle's underground abode. But this process (for a detailed description of which see Halffter and Matthews p. 108f.) is not very similar to what Aristophanes' slaves describe, and why should it be confused with eating? On the other hand, the ball-making process, as described by Halffter and Matthews (p. 102f.), has two phases. In the first (that of cutting) 'the beetle places itself on top of the dung, bends the forebody down so that head and fore tibiae cut into the mass, and then proceeds to execute three simultaneous movements: a bending and unbending of the fore body in relation to the hind body, a back-and-forth movement of the fore tibiae toward and away from the head, and a rotation of the whole body about the vertical axis. In this way the beetle pivots about in a circle and rapidly builds up a mass of dung beneath itself.' In the second phase (that of shaping) 'the crude ball is converted to a more or less perfect sphere by repeated patting of its surface with the fore tibiae and by trimming with the head and tibiae'. Either of these phases could be mistaken for the process of eating, and the former in particular seems quite close to what Aristophanes describes at ll. 34ff.

Chrysokantharos

'Golden beetle': a word used to gloss *mêlolonthê* by scholia on Aristophanes *Clouds* 763 (*Schol. Ar.* 1.III.1 p. 159 and 1.III.2 p. 114 Koster). This may represent no more than an arbitrary guess based on the other striking reference to this type of insect in Aristophanes, *Wasps* 1341 where a flute girl is called a 'golden cockchafer' (*chrysomêlolonthê*: see the next entry). Note in this context that the other instance of the word preserved by *LSJ* s.v. is feminine: *chrysokantharis*. The very existence of the word (and the insect) is therefore in doubt.

Mêlolonthê

For the different forms (*mêlolonthê*, *mêlolanthê*, *mêlonthê* etc.) offered by the ancient grammarians see J. Taillardat's edition of Suetonius' *peri paidiôn* (Paris 1967) p.39f. Etymology: extremely problematical. Strömberg pp.5ff. has a detailed account of the question. He prefers to explain it as *mêl-olonthê*[50] from *mêlon* ('sheep': an animal that grazes) and *olonthos* ('wild fig'), comparing, for the principle of words constructed from two separate nouns, hippo-potamus (cf. *kyna-muia* considered below p. 155) and similar insect names in other European tongues (*'cow-lady'*, an English name for the lady-bird) and supposes that the name originally applied to an insect that lived on wild figs and was later extended. He compares Theocritus *Id.* 5.114f. (mention of a beetle that nibbles figs and can fly)[51] a passage also cited by Gossen, *Sudhoffs Archiv für Geschichte der Medizin und der Naturwissenschaften* 30 (1938) 322 who independently refers it to the *mêlolonthê* and notes that Theocritus could not have worked that actual name into an hexameter.

Aristotle *HA* 552a16ff. says that *mêlolonthai* come from larvae found in the dung of oxen and asses: this probably refers to the dung beetle.

Treating these insects as pets or part of a game

The practice of tethering them by a thin thread and letting them buzz, is implied by two passages in Aristophanes (*Clouds* 763, *Wasps* 1341) and one in Herodas (12.2),[52] specifically stated by scholia on the Aristophanic lines (*Clouds*: *Schol. Ar.* 1.III.1 p.158 and 1.III.2 p. 114 Koster; *Wasps: Schol. Ar.* II.1 p. 212 Koster). See too *Suda* s.v. *mêlolonthê* (3.386 Adler).

Chrysomêlolonthê

'Golden cockchafer': implied by the scholion on Aristophanes *Wasps* 1341b (*Ar. Schol.* II.1 p. 213 Koster) to be the word of which that verse's *chrysomêlolonthion* is the diminutive used by an amorous old man of a flute girl. 'Beetle' was once used as a similar term of endearment in German ('ein netter Käfer'); cf. Shakespeare's *Romeo and Juliet* 1.3.3 (Nurse to Juliet): 'What,

---

[50] Eustathius *Il.* 1329.25 oddly states that *mêlonthê* (an abbreviated or 'dissimilated' form) is the Attic version: cf. Gil Fernández p. 231 nn. 15 and 16.

[51] Gow ad loc. (2.112) suggests that Theocritus is referring to the *kantharis* (see below p. 92).

[52] Misunderstood by Cunningham ad loc. who talks of young boys 'releasing [insects] so that the thread comes off as they fly', a pointless procedure which is not, in fact, suggested by the available evidence.

4. Beetle/cockchafer

lamb. What, ladybird.'

For the use of beetles and cockchafers as pets see above p. 90. 'Golden' or 'with gold wings' add the scholia, and such a beetle as *Melontha aurata* has been seriously suggested as the object of the reference (compare, e.g. Gossen, *RE* Suppl. 8. (1956) 237, 241). Note, however, that in Greek and Latin writers the adjective 'golden' is 'a lover's word' (Nisbet and Hubbard on Horace *Odes* 1.5.9) used of the object of affection without necessarily conveying a literal statement as to colour. Gil Fernández p. 101f. likewise supposes we have here 'un neologismo acuñado por el cómico, con el fin de provocar la hilaridad del auditorio', though he thinks in terms of a humorous crossing of *mêlolonthê* with *chrysokantharos*.

Bouprêstis

The name is derived from the noun *bous* and the verb *pimpranai* (cf. *prêstês*, fem. *prêstis*) and means 'cow-inflater', an insect that lurks amid the grass where it is inadvertently swallowed by grazing cattle which then swell up and burst. The toxic substance responsible for this can also be brewed into a concoction of the same name. Our main source for this creature is Nicander *Alex.* 335ff. Scholia ad loc. (p.128 Geymonat) identify it with the *staphylinos* (grape-beetle) mentioned by Aristotle *HA* 604b19 as similarly injuring horses. Other sources too connect it with various types of beetle: Pliny *NH* 30.30 says it is like a scarab-beetle with long legs; Dioscorides (see below) says it is a type of beetle; Galen 19.89 (*Exegesis of Hippocratic words*) and Dioscorides *de mat. medicin.* 2.61.1 both claim that it is a type of or like the *kantharis* (see below p. 92). On the other hand Galen elsewhere (19.726 (*Synonyms*)) says it looks like a cockroach or leech; and Vegetius (*Mulomedicina* 2.142) says it looks like a spider. For other mentions of it in Antiquity and for modern attempts at identification see Gow-Scholfield on the Nicandrian line and J. Scarborough, *Pharmacy in History* 21 (1979) 20f. (with notes). The latter approves the identification with *Meloe variegatus* Donov. (a blister beetle) made by Gossen (*RE* s.v. Käfer (10 (1919) 1480) and others, on the grounds that it has a good deal of cantharidin in its elytra, and since the latter are short and the insect has a bronzed-black body, it is roughly the right shape and colour for comparison with cockroach or leech. This is one of the likelier of such identifications.

Perhaps identical with *kyno-prêstis*: cf. Hesychius s.v. (2.549 Latte): 'dog-inflater', the name of 'an animal'.

On the various remedies against *bouprêstis* alleged by Nicander see Scarborough p. 79f.

Kantharis

[Grammatically the diminutive form of *kantharos* (cf. Plato Comicus cited above p. 86) a signification that cannot always be excluded (cf. Gil Fernández p. 65) in favour of the following technical sense.]

'Blister-beetle': so-called because a producer of the blistering agent cantharidin; Antiquity was divided as to which part of the insect's body produced this substance; Pliny rightly guessed the elytra (see J. Scarborough, *Coleopterist's Bulletin* 31 (1977) 295). Its appearance here has, therefore, an appropriateness extending beyond the alphabetical since, as we have seen, the previous entry produces the same agent and is sometimes associated with the *kantharis*.

Aristotle (*HA* 542a9ff., 552b1ff., *GA* 721a6ff.) does not distinguish between different types. Pliny, however (*NH* 29.94), lists five varieties (cf. Scarborough p. 294f.). Not all of these need be genuine blister beetles. The most convincing and interesting (also mentioned by Dioscorides *de mat. medicin.* 2.6 and Galen in a variety of passages) is the *poikilê* (or 'variegated') *kantharis*, which gets its name from yellow bands running across its wings (identified with the genus *Mylabris* by e.g. Keller, *Antike Tierwelt* 2.414) and is recognisable in several illustrations in the illuminated MSS of Dioscorides (see Kádár p.60 and pls. 68.3, 88.1 (our Fig. 20), 93). Hesychius s.v. *chelônias* glosses that animal as *poikilê kantharis* but (cf. Gossen, *RE* Suppl. 8 (1956) 238) that name derives from the Greek for tortoise and may well refer to the ladybird (also appropriately called *poikilê*). Note that in the Greek nursery rhyme 'fly beetles – a savage wolf is after you' (Pliny *NH* 27.100: Bergk, *Poetae Lyrici Graeci* 3.665) the name for the insect is *kantharis* and the song is compared with our 'Lady-bird, lady-bird' by W.R. Halliday, *Folklore Studies, Ancient and Modern* (London 1924) p. 115.

The first of Pliny's varieties of *kantharis* is said to develop out of a little worm, found on wild rose gall: it is equivalent to

4. Beetle/cockchafer

20. Blister-beetle (?) in illustration in Byzantine Manuscript of Dioscorides (Vat. gr. 284 codex fol. 225^V: from Z. Kádár, *Survivals of Greek Zoological Illuminations in Byzantine MSS* (Budapest 1978) pl. 88.1).

Aristotle's *kampê* (see below p. 102) of this insect which feeds on the wild rose (*HA* 552b1ff. → Plutarch *moral*. 874B), the fig, pear or fir: cf. Aelian *NA* 9.39: the *kantharis* generated among fig, wheat, poplar, Theophrastus *HP* 8.10.1 (with a suggestion of spontaneous generation); the creature is a pest of wheat (similarly Nicander *Alex*. 115); with the menstruating woman prescribed as a method for removing this pest by Pliny (*NH* 18.152 citing Metrodorus of Scepsis *F.Gr.Hist.* 184 F11) compare p. 103 below. With the notion (Aristotle fr. 372 Rose) that vipers restore their venom by feeding on this insect compare p. 77 above.

As a result of their cantharidin these insects were used medicinally as a blisterer and counter agent when externally applied (see e.g. Hippocrates T32 (in H. Grensemann, *Knidische Medizin* 1 (1975) p.44); also internally as a poison (cf. Nicander *Alex*. 115ff. and (on remedies) 128ff.: for a list and critique of these remedies see J. Scarborough in *Pharmacy in History* 21 (1979) 73ff., for an account of the effects of the poison ib. 13f.). There is no evidence from antiquity of the belief later so popular that minute doses of the substance would act as an aphrodisiac (cf. the notorious *Lytta (Cantharis) vesicatoria* or 'Spanish-fly': this notion is first attested in the sixteenth century (see B. Karle ap. *Bächtold-Stäubli, Handwörterbuch des deutschen Aberglaubens* 4.964), though cf. Scarborough pp. 74 and 79 and for a general survey of the medical and aphrodisiac application P.V. Taberner, *Aphrodisiacs: the science and the myth* (1985) pp. 102ff.

On the following insect names derived from the Greek word for 'horn' (*keras*) see A.J. Nussbaum, *Head and Horn in Indo-European* (1986) p. 7 n.15.

Kerambêlon

Hesychius s.v. (2.462 Latte) identifies as either a type of beetle with horns or a small creature which, when tied on to fig trees, will drive away *knipes* (see below p. 97f.) by its noise. The first definition and the word's form remind one of the two following entries; the possible reference to stridulation (cf. Keller, *Antike Tierwelt* 2.408) suggests a connection with the Cerambycids, which produce sound by rubbing together two parts of the thorax; or by friction of their hind legs against their wing cases (cf. Imms, *Textbook of Entomology*³ p. 809).

Kara(m)bus

According to Aristotle *HA* 531b25 a kind of beetle with large antennae (*HA*532a27) that develops out of larvae found in dry wood (*HA*551b17ff.; cf. Hesychius s.v. (2.412 Latte) who defines as the *skôlêkia* in dry timber). The word is also applied to the spiny lobster or crawfish (see D'Arcy Thompson, *Greek Fishes* s.v. (p. 102f.)): perhaps the common feature of both is supposed to be their large 'antennae' (on the word's etymology see Gil Fernández pp. 228ff.).

Kerambux

Nicander fr. 38 Schneider cited by Antonius Liberalis *Metam.* 22.5 tells the story of an individual called Kerambus who was transformed into a *kerambux*, a large beetle (cf. Hesychius s.v. (2.462 Latte)) with head and horns together resembling a tortoiseshell lyre which is also called *xylophagus bous* ('wood-eating ox' – presumably a reference to the larval stage). Children use it as a toy (cf. p. 90). The name obviously derives from the Greek word for horn (*keras*: cf. Gil Fernández pp. 78ff.). R. Goossens, *L'Antiquité classique* 19 (1948) 263ff. like Keller before him (*Antike Tierwelt* 2.408) plausibly sees a reference to the curving mandibles of the Lucanidae.

4. Beetle/cockchafer

Kerastês

Theophrastus *HP* 4.14.5, 5.4.5 (→ Pliny *NH* 16.220, 17.221) defines this as the adult stage of the *skôlêx* (see below p. 102 n.60) that attacks trees (especially fig) and cut timber. His former passage, by an apparent reference to stridulation, would encourage an identification with the Cerambycids or horned beetles (see under *kerambêlon* above) as would the etymology of the word (see under *kerambux* above). For varieties particularly hostile to figs (*Hesperophanes grieseus* (Fab.) and *H. fasciculatus* Eald.) see Bodenheimer, *Animal and Man* p. 78.

Sp(h)ondulê

Etymology: probably from *sphondulos* ('vertebra'): see Gil Fernández p. 242, Chantraine s.v. (4.1078). Mentioned by Aristotle *HA* 542a11, Theophrastus *HP* 9.14.3 (cf. Aelian *NA* 8.13) as a type of beetle which emits a foul odour when alarmed, in the manner familiar from e.g. the 'bombadier' beetle. Compared to *bouprêstis* by schol. Nicand. *Alex.* 335 (p. 128 Geymonat). The name is used of a creature producing a fart in a mock-oracle at Aristophanes' *Peace* 1017, where E.K. Borthwick, *CR* 18 (1968) 138 argues that it can also refer to a *weasel*, an animal familiar (cf. S. Benton, *CR* 19 (1969) 260ff.) to Athenian houses and also rather noisesome.

Beetles and religion

Such a heading may seem eccentric to us, but it would not have seemed so to many ancient peoples, including the Greeks.

Naturalistic models of beetles have been found in Minoan sanctuaries on the tops of mountains: for their presumed significance see e.g. Dietrich, *Origins of Greek Religion* (1974) p.292 n.15, *Tradition in Greek Religion* (1986) p. 26.

It was in the civilisation and religion of ancient Egypt, of course, that the beetle, or rather, sacred scarab (*Scarabaeus sacer*), played so large a part (see e.g. Harpaz ap. *History of Entomology* (ed. Smith et al.) pp. 23ff., W.A. Ward, *Studies on Scarab Seals* 1 (1978) pp. 87ff.).

This does not concern us directly here, but it is mentioned by several Greek writers, in particular Plutarch in his work on *Isis and Osiris*, who tells us that soldiers had a scarab-beetle as their stamped badge (10 (*moralia* 355A): for the religious significance see J. Gwyn Griffiths' commentary ad loc. (p. 289)) and that the scarab-beetle was honoured by the Egyptians because it preserved a faint trace of the powers of the gods (74 (381A)). In particular the beetle's habit of rolling its dung ball backwards is said to resemble the way in which the sun seems to turn the sky around in the opposite direction when moving from west to east (see again J. Gwyn Griffiths ad loc. (p. 555f.) for other Greek authors who connect the scarab-beetle with the sun). For the beetle as a paradigm of wisdom see Diogenian *cent.* 5.40 (1.259 Leutsch-Schneidewin).

Scarab-rings

For the significance of the shape of such rings see P. Zazoff, *Die Antiken Gemmen* (Munich 1983) p. 246f.

5. BORERS OF WOOD

The larva of wood-boring insects (believed, not altogether unintelligently (see above p. 21), to be spontaneously generated from the wood it feeds on) is generally called *skôlêx*, a word which bears other significations (see below p. 102 n.60). So, for instance, Aristotle *HA* 551b17ff., and 614b1 (cf. *Marvels Heard*[13] (831b5ff.)). Theophrastus *HP* 5.4.5. → Pliny *NH* 16.220 distinguishes three classes of timber pests, the marine *terêdôn*; the *thrips*; and the *skôlêx*; but he regularly uses the last of larvae except in *HP* 5.1.2 where he employs it of a *thrips* (cf. Pausanias Atticistes s.v. *terêdôn* (Erbse, *Untersuchungen zu den Attizistischen Lexika* (1950) p. 212: a wood-chewing *skôlêx* that lives in timber; see Erbse ad loc. for other testimonia to this effect). In the Greek translation of Proverbs 12:4 and 25:20 *skôlêx* is the archetypal enemy of wood, *sês* of clothing: cf. below p. 110f. Other terms for the larvae of wood-boring insects are *eulê* (Aelian *NA* 16.14 of creatures extracted from plants which are worm-eaten), a word more usually applied (cf. below p. 151) to fly larvae; *romos* or *romox* (defined by Hesychius s.v. as a *skôlêx* in timber); and *dêx* (Tzetzes' commentary on Hesiod *Works and Days* 418).

Ammonius, *de adfinium vocabulorum differentia* 244 (p. 64 Nickau) is at pains to distinguish four animals: *ips*, *thrips*, *ix*, and (see p. 111; cf. Theophrastus *CP* 4.15.4) *kis*.

5. Borers of wood

Ips

Etymology: see Gil Fernández p. 116f. Perhaps connected with the verbs *ipoun* ('press hard upon'); cf. the noun *ipos* (that part of a mousetrap which springs down on the mouse); compare the etymologies of *terêdôn* and *thrips* cited below. For the formation see *thrips* (below p. 99), *(s)knips* (below p. 97f.).

Mentioned in the *Odyssey* (21.395) in connection with Odysseus' bow (see above p. 8 n.26). Theophrastus *de lapidibus (On Stones)* 49 (p. 74 Eicholz) states that in Cilicia there is a sort of earth which grows viscous when heated and is used instead of *ix* ('bird-lime') to dress vines against *ipes* (this earth was probably a hard variety of asphalt: for further details see the commentaries of Caley and Richards (p. 168f.) and Eicholz (p. 122) ad loc.). Cf. id. *CP* 3.22.5, *HP* 8.10.5 (*ipes* perish when their food is exhausted). Strabo 13.613 says the inhabitants of Erythra call Heracles *Ipo-ktonos* ('*Ips* killer') for ensuring the creature's absence from their part of the world.

Ix

Etymology (see Gil Fernández p. 115f.) problematic: perhaps to be connected with words like Latin *ic(i)o*, *ictus*, meaning strike, Greek *igdis* (a mortar, i.e. a tool for *grinding*) or *aikhmê* (spear (-tip)) all sharing the general concept of striking or piercing.

The early lyric poet Alcman (fr. 93 P) apparently mentioned them as destroyers of vines and this has led most scholars (e.g. Gil Fernández p. 115f., *LSJ* s.v.) to class them as insects. But a newly discovered papyrus of Alcman's fragment (see S. Daris, *Actes du XVe Congrès International de Papyrologie* 2 (1979) pp. 9ff., C. Calame, *Alcman* p. 152f.) seems to gloss them as a sort of bird (for attempts at identification see W.G. Arnott ap. Daris p. 9 n.3).

(S)knips

Etymology: compare such verbs as *knizein* ('scratch, grate'), *skniptein* ('pinch, nip'); an attempt to interpret as an Egyptian borrowing (Hemmerdinger, *Glotta* 46 (1968) 242) hardly convinces. D. Moutsos, *Zeitschrift für Vergleichende Sprachforschung* 94 (1980) 150 distinguishes two senses:

(a) *Small creatures which infest the fig- and the oak-tree*: Aristophanes *Birds* 590 associates them with attacks on the former. Aristotle *HA* 534b19 mentions them by name only as capable of perceiving honey from a distance (like bees); but he may mean them when he refers to unnamed insects beneath the bark of trees and says birds eat them (*HA* 593a2, 614b1 → Pliny *NH* 10.40 and 11.19; Theophrastus *HP* 2.8.3, 6.10.8, *CP* 6.5.3; and compare with *empis* (see below p. 165). Cf. Hesychius s.v. *knips* and *knipes* (2.494 Latte).

(b) *Small ants*: Aristotle *de sens*. 444b12. Used as a translation for one of the plagues of Egypt by the Greek translator of Exodus 8:16 ('lice' in the Authorised Version) and by Ezekiel in his *Exagoge* (*Tr.G.F.* 1 (128) 135ª), a dramatisation of the events of Exodus composed by an Alexandrian Jew.

Also abusive slang for an old woman according to Suetonius *peri blasphêmiôn* 8 (p. 61 Taillardat): see Taillardat's commentary ad loc. (Paris 1967, p. 146) and below p. 177.

Terêdôn

Etymology: see Gil Fernández p. 115; presumably from the Greek verb *teirein* (cf. Latin *tero, trivi, tritum*; English 'attrition' etc.) meaning to wear away or down: compare the Greek noun *teretron* (a tool for boring). For the formation cf. *anthrêdôn, tenthrêdôn* etc. (see above p. 79).

Aristotle *HA* 605b17 mentions it as being engendered in hives (see above p. 64); Theophrastus *HP* 5.4.4 says it feeds on decaying wood in sea water and though small has a large head and teeth. Similarly Pliny *NH* 16.220 who elsewhere, however, uses it of terrestrial pests (see H. Leitner, *Zoologische Terminologie bei Älteren Plinius* (1972) p. 231f.). On the evidence of Pausanias Atticistes see above p. 96. Such passages suggest some dispute as to whether it represents something specific such as the marine shipworm or is merely a general term.

Strato in *AP* 12.190.3f extravagantly wishes that he were a *terêdôn* or *thrips* that he might feed on a wooden tablet containing (on wax) the image of his beloved. At Arist. *Thesm.* 1175 *Terêdôn* is probably a woman's (nick-)name (cf. below pp. 156 and 177).

Thrips

Etymology: see Gil Fernández p. 114f., Chantraine s.v. (2.442). Perhaps derived from the Greek verb *tribô* meaning 'to wear down' (cf. Latin *tritum* and the remarks on *terêdôn* above). For the form cf. *ips* (above p. 97), (*s*)*knips* (above p. 97f.).

Theophrastus *HP* 5.4.5 says it is similar to a *skôlêx* (see below p. 102) and gradually eats away wood decaying on land (contrast his remarks on the *terêdôn* cited above).

On Strato's reference to a *thrips* in *AP* 12.190 see above on *terêdôn* (p. 98).

6. BUTTERFLY/MOTH

The regular Greek name for this (first attested in Aristotle *HA* 551a14) is *psychê*, the word for soul: the adult's emergence from

21. Butterfly on a late Minoan gem from Knossos (Ashmolean Museum, Oxford): V.E.G. Kenna, *Cretan Seals: with a catalogue of the Minoan gems in the Ashmolean Museum* (Oxford 1960) no.234 (p.123).

Greek Insects

the darkness of the pupa (see below p. 103: called in Greek *nekydallos* or 'little corpse' (cf. Gil Fernández p. 202)) is presumably the key to the metaphor[53] (together with the popularity of the concept of winged souls)[54] on which see further below p. 103f. The word *psychê* also embraced moths (see below p. 109), and Latin *anim(ul)a* is similarly used of both soul and butterfly (cf. J. André, *Rev. Phil.* 36 (1962) 23). In Yorkshire and Gloucestershire a 'soul' 'is a night-flying white moth' according to E.M. Wright, *Rustic Speech and Folk-lore* (1913) p. 116.

Modern poets have put to good use the metaphorical capacities of this insect: see e.g. Dante's *Purgatorio* 10.124ff. ('noi siam vermi/nati a formar l'angelica farfalla'), on which see e.g. P. Boyde, *Dante Philomythes and Philosopher* (Cambridge 1981) pp. 291ff., or Spenser's *Muiopotmos* on which see D.C. Allen, *Image and Meaning: metaphoric traditions in Renaissance poetry*[2] (1968) pp. 30ff. By contrast, several writers have remarked upon the strange paucity of references in ancient literature to this creature which more modern taste has found so attractive or symbolic. Thus Otto Keller (*Antike Tierwelt* 2.436f.) notes its total absence from Homer, Lyric, Drama, Aesop's *Fables*[55] and the *Greek Anthology*[56], and D'Arcy W. Thompson (ap. *The Legacy of Greece* p. 153 ≃ *Die Naturphilosophie des Aristoteles* p. 18f.) observes that 'allusions to the butterfly are scanty and rare' in Greek literature (especially poetry) and appends the explanation 'I think the Greeks found something ominous or uncanny, something not to be lightly spoken of, in that all but disembodied spirit which we call

---

[53] For 'the caterpillar (as) an emblem of the Resurrection' as late as seventeenth-century England see Thomas, *Man and the Natural World* p. 64 and n.78.

[54] See on this topic Waser ap. Roschers *Ausführliches Lexikon d. gr. und röm. Mythologie* s.v. 'Psyche' (3.3213ff.), Nilsson, *Geschichte der gr. Religion* 1³ 197f., R. Lattimore, *Themes in Greek and Latin Epitaphs* (1942) p. 30 and n. 77, and J. Bremmer, *The Early Greek Concept of the Soul* (1983) p. 93f. and n. 61. On the winged soul in general see Gaster, *Myth, Legend and Custom in the Old Testament* p. 769.

[55] But cf. fable 31 in Perotti's Appendix (p. 414 Perry), on which see Perry's Introduction p. xcviif. (= 556 in Perry's Appendix) on the butterfly and the wasp.

[56] Though Meleager *AP* 5.57 = *HE* 4074f. on the winged *psychê* is interpreted by Gow-Page ad loc. (2.617) as referring to both soul and butterfly. One might further note the butterfly's absence from the list of Plato's animal symbols for the soul given by U. Dierauer, *Tier und Mensch im Denken der Antike* (Amsterdam 1977) pp. 66ff.

6. Butterfly/moth

butterfly, and they called by the name of *psychê*, the Soul'.[57] It must be added, however, that visual artists seem to have laboured under no such inhibitions as to the depiction of the creature, and often exploit the opportunities for symbolism offered by its ambiguous name (see below pp. 103ff.).

22. Butterfly with pupa above and caterpillar below, on a gem from a private Swiss collection [Leo Merz], first century B.C.: see M.-L. Vollenweider, *Deliciae Leonis: Antike geschnittene Steine und Ringe aus einer Privatsammlung* (Mainz 1984) no.106 (p.71).

---

[57] Thompson's explanation may seem fanciful (though no more so than Gossen's idea (*RE* 2A (1923) 571.45f.) that to do full justice to the butterfly one requires a teutonic temperament ('germanisches Gemüt') and that Greece has conspicuously fewer butterflies than North Europe) but it becomes less so when considered in the light of the general principle of a taboo on names of those animals conceived as having human intelligence (cf. Frazer, *The Golden Bough* 3 (*Taboo* etc.) pp. 392ff. esp. 416ff., E. Clodd, *Magic in Names and in Other Things* (London 1920) pp. 89ff.), and the particular taboo on the naming of bees studied by R. Gauthiot, *Mémoires de la Société de Linguistique de Paris* 16 (1925) 264ff.

Generation and life cycle

Aristotle, his pupil Theophrastus after him, and, indeed, the whole of Antiquity down through the Middle Ages, suffered from a misconception as to this process, since they were ignorant about the initial stage whereby male and female butterflies mate to produce eggs[58] from which the larvae or grubs emerge. For ancient writers, the sequence begins with the direct generation of larvae the size of a millet grain, which receive their nourishment from adjacent plants, especially cabbages (cf. in general W. Capelle, *Rh. Mus.* 105 (1962) 57). Aristotle *HA* 551a14ff. (cf. 551a2f., Theophr. *HP* 2.4.4, Pliny *NH* 11.112 (cf. Arist. Byz. *hist. an. ep.* 1.36)) states that the butterfly is produced on a leaf out of dew condensed by the sun to the size of a millet seed from which the grub develops).[59] The fact that the Greek word for dew (*drosos*) can be used of seminal fluid (see Callimachus fr. 260.19 and Pfeiffer ad loc. (1.248)) is likely to be relevant here (at least in terms of popular association) as Cook, *Zeus* 2 (1) p. 645f. n.4 implied. For the connection between butterflies and semen see below p. 104f. and cf. below p. 171 on the generation of lice. For Aristotle, then, the first stage of the butterfly is the grub/larva from which the pupa/chrysalis develops; out of this in turn the butterfly itself emerges after an interval of days or months. Aristotle calls the grub/larva stage the *kampê* ('caterpillar'); so too Plutarch (*moralia* 611F (as explained by Pearson, *Journ. Philol.* 30 (1907) 214) and 636C etc. (though there is ambiguity as to the distinction between *kampê* and *skôlêx* (cf. *LSJ* s.v. 2)).[60] At *HA* 551b12 (perhaps a description of the moth *Lasiocampa otus*: see below p.113) the sequence is *skôlêx→kampê→bombyl(i)os* ('cocoon': see above p.73 n. 83)→*nekydallos* which is matched by Clement of Alexandria *Paed.* 2.10.107 (1.21 Stählin) who, however, quotes the last as a synonym for the penultimate. The identification of *skôlêx* and *nekydallos* at Arist. Byz.

---

[58] An ignorance which extended to other insects (see above p. 20) because of the extreme smallness of the eggs in question.

[59] Aristotle *HA* 539b12 lists the various progeny produced by various insects: egg-like *skôlêkes* (see next note) are engendered by insects which appear in some MSS as *psyllai* ('fleas': see below p. 149) in others as *psychai*.

[60] For a more detailed account of Aristotle's (and others') use of *skôlêx* cf. W. Capelle, *Rh. Mus.* 98 (1955) 153, who points out that it can mean (depending on the context) (1) worm; (2) caterpillar (i.e. butterfly-larva); (3) the larva of any insect; and claims that as (2) Aristotle uses it more often than *kampê*.

6. Butterfly/moth

hist.an.ep. 9.6 may be the result of excessively compressed epitomisation. At *de incessu animalium* 705b26f. Aristotle erroneously states that *kampai* have no feet.

In discussing the sorb, Theophrastus (*HP* 3.12.8) observes that the unripe fruit is eaten on the tree by the *skôlêx*, as is the tree itself, and in this latter case the *skôlêx* is 'red and hairy' (cf. Pliny *NH* 17.221). Theophrastus *CP* 5.10, 3.22.3ff., 4.14.4f., *HP* 8.10.5 and 11.2 strictly observes the distinction between *skôlêx* and *kampê*.

Such *kampai* were proverbially greedy for vegetables (see e.g. Aristophon fr. 10.4 K-A (*PCG* 4.8)). A fascinating piece of superstition is preserved by Aelian *NA* 6.36 when he tells us that the threat posed to vegetables by *kampai* can be ended by getting a menstruating woman to walk through the vegetables and thus kill the insects. This practice was explained by H.J. Rose, *CR* 38 (1924) 65, 112, 171f. who cites several similar prescriptions largely in connection with Martial 4.64.[61]

Butterflies' antennae conceived in terms of horns in front of the eyes: Aristotle *HA* 532a26, Pliny *NH* 11.100 (categorising them as 'useless').

Metaphor and symbolism

Since the same Greek word (*psychê*) means both 'soul' and 'butterfly', late antiquity and (in particular) Christian writers such as St. Basil and other Church Fathers exploit the ambiguity as an allegory of the Resurrection. It has been argued by several scholars that in contrast there is no evidence for such symbolism in earlier antiquity, and the data we shall shortly examine are admittedly not wholly explicit. On the other hand, we are dealing with an idea that has parallels in many cultures (see, for instance, Stith Thompson's *Motif-Index of Folk-Literature*[2] E 734.1 ('soul in form of butterfly'), Cook, *Zeus* 2(1) p. 645 n.4, Frazer, *Golden Bough*, general index s.v. 'Butterfly, Souls of Dead in' and 'Butterfly, the soul as a'; *Totemism and Exogamy* 2.81; R. Riegler ap. *Bächtold-Stäubli, Handwörterbuch des deutschen Aberglaubens* 6.594f., 7.1241ff.; J.P. Mills, *The Ao Nagas* (1926) p. 226 n.3. As for ancient Greece the following

---

[61] For analogous traditions as to the magical (usually destructive) properties of menstrual blood see R.C.T. Parker, *Miasma* (Oxford 1983) p. 102f.

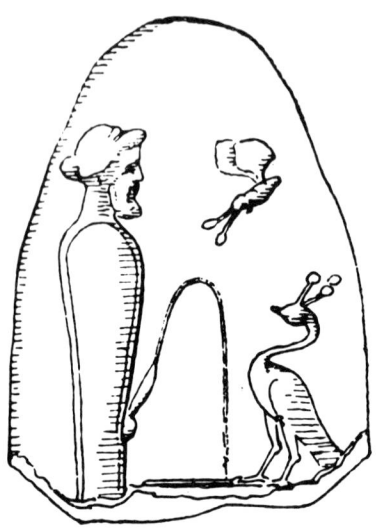

23. Butterfly and semen on a Roman gem in Copenhagen: P. Fossing, *The Thorvaldsen Museum: Catalogue* etc. (1929) no.504 (from Cook, *Zeus* 2(1) p.645 fig.563).

artefacts from widely varying places and times must be considered.[62]

Several gems depict a butterfly hovering over a human skull (so, for instance, a first-century B.C. onyx now in Munich (A1708: for full description and other examples see E. Brandt, *Antike Gemmen in Deutschen Sammlungen. I.2: München* (Munich 1970) p. 67f.; cf. O. Brendel, *Mitteilungen des deutsch. Arch. Inst. (Röm. Abt.)* 49 (1934) 160ff.) and in antiquity the soul was often thought to reside in the head (see Onians, *Origins of European Thought* pp. 102ff.). Hermes, a deity variously associated with the soul (see Onians p. 122, H. Herter, *Rh. Mus.* 119 (1976) 217ff.) has a butterfly at his shoulder on an Etruscan

---

[62] On these O. Jahn, *Archäol. Beiträge* (Berlin 1847) pp. 137ff. is still worth consulting. For more recent views see in particular the contributions and discussions by Waser, *Archiv für Religionswissenschaft* 16 (1913) 382ff. and in *Roscher* 3.3234ff., H. Guntert, *Kalypso* 2 pp. 213ff., O. Immisch, *Glotta* 6 (1915) 193ff. M. Nilsson, *Geschichte der gr. Religion* 1³ 198 is cautious as to the earliness of the concept but cf. Bremmer, *The Early Greek Concept of the Soul* p. 82 (stressing the probability that the use of *psyché* to mean butterfly antedates its first occurrence in Aristotle).

6. *Butterfly/moth* 105

24. Butterfly and semen on an Attic black-figure amphora of the sixth century B.C. (Pergamon Museum, East Berlin 1684).

gem (P. Zazoff, *Etrusk. Skarabäen* (1968) no. 724 (p.167)). Hermes is also associated with the phallus (Onians p. 122, Herter pp. 220ff.) and therefore gives his name to the herm (a squared pillar with his head at top and genital organs, including erect phallus, in middle: cf. Herter pp. 200ff.): a Roman gem shows one such from whose penis emerges a curving jet at the crest of which flutters a butterfly (details in P. Fossing, *The Thorvaldsen Museum: Catalogue of the antique engraved gems and cameos* (Copenhagen 1929) no. 504 (p.91). For other gems combining 'a large phallus with a butterfly and snail' see Cook, *Zeus* 2(1) p. 645 n.4). Several scholars have compared with this an artefact from a very different time and place, the Attic black-figure amphora (sixth century B.C.: East Berlin 1684) which shows two naked men facing each other; the one on the left is playing the *aulos* (a reed instrument rather like our oboe) and from his erect penis drip four drops of semen beneath which a butterfly can be seen fluttering. Heraclitus thought soul an exhalation from liquid (Onians p. 252), the Hippocratic treatise *On Regimen* 1.6f. and 29.2 (*Corp. Medic. Graec.* 1.2.4 (Joly) pp.128f. and 146) identified soul and sperm (cf. R. Joly, *Recherches sur le traité*

25. Athena holding a soul in the shape of a butterfly: detail of the Prometheus sarcophagus, A.D. 290/300 (Rome: Museo Capitolino, Sala delle Colombe): H. Sichtermann and G. Koch, *Griechische Mythen auf römischen Sarkophagen* (1975) no.68 (p.63f.).

pseudo-hippocratique Du Régime (Paris 1960) p. 30f.), Aristotle treated the question 'does the soul have semen?' (cf. A. Preus, *Journal of the History of Biology* 3 (1970) 23ff.), Plato connected the soul with seed (cf. Onians p. 119). Gem and vase, then, may represent an analogous picture on the popular level (cf. Onians pp. 108ff., Cook, *Zeus* 2(1) p. 645f. n.4). The juxtaposition of semen and butterfly may also remind us that some modern European names for this insect similarly connect it with liquid *vel sim.* that possesses nutritive power (English *butter*-fly, German *Molkendieb* (whey-thief) etc.).[63] However, Fossing ibid. thinks that on both the butterfly is attracted by the phallus 'as a

[63] See Immisch, *Glotta* 6 (1915) 197, R. Riegler ap. Bächtold-Stäubli, *Handwörterbuch des deutschen Aberglaubens* 7.1246. English etymology seems baffled by *butterfly* (OED and Onions, *Dictionary of English Etymology* can only suggest a derivation from the appearance of the creature's excrement in view of the Dutch synonym Boterschijte, though the latter cites the German terms mentioned above). In one of William Blake's illustrations to his *Songs of Innocence and Experience* we see 'The organ of generation ... with the generative principle breaking from its crest in the form of tiny winged ... figures' (G. Keynes in his edition (Oxford 1970) on pl. 11).

6. Butterfly/moth

female being' (cf. Immisch, *Glotta* 6 (1915) 197), and Cook ibid. suggests a pun on phallus and *phallê* (glossed by Hesych. s.v. as 'the flying *psychê*').

Many a late Roman artefact (in particular the sarcophagus) depicts Prometheus creating man with Athena the goddess of wisdom standing by holding a butterfly that represents man's soul. For a full survey of these depictions see H. Kaiser-Minn, *Die Erschaffung des Menschen auf den spätantiken Monumenten des 3. und 4. Jahrhunderts (Jhb. für Antike und Christentum Ergänzungsband* 6 (1981)) pp. 34ff. (cf. p. 103) and plates 14ff. For further bibliography on the sarcophagi see G. Koch and H. Sichtermann, *Römische Sarkophagen* (Munich 1982) p. 183.

There remains the question of the creature's possible significance in Minoan and Mycenaean religion. Painted butterflies and chrysalises have been found on the wall of a shrine in Minoan Crete, butterfly designs on gold leaves and gold models of balances in shaft graves at Mycenae. The exact religious significance of these and their connection with the beliefs implied by the aforementioned artefacts is uncertain: for full details see Nilsson, *The Minoan-Mycenaean Religion and its Survival in Greek Religion* (1950) pp. 45ff., Dietrich, *Origins of Greek Religion* (1974) pp. 119ff. The famous story of Cupid and Psyche as depicted visually often alludes to the heroine by picturing a butterfly or giving her butterfly wings: see, for instance, R. Merkelbach, *Roman und Mysterium in der Antike* (1962) p. 27f. and n.1, E. Zwierlein-Diehl, *Die Antiken Gemmen des Kunsthistorischen Museums in Wien* 1 Index (p.276) s.v. 'Psyche-Schmetterling', M.-L. Vollenweider, *Deliciae Leonis: Antike geschnittene Steine und Ringe aus einer Privatsammlung* [Leo Mertz] (Mainz 1984) pp. 65f and 70. This particular detail was probably Hellenistic in origin as Wilamowitz (*Glaube d. Hellenen* 1.377) stressed.

Miscellanea

Allegedly the earliest reference to a butterfly in Greek literature[64]

---

[64] Cited by W. Capelle, *Rh. Mus.* 105 (1962) 56f. who also detects a possible reference to the butterfly (or rather the caterpillar) in Democritus 68B fr. 126 DK with its reference to 'creatures which proceed along their path with a wave-like motion'. *Kampê*, the word for caterpillar, is cognate with *kampê* meaning 'bend, turn' etc.

has been discerned in the Hippocratic *peri epikuêsios* (*On Superfetation*)[65] as part of a suggested remedy for a suppurating womb: apparently one must cut up (carefully, so that the goodness (*phorbê:* lit. 'food', 'nourishment') does not escape) the *kampai* (see above p. 102) of the *tithumallis* and then dry and pound them. One is to do likewise with *skôlêkes koprinoi* ('worms in excrement' *sec. LSJ* s.v. *koprinos:* but cf. above p. 102) and blend the results in a potion that includes other elements (such as white wine to counteract the foul odour!). The drink thus administered will (perhaps not surprisingly) produce a torpor in the belly. The *kampai* of the *tithumallis* are said to possess *kentra* (spikes) and W. Capelle, *Rh. Mus.* 105 (1962) 56f. identifies them with the larvae of *Sphinx euphorbiae* L. (generic name now[66] actually *Hyles*), the Spurge Hawkmoth (*tithumallos* being the spurge: cf. e.g. J. Scarborough, *Journ. Hist. Biol.* 11 (1978) 368) whose larva (like all the Hawkmoths) has one horn at the back.

Phalaina

A moth mentioned at Nicander *Ther.* 760 and alleged by a scholion ad loc. to be a Rhodian name (p. 274 Crugnola). O. Immisch attempted (*Glotta* 6 (1915) 197) to derive the word from *phallus* (of which it looks the feminine) in view of the butterfly's association with that object on various artefacts (see above p. 104f., and for winged *phalloi* on a number of Greek vases see, for instance, Dover, *Greek Homosexuality* p.133 on what he calls the 'phallus-bird'). This is not impossible, but seems less convincing than the alternative approach (see most recently Gil Fernández pp. 204ff., Chantraine, s.v. (4.1175)) which associates the name with various words centering around the concept of 'light' (*phaos,* cf. *phanos* ('torch') etc.) and referring to its whitish colour or its attraction to lamps. Otto Keller (*Antike Tierwelt* 2.437f.) has an imaginative and evocative description of how such a specimen as the Death's-head Hawkmoth (common in Southern Europe) fluttering in sufficient numbers around garden tombs on a summer's evening and emitting its characteristic

---

[65] Hippocr. *de superf.* 28.2 (*Corp. Medic. Graec.* I.2.2. (Lienau) p. 84): on the exact text see Lienau ad loc. (p. 115).

[66] Since 1819.

6. Butterfly/moth   109

uncanny squeak[67] might well have encouraged that connection between moth/butterfly and soul considered above (p. 103). Nicander proceeds to a description of how the *phalaina* nods its head in grim manner and plants its sting in a man's head or neck. Not surprisingly Gow and Scholfield ad loc. suppose this part of the description to be quite mythical (perhaps referring to the mythical 'winged scorpion'). On this and the possibility that features of both moth and wasp have been combined see J. Scarborough, *Pharmacy in History* 21 (1979) 14f.

Psôra

Another name for *phalaina* according to schol. Nicand. *Ther.* 760 (p. 274 Crugnola). Since the word *psôra* usually refers to a disease known as the scab, scurvey or mange, Immisch (*Glotta* 6 (1915) 194) ingeniously suggested that its extension to the moth in question implies an otherwise unattested popular belief that the insect caused the aforesaid disease. Gil Fernández p. 39f. prefers the simpler explanation in terms of the texture and appearance of the insect itself, to whose wings it is not at all implausible that the corresponding adjective *psóros* ('rough, scaly') might have been applied. For the 'mealy' wings of 'butterflies' cf. Shakespeare *Troilus and Cressida* 3.3.78f and K. Palmer's Arden edition ad loc. For the butterfly as a 'Krankheitsdämon' see R. Riegler ap. *Bächtold-Stäubli, Handwörterbuch des deutschen Aberglaubens* 7.1247f.

Pyraustês

As its name suggests, a type of moth that is attracted to the candle's flame and flies closer to it until it is scorched (see further Strömberg p.21, Gil Fernández p. 154f.). Mentioned by Aeschylus (*Tr.G.F.* 3 F288 Radt), the fate of this creature became (not surprisingly) proverbial for the brevity of life: see the passages collected by Radt ad loc. (p. 357f.). The picture is common in other milieux too: thus for Biblical examples see M.H. Pope's commentary (New York 1965) on Job 4:19. and for English Tilley, *Dictionary of Proverbs* F394 and J89, P. Ansell

---

[67] For the spirits of the dead represented as squeaking or gibbering see Gaster, *Myth, Legend and Custom in the Old Testament* p. 570.

Robin, *Animal Lore in English Literature* (London 1932) p. 112f.

The animal is mentioned at *HA* 605b11 where there is some uncertainty as to its connection with *klêros*, the grub that harms honey-combs (see above p. 63f.). As the text stands, *pyraustês* is a synonym of *klêros*. Schneider, followed, for instance, by Thompson, transferred the mention of *pyraustês* to a different portion of the text. *Klêros* is usually taken to be a beetle. However, we may be given pause by an entry in Hesychius s.v. *sklêros*, a disease caused by spiders in the hive which Strömberg p.21 equated with the *klêros* of *HA*. If *sklêros* is indeed a legitimate variant form of *klêros*, then *(s)klêros* would indeed be a suitable synonym for a moth, or at least for the moth's pupal stage, since as an adjective *sklêros* means 'hard, brittle'.

The word for moth used by Aristotle in explaining the term *pyraustês* is *hêpiolos* (variant reading *-olês*) which the majority of scholars have connected with *êpialos*, the Greek for fever.[68] This name for a moth occurs nowhere else, though we should note Hesychius s.v. *êpialos* (2.290 Latte) which refers to cold and fever and goes on to say that this was the name of *hoi psychroi* ('the cold men': but the slight emendation *hai psychai* 'the butterflies/moths' (cf. Gil Fernández p. 197) would be attractive). For the connection in another language between words for 'fever' and for 'butterfly/moth' see Boisacq, *Dictionnaire étymologique* s.v. *hêpiolos*, Gil Fernández p. 197.

Sês (clothes-moth)

Etymology: very uncertain. See Gil Fernández p. 119f. suggesting a derivation from the verb *sinesthai* ('destroy'), compare Latin *tinea* meaning moth; cf. Chantraine s.v. (4.999). Recognised by Aristotle (*HA* 557b1ff.) who states that it is engendered in wool and woollens, particularly if the latter are dusty and a spider has been shut up inside them to use up the moisture. This type of moth appears as a devourer of *books* in Lucian's *Ignorant Book Collector* 1 (2.121 Macleod).

---

[68] Cf. H. Herter, *Rheinische Jahrbuch für Volkskunde* 1 (1950) p. 126 = *Kl. Schr.* p. 57 and n.42f. Pliny *NH* 11.65 in a passage based on Aristotle calls the creature *'pestifer'*. For the butterfly's link with 'Pest und Fieber' cf. R. Riegler ap. *Bächtold-Stäubli* 7.1247f.

6. Butterfly/moth

Metaphor

Mentioned by Pindar fr. 222 Snell (together with *kis* (weevil)) as a paradigm of those destructive agents which are unable to overcome the shining permanence of gold. (Compared with the Biblical reference to 'moth and rust' (Matthew 6:20) by W.T. Lendrum, *CR* 20 (1906) 307.) A similarly proverbial reference to the creature in Menander fr. 538.5f. Sandbach (rust rots iron, the *sês* clothes, and the *thrips* (see above p. 99) wood). The name is used disparagingly of grammarians in several epigrams from the *Greek Anthology*: thus Philip (*AP* 11.321.1 = *GP* 3033) calls them *sêtes akanthôn* ('thorn-moths') because they browse on thorny passages in books; Antiphanes (*AP* 11.322.2 = *GP* 772) calls them *sêtes akanthobatai* ('clamberers about thorns') for the same reason; and Philip again (*AP* 11.347.2 = *GP* 3042) *akanthologoi* ('fond of thorny questions'). For 'thorn' used thus metaphorically see Gow-Page, *GP* 2.38. In the same spirit Shelley called 'epitomes ... the moths of just history; they eat out the poetry of it' (*A Defence of Poetry* Part 1). For the general principle of insect names used in contempt see Headlam's note on Herodas 2.73 (p. 96f.), Shakespeare's use of the term 'water-fly' (*Hamlet* 5.2.82, *Troilus* 5.1.38ff.), Pope's 'bug with gilded wings' etc. and for opprobrious animal names applied to grammarians compare Timon of Phlius fr. 786 *Suppl. Hell.*: 'Many are feeding in populous Egypt, scribblers on papyrus, ceaselessly wrangling in the bird-cage of the Muses',[69] Herodicus of Babylon fr. 494.3 *Suppl.Hell.* who calls the followers of Aristarchus *gônio-bombukes* ('creatures that buzz in corners': cf. above p. 72f.) and see in general R. Kassel, *Winkelbrummer: Antike Kritik an Philologie und Philologen* (Berlin 1973). One may compare Tennyson's description of the critic Churton Collins: 'a louse on the locks of literature' (Charteris, *Life of Gosse* p.132).

Hyperon and pênion

Juxtaposed by Aristotle *HA* 551b6ff. as insects derived from similar caterpillars and of like colour, which move in an

---

[69] Translation taken from Pfeiffer, *History of Classical Scholarship* 1.97f., who has an interesting discussion of the image and the attitude to scholarship that underlies it (but cf. Lloyd-Jones and Parsons' note ad loc. in *Supplementum Hellenisticum* (p. 372f.)).

undulating manner, with one part advancing forward and then the hind part pulled up by a bend in the body. The names are etymologically crystal clear, being identical to the Greek for pestle (*hyperon*) and spindle (*pênion*). Thompson ad loc. (n.5) claims they are chrysalids of the 'looper' caterpillars of the Geometridae and finds the reference to colour 'suggestive of the common currant-moth *Abraxas grossulariata*'. He also suggests emending the entry of the *Suda* s.v. *pênion* ((4.126 Adler) = Photius) 'a creature similar to a *kônôps*' to 'a creature similar to a *kampê*' (i.e. 'to a caterpillar': see above p. 102). This would fit Aristotle's remarks, but it cannot be right, as the rest of the *Suda*'s article shows: first of all a fragment of the now lost *first* version of Aristophanes' *Clouds* is quoted which mentions a *pênion* (or, rather, compares some individuals to two *pênia* in motion (fr. 393 K-A (*PCG* 3.2.217)): a difficult passage: for an interpretation see Taillardat, *Images d'Aristophane*[2] p.128f. supposing an allusion to the meagre and emaciated appearance of the followers of Socrates). And then Speusippus of Athens, the nephew and pupil of the philosopher Plato, is cited as commenting on the similarity of the insects *pênion, empis* and *kônôps* (fr. 11 Tarán).[70] *Kônôps* cannot be a corruption here too because it and *empis* appear elsewhere together as equivalents or near-synonyms (see below p. 165).

Aristotle *HA* 551b10ff. describes a large grub with, 'as it were', horns, which metamorphoses via caterpillar and cocoon into the *nekydallos* within six months (see above p. 102). Women unwind the cocoons and weave the threads into a fabric in a manner invented by Pamphila of Cos, daughter of Plateus. Pliny *NH* 11.22f. has a confused but fuller account which adds that the insect in question lives on the ash, the oak and the cypress tree. Clement of Alexandria *Paed.* 2.10.107 (1.221 Stählin) shares with him the details that the grub is covered in thick-set hairs and the cocoon is constructed of a loose material like a spider's web (cf. Heliodorus *Aethiopica* 10.25.2).

These writers are hardly likely to be perpetrating an inaccurate description of the silk-worm (*Bombyx mori*)[71] since

---

[70] The fr. comes from Speusippus' work *On Similarities* (on which see Tarán's commentary pp. 235ff.). On the precise relationship that is likely to have been said to exist between the relevant insects see Tarán again p. 249f.

[71] Though W. Capelle, *Rh. Mus.* 105 (1962) 58 still takes the Aristotelian passage to refer to this, as does *LSJ* s.v. *kampê*. An Assyrian silk moth is referred to by Pliny *NH* 11.74; see further W.T.M. Forbes, *Classical Philology* 25 (1930)

7. Cicada

this was first introduced into Europe from the East slightly before the reign of Justinian in c. 550 A.D.[72] D'Arcy Thompson (ad loc. (n.2) and ap. *Legacy of Greece* p. 153f. ≃ *Naturphilosophie des Aristoteles* p.19) suggests we have here a reference to *Lasiocampa otus*,[73] a large moth from South-East Europe which spins a rough cocoon quite similar to the Emperor moth's whence came such rough silky fabric as the 'Tussore silk' of India which was only superseded when the genuine silk moth entered Europe. It has a horn-like protuberance.

Aristotle *HA* 557b13ff. describes as an odd creature a grub known as the 'faggot-bearer' because the greater part of its body (save for head and feet at either end) is cased in a tunic like a spider's web to which are connected twig-like formations. This is identified with a South European species of moth, the 'basket-worm' or caterpillar of Psyche by D'Arcy Thompson in his translation (n.4) and by W. Capelle, *Rh. Mus.* 105 (1962) 58ff. who claimed the passage had not yet been explained (see contra Peck on the Aristotelian passage (2 p.214 n.b)) and observed that the insect was unknown to the great Linnaeus owing to its absence from his native Sweden.

7. CICADA (tettix)

Etymology: an onomatopoeic attempt to reproduce the insect's characteristic sound (on which see below pp. 114ff.): cf. the relevant verb *te(ra)tisdô* on which see E.K. Borthwick, *CR* 15 (1965) 253. Several scholars (cf. Gil Fernández p. 130f.) have therefore assumed that the original form was *tittix* (compare Modern Greek *tzitzikas* (cf. Cook, *Zeus* 3 p. 257 n.2 for analogous names in modern languages and on the general principle involved see F. Skoda, *Le Redoublement expressif: un universal linguistique* (Paris 1982) pp. 45 and 71). Compare *kerka* (below

---

22ff., G.M.A. Richter, *AJA* 33 (1929) 27ff. For an account of the Coan silk-trade see S. Sherwin-White, *Ancient Cos* (*Hypomnemata* 51 (1978)) pp. 378ff.

[72] It was, however, known to and described by earlier writers: see, for instance, Pausanias 6.26.6ff., Nearchus *F.Gr.Hist.* 133 F 19; cf. K. Zádár, *Acta Classica Universitatis Debreceniensis* 3 (1967) 96 and (on the silk trade between China and the Roman Empire c. 90-130 A.D.) J. Thorley, *Greece and Rome* 18 (1971) 71ff.

[73] *Pachypasa otus* (Drury) had, indeed, already been suggested by Keller, *Antike Tierwelt* 2.443ff. For further bibliography for and against the suggestion see Sherwin-White, *Ancient Cos* p. 378 n.3.

26. Cicada on the omphalos of an Attic white-ground phiale by Sotades, c. 460 B.C. (Boston Museum of Fine Arts 98.886: $ARV^2$772).

p. 146) etc., English cricket, French criquet, Dutch krekel etc.

'Hardly any other insect stirred the ancients' feeling for nature more than the cicada', says Steier, RE s.v. *tettix* (5A.1 (1934) 1113f.) rightly. Two particularly important documents for this attitude are Plato's dialogue *Phaedrus* (esp. 230C, 258E), where a philosophical discourse upon love takes place against the backdrop of an idyllic landscape of which the cicadas' chirruping is an essential ingredient; and the famous and uniquely charming poem on the cicada by an anonymous hand (*Anacreonteum* 34: on this see A. Dihle, *HSCP* 71 (1966) 107ff.) which was memorably translated into German by Goethe ('Selig bist du, liebe Kleine, / Die du auf der Baume Zweigen') and

7. Cicada

Eduard Mörike (cf. *Epochen der deutschen Lyrik: Übersetzungen (Deutscher Taschenbuch Verlag)* 1.205 and 2.481 respectively).[74] For a bibliography of treatments of the cicada in medieval and modern literature see R.B. Egan, *Classical World* 77 (1984) p.175 n.2.

Cicadas and trees

Cicadas, the poets tell us, sit in trees.[75] Homer *Il.* 3.152, Hesiod *Works and Days* 583 (cf. Alcaeus fr. 347.3 LP), Aristophanes *Birds* 1f., 39f. (specified as a *fig*-tree: see E.K. Borthwick, *CR* 17 (1967) 248f.), Theocritus *Id.* 16.95f.; *Anacreonteum* 34.2, Leonidas *AP* 6.120.1f. = *HE* 2521f., Pamphilus *AP* 7.201.1 = *HE* 2839, Meleager *AP* 7.196.3 = *HE* 4068; Apollonides *AP* 9.264.1 = *GP* 1223; Nicias *AP* 7.200.1ff. = *HE* 2767ff. (the insect here *is* probably a cicada: see Gow-Page's note ad loc. (2.431)); note that Antiphilus *AP* 9.71.1ff. = *GP* 985ff. specifies an oak;[76] cf. Timon of Phlius fr. 804 *Suppl. Hell.*, Gregory of Nazianza *carm. mor.* 14.17ff.). Aristotle confirms this (*HA* 556a22ff.: 'cicadas do not occur where there are no trees'), adding that they are particularly fond of the olive tree as not producing too deep a shade[77] (cf. *HA* 601a7). This brings us to the next point.

Association with heat.

Cicadas do not crop up in cold places, says Aristotle (*HA* 556a24f. → Pliny *NH* 11.95). On the contrary, they are closely connected with the season of summer ([Hesiod] *Shield* 394, Alcaeus fr. 347.4 LP (cf. Alcaeus fr. 347B LP = Sappho fr. 101^a

---

[74] Also translated into English by Abraham Cowley and adapted in Lovelace's 'The Grasse-Hopper'. On this latter see D.C. Allen, *Modern Language Quarterly* 18 (1957) 35ff. ≃ *Image and Meaning: Metaphoric Traditions in Renaissance Poetry*² (1968) pp. 152ff. who also documents English confusion between cicada and grasshopper.

[75] Hence the proverbial expression about cicadas singing from the ground (Ar. *Rhet.* 1394bf. etc.) indicates a land's total desolation.

[76] Anyte *AP* 7.190.1f = *HE* 742f. also refers to the cicada as reposing in an oak (the word could merely mean 'reposing in a tree', and this non-specific signification is preferred by Gow and Page ad loc. (2.101) who fail to quote Antiphilus).

[77] Archias *AP* 7.213.1f. = *GP* 3716f., however, specifies 'fir or shady pine' as the insect's abode; on the association between cicada and shade in Theocr. *Id.* 7.138 see Gow ad loc. (2.164).

V), Plato *Phaedrus* 230C, Leonidas *AP* 6.120.2 = *HE* 2522, Bianor *AP* 9.273.1 = *GP* 1707, Epictetus *Gnom.* 26, [Lucian] *amores* 18, Longus *Daphnis and Chloe* 1.25, *Anacreonteum* 34.11, Ovid *ars amatoria* 1. 271, Juvenal *Sat.* 9.69; Theocritus *Id.* 7.138 uses the term *aithalion* of cicadas, which the scholia ad loc. (p. 110 Wendel) explain as from the verb *aithesthai* meaning 'to burn, to be heated by the sun') especially the mid-day heat (Aristophanes *Birds* 1095f. ('mad with the sun'), Aristophon fr. 10.6f. K-A (*PCG* 4.8), Aelian *NA* 1.20, Meleager *AP* 7.196.7 = *HE* 4072, Apollonides (?) *AP* 9.264.2 = *GP* 1224, Bianor *AP* 9.273.1 = *GP* 1707, Tiberius Ilus *AP* 9.373.3 = *FGE* 2070, *AP* 9.584.11 (anon.), Clem. Alexandr. *Protr.* 1.1ff. (1.3 Stählin)), when their chirruping is a reminder that all other creatures (not least man) are at rest (for the contrast see Gow's note on Theocr. *Id.* 5.110f. (2.112: note especially Plato *Phaedrus* 258E) adding Longus *Daphnis and Chloe* 1.25, Vergil *Eclogues* 2.12f. etc. (for other Latin authors see Steier 1115.18ff.)).

Loud sound

One South American species of cicada is said to be audible a mile away; another has been likened in noise to the screech of a steam-whistle. This reminds us that, even in Europe, visitors from more northerly climes have proved unappreciative of the cicada's charms, a fact that is particularly true of the English: Shaw, *Travels* (or *Observations referring to several parts of Barbary and The Levant*) (Oxford 1783) p. 186 refers to its 'excessively shrill and ungrateful noise' (cf. Byron's 'shrill cicadas', Browning's 'the stunning cicada is shrill', this latter the distinctly prejudiced view of an Italian who prefers down in the city to up at a villa). Dodwell found 'nothing so tiresome and inharmonious as the musical tettix' (*A Classical and Topographical Tour through Greece* (London 1819) vol. 2. ch. 4). A.S.F. Gow characterised their sound as 'a rasping din' (*CQ* 29 (1935) 68). A character holidaying on a Greek island in a recent play by Dennis Potter (*Sufficient Carbohydrate* (1983)) reveals considerable animosity: 'Any moment now the sun will burn a hole in the sky. And the bloody cicadas will start rubbing their bloody legs against their bodies. It's a bloody complicated form of masturbation, don't you think?' See further Patrick Leigh Fermor, *Mani* (London 1958) p. 41: 'the roar of millions of

7. Cicada

cicadas ... rhythmic grating ... metallic waves ... electric rattle ... a whirling canister of iron filings'; L. Bodson, *L'Antiquité classique* 45 (1976) p. 76 n.4. Vergil's *et cantu querulae rumpent arbusta cicadae* (*Georgics* 3.328; cf. *Eclogues* 2.13f.: *raucis ... cicadis*) presupposes similar irritation.[78] It would seem that the Greeks thought differently:[79] the cicada's chirrup is deemed 'sweet' by Aristophanes *Peace* 1160, Apollonides (?) *AP* 9.264.3 = *GP* 1225, Pamphilus *AP* 7.201.2 = *HE* 2840, Longus *Daphnis and Chloe* 1.25 (a second-century A.D. verse inscription (2027.10 Peek) refers to its sweet lips (see below p. 119 n.83)). Theaetetus *AP* 10.16.4 says harvesters are lulled by the sound of the cicadas, Meleager *AP* 7.196.5ff. = *HE* 4070ff. that even the restless lover can be put to sleep by them. It is striking (cf. Cook, *Zeus* 3 p. 62 n.1) that the only play by Aristophanes to name these insects at all often is his *Birds*. Other writers name cicadas in the same breath as *song-birds* (Himerius *orat.* 48.11 (p.201 Colonna) = Alcaeus fr. 307^c LP, Antipater *AP* 9.92.1f. = *GP* 81f., anon. *AP* 9.122, Aristotle *de aud.* 804a22, Plutarch *Quaest. Conv.* 8.7.3 (*moralia* 727E), Aelian *NA* 1.20, Achilles Tatius 1.15.8, Clem. Alexandr. *Strom.* 5.5 (2.343 Stählin), Kaibel *Epigr.* 546.10); cf. the fable mentioned below p. 122 and Menander Rhetor *peri epideikt.* 2.391.13 (p. 118 Russell-Wilson) with Russell-Wilson's note ad loc. (p. 299). Even the gods (or at least Eos: see below p. 126f.) are charmed by their sound: see Hieronymus fr. 15 Wehrli (10.13). Several authors (see West's note on Hesiod's *Works and Days* 583, E.K. Borthwick, *CR* 15 (1965) 255, Aristotle *de aud.* 804a22 etc.) call this sound *liguros* (on whose meaning see Davies on Stesichorus fr. 240 P) a word that poets also apply to the Muse(s) (see Davies loc. cit.) whence the entry in Hesychius s.v. *ligantôr* (2.596 Latte): 'a type of cicada (according to the Laconians)'; cf. Strömberg p.18 citing the verb *ligainein* ('to make a shrill din'). Compare Meleager *AP* 7.195.2 = *HE* 4059 where the terms 'Muse' and '*ligupterugos*' are

---

[78] For other Latin authors who call the cicada's song *raucus* see D.F. Dorsey, *CR* 20 (1970) 138.

[79] Some ingenious psychological speculation on this ('the ancients possessed ears different from our own, ears both coarser and more refined ... [they] loved noise as such') in Douglas, *Birds and Beasts of the Greek Anthology* pp. 190ff. See further W.B. Stanford, *Phoenix* 23 (1969) 6 ('the Greeks seem to have liked shrillness in tone better than we do') and 8 (stressing the absence of metal machinery – with its unpleasant associations – from the ancient world).

applied to an *akris*, to which the characteristics of a *tettix* are being transferred (see below p. 134).[80] A cicada calls itself 'the wayside nightingale of the Nymphs' in Tiberius Ilus *AP* 9.373.3 = *FGE* 2070; Posidippus calls his own soul the cicada of the Muses (*AP* 12.98.1 = *HE* 3074). Cicadas are loved by the Muses says Leonidas of Tarentum (*AP* 6.120.7 = *HE* 2527), by the Muses and Apollo according to *Anacreonteum* 34.12f., Plutarch *Quaest. Conv.* 8.7.3 (*moralia* 727E) and Aelius Dionysius Atticist. (Erbse, *Untersuchungen zu den Attizistischen Lexika* p. 143). Schol. Hermogenes (Walz, *Rhet. Gr.* 4.79 n. 40) and Clem. Alexandr. *Strom.* 5.5 (2.343 Stählin); cf. schol. Thucyd. 1.6.3 (p. 8 Hude)) call them *mousikoi* (something more than merely 'musical': cf. Clem. Alex. *Protr.* 1.1ff. (1.3 Stählin) and Tiberius Ilus *AP* 9.372.6 = *FGE* 2067 where a cicada's song is *mouseios*).[81] Philostratus *epist.* 71 therefore compares a poet-musician to a cicada. For other comparisons of singers on the public stage to cicadas see E.K. Borthwick, *CR* 15 (1965) p. 256 n.5. The emperor Nero, in the context of one of his own public performances, seems to have likened his singing to a cicada's: see Suetonius' biography of him (20.2) as interpreted by Borthwick, *CR* 15 (1965) pp. 252 ff. especially 256. Timaeus *F.Gr.Hist.* 566F43 relates how, at a musical contest once, when a competitor's cithara string snapped, a cicada hopped on to the instrument and supplied the missing note. The consequently victorious bard gratefully included the insect in the commemorative statue of himself and his instrument (for other authors who mention or imply this story see Borthwick, *CQ* 16 (1966) p. 106f. and n.8). Archias, indeed (*AP* 7.213.4 = *GP* 3719), finds the creature's 'melody more joy-giving than the lyre'.[82] Its constant singing is an index of happiness (*Anacreonteum* 34.1,

---

[80] Likewise with the *akris* that sings with *liguphthongos* wings in Mnasalces *AP* 7.192.1 = *HE* 2647 and the *akris* that once exhibited a *ligura mousa* in connection with its wings (Phaennus *AP* 7.197.1f. = *HE* 2931f.). Cf. Aristodicus *AP* 7.189.1f. = *HE* 772f. (an akris' song *ligus*), Kaibel *Epigr.* 546.11f. (an akris called *ligupnoos*).

[81] A type of cicada that was silent thus became a symbol for lack of musical talent: Simonides 610 P with Page ad loc.

[82] 'The cicada has this in common with the dolphin, that both creatures are supposed to be endowed with sentiments towards humanity of the same nature as those which humanity cherished for them. There was a link of affection between the two. Men loved the cicada; what more reasonable than that it should requite the feeling?' (Douglas, *Birds and Beasts of the Greek Anthology* p. 195).

7. Cicada

Philostratus *VA* 7.11; cf. Xenarchus fr. 14 (2.473 K) cited below p. 120 n.86).

Several authors (many listed by West in his note on Hesiod *Works and Days* 583) refer to the cicada's sound as a 'song', though they are perfectly well aware that it does not proceed from the insect's mouth[83] – so, in particular, Aristotle, who mentions the cicadas as singing (*HA* 556a20 and b11f.; cf. 535b6), though elsewhere he says they alone of animals have no mouth, merely a tongue-like organ (*HA* 532b11ff., → Pliny *NH* 11.93); cf. *PA* 682a18ff. (mouth and tongue fused into one part: contrast Bianor *AP* 9.273.2 = *GP* 1708 which *may* (see Gow and Page ad loc. (2.204)) mean the insect has a forked tongue, Simias *AP* 7.193.4 = *HE* 3275 on an *akris'* tongueless mouth). This is a perfect legitimate idiom (see West ib.). Other writers use the verb *êkheô* (see Gow on Theocritus *Id.* 1.148 (2.31), Alcaeus fr. 347.3, Theocr. *Id.* 16.96, Longus *Daphnis and Chloe* 1.25f., 3.24.2) and the corresponding noun *êkhê* of their sound (Longus ib. 1.23.1) the adjective or noun *êkhetês* (cf. Gil Fernández p.122) of the cicadas themselves (Hesiod *Works and Days* 582, [Hesiod] *Shield* 393, Aristophanes *Peace* 1159, *Birds* 1095, Aristotle *HA* 556a20, 532b16, Archias *AP* 7.213.3 = *GP* 3718, cf. 191.3 = *GP* 3712, Pamphilus *AP* 7.201.3 = *HE* 2840, Meleager *AP* 7.196.1 = *HE* 4066).[84] On these words see further Borthwick, *CR* 15 (1965) p. 256 n.3. Others beside talk of 'garrulous chatter' (cf. Gow on Theocritus *Id.* 5.34 (2.101), adding Aristophanes *Birds* 39, Silentarius *AP* 6.54.9, Aelian *NA* 1.20 etc.). This point perhaps underlies the use of *tettix* as a nickname for foreign cooks (Athenaeus 659A, Hesychius s.v. *tettix*: compare the similar use of the word 'swallow' (Aristophanes *Frogs* 1679ff. etc.)).[85] The fact that the cicadas of the neighbouring towns Rhegium and Locris were silent in each other's territory was a sign of their great mutual antipathy (Aelian *NA* 5.9).

---

[83] However, a second-century A.D. verse inscription (2027.10 Peek) has the cicada pouring its song (cf. Hesiod *Works and Days* 583, Alcaeus fr. 347.4 LP, Pamphilus *AP* 7.201.2 = *HE* 2840) 'from its lips'.

[84] To be more precise the adjective *êkhêeis* is employed by Meleager, and D.F. Dorsey, *CR* 20(1970) 137 argues that his use of the word (which literally means 'clanging' or 'roaring') is intentionally 'hyperbolic, inappropriate, and perhaps unkind'. Wasp's buzz and cicada's song contrasted: cf. V. Schmidt, *ZPE* 30 (1978) 17.

[85] For further discussion of this question and citation of relevant sources see H. Dohm, *Mageiros* (*Zetemata* 32 (1964)) pp. 11ff. esp. 17f.

27. The cicada's sound-producing muscles (from Pringle, *Proc. Lin. Soc.* 167 (1957) 145, fig.1).

The sound is produced by the male cicada only (Aristotle *HA* 535b7 → Pliny *NH* 11.92: cf. *Anacreonteum* 34.1, Philostr. *VA* 7.11; his wife (as silent as a bashful young girl says Aelian *NA* 1.20) cannot utter a word[86] (schol. Homer *Il.* 3.15 (1.386 Erbse)) who (as a sexual signal) vibrates a membrane in his thorax. The facts were known to Aristotle (*HA* 532b17, 535b7 → Pliny *NH* 11.266 (93 and 107 are less clear); Aelian *NA* 1.20 merely says they vociferate 'from their waists': cf. Archias *AP* 7.213.3 = *GP* 3718: 'along your fine-winged[87] waist[88]'; Timaeus

[86] Aristotle *HA* 532b17, 556a21 uses the word *tettigonion* of the small and voiceless female. This word was used as the nickname of a prostitute from whom a comedy by Alexander (3.373K) got its title (for insulting insect names cf. above p. 111, below p. 156). Xenarchus fr. 14 (2.473K) jokingly congratulates the cicada since, alone of husbands, he has a silent wife.

[87] On this epithet see Bodson, *L'Antiquité classique* 44 (1975) 632ff.

[88] Aristotle *HA* 556a17ff. states that of the large and small kinds of cicada some are divided at the *hypozōma* (these are the singing ones) and some undivided. And at *HA* 532b16 he describes how the *ekhetēs* (the male: see above p. 119) has an opening under the *hypozōma* where a membrane (the tympanum: see below p. 121) is clearly visible. *LSJ* s.v. translates *hypozōma* in these passages as 'waist', but A. Preus, *CQ* 18 (1968) 272ff. shows that the question of the word's meaning here and elsewhere is considerably more complex.

7. Cicada

F.Gr.Hist. 566 F 43 speaks of them as 'expanding their membranes'. A would-be learned scholion on Aristophanes *Clouds* 158 (*Schol. Ar.* I.III.1 p.45 Holwerda) insists that 'they vociferate from the chest'). A.S.F. Gow (*CR* 6 (1956) p. 93 n.4) has briefly but clearly explained things for the benefit of classicists (as has Bodson, *L'Antiquité classique* 45 (1976) 77ff. with more detail and in French). Nevertheless, a slightly fuller account (with illustration) may be helpful here. Much pioneering work was done by J.W.S. Pringle: note especially his paper 'The structure and evolution of the organs of sound production in cicadas' (*Proceedings of the Linnaean Soc.* 167 (1957) 144ff. with illustration of muscle structure on p. 145) which is fundamental for all later studies.

'The tymbals, or drums, of the cicadas ... consist of a pair of ridged areas of cuticle, each often covered by a flap or *operculum*, on the dorsolateral part of the abdomen ... A strong muscle which has its origin on the ventral abdominal wall, is attached by an apodeme to the inner surface of each tymbal. The muscles are surrounded by tracheal delatations, and thus lie in an air space. This organ also acts by a "click" mechanism. Contraction of the muscle builds up tension in the tymbal to a critical level at which it suddenly deforms, emitting a pulse of sound, releasing tension in the muscle, and temporarily deactivating it. The elasticity of the tymbal then causes it to return to its original shape, whereupon the muscle once more starts to exert tension' (D. Gilmour ap. *The Insects of Australia* (Melbourne 1970) p. 53).

Earlier (and some not so early) authors in antiquity mistakenly refer to the wings as the source of sound ('from under their wings' Hesiod *Works and Days* 584 (paraphrased by Alcaeus fr. 347 LP: cf. Alcaeus fr. 347B LP = Sappho fr. 101^a V), 'from forth their wings' Nicias *AP* 7.200.2 = *HE* 2768 of an unnamed tree-haunting insect which the epigram's lemma (title added at a date later than composition) identifies as a cicada; 'from forth your wings' Mnasalces *AP* 7.192.4 = *HE* 2650 addressed to an *akris* to which the cicada's characteristics are being transferred (see p. 134); 'from my wings' says the anonymous insect at Nicias *AP* 7.200.2 = *HE* 2768 (probably a cicada: see Gow-Page ad loc. (2.431)); Apollonides (?) *AP* 9.264.3 = *GP* 1225 has the cicada beating its belly with its wings to produce the sound) either because they knew the relevant sound-producing membrane was close to the root of the wings, or (more probably (cf. Gow, *CR* 6 (1956) p. 93 n.4) since the membrane is externally invisible) through assimilation to the otherwise dissimilar grasshoppers and locusts which rub their forewings with their legs to produce sound (see below p. 135). Meleager *AP* 7.196.3f = *HE* 4068 has the cicada sitting and producing its sound with 'serrated limbs' (an odd phrase on which cf. D.F. Dorsey, *CR* 20 (1970) 138) presumably by virtue of this same assimilation.

Theophrastus fr. 187 as preserved by Aelian *NA* 3.38 believed it was because cicadas are constitutionally cold that when warmed by the sun they sing. (By contrast, Aristotle *de resp.* 474b31ff. associates their singing with a need to get cool: cf. Peck's note on *HA* 535b10 (2 p.74f. n.c).) It is, in fact, the case that cicadas will not sing (or reproduce) below a certain temperature (65°F, for instance, in the case of England's only species of cicada: see J.A. Grant, *Countryside: the Journal of the British Naturalists' Association* 21 (Summer 1970) 302; compare W.W. Frogatt, *Agricultural Gazette of New South Wales* April 1903 p. 334 (of Australian cicadas: 'The only thing that stops the noise between sunrise and sunset is a sudden rain or wind storm')).

The cicada's link with the Muses and Apollo is first explicitly stated in the exquisite aetiological myth which we find in Plato's *Phaedrus* 259C (= Perry's Appendix 470) and which most scholars have rightly attributed to the inventive powers of Plato himself.[89] According to this story, cicadas were originally men, or at least descended from men who, when the Muses were born and music invented, became carried away and kept on singing until they died. From these men sprang the race of cicadas, who were granted by the Muses the power to exist without food and drink: when they die they come to the Muses and tell them who honours them on earth. (Compare Leonidas *AP* 6.120.7 = *HE* 2527 and *Anacreonteum* 34.12f. where the cicada is beloved of Apollo (or Athena) and the Muses; also the application to the cicada of the adjective *liguros* (see above p. 117).)

---

[89] This rules out the anyway unlikely theory of R. Böhme, *Jhb.d.deutsch. Arch. Inst.* 69 (1954) 53f. that Plato and the simile in *Il.* 3.149ff. are drawing on an early Orphic myth about the cicada. On Plato's myth see further Karadagli, *Fabel und Ainos* pp. 181ff.; cf. K.J. Dover, *JHS* 86 (1966) p.43 n.14.

7. Cicada

Food

Plato's lovely tale was not invented out of thin air. Its underlying notion that cicadas survive without food or drink has clearly been inspired by the popular belief that these insects lived on dew. Our earliest extant source for this is [Hesiod] *Shield* 393. See too *Anacreonteum* 34.3,[90] Synesius *Hymn* 9.45 and the amusing fable (Perry's Appendix 184) which relates how an ass, envying the cicadas' voices, asked them what they fed on; hearing that their diet consisted of nothing but dew he adopted it and very soon died of starvation. For other authors who relate the tradition that the cicada eats only dew see Gow's note on Theocritus *Id.* 4.16 (2.80), Pfeiffer, *Hermes* 63 (1928) 324 = *Ausgewählte Schriften* p. 117f. and Borthwick, *CQ* 16 (1966) 107 and 110 (who ingeniously interprets Eubulus fr. 10 Hunter as presupposing it (108ff.)). Even Aristotle accepts the idea (*HA* 532b13, 556b16; cf. also *PA* 682a25;[91] Pliny *NH* 11.94 is more sceptical) and Meleager developed it into a poetic fantasy with his pleasing picture (*AP* 7.196 = *HE* 4066ff.) of cicadas intoxicated by dew (copied by Antipater of Thessalonica *AP* 9.92.1 = *GP* 81).[92] In fact their diet is vegetable, they feed on the sap of plants by boring through the bark of trees with a sucker. The reason for the popular fancy which prevailed in antiquity may be, as Steier suggests, that cicadas (like many Homoptera) excrete surplus water and relatively small molecules such as sugars and amino acids, through their hind gut as 'honeydew' (a fact known to Aristotle *HA* 556b14ff., though denied by Pliny *NH* 11.32.92 who says they have no aperture for excrement (cf. Aristotle *HA* 532b14: 'no excretion found in their stomach')). This liquid is often clearly discernible on trees where cicadas have been. Of course the poetic connotations of dew are also relevant. The underlying idea is that the cicada drinks the (dawn) dew and then sings (at mid-day). Particularly explicit as to this sequence are [Hesiod] *Shield* 395, Antipater *AP* 9.92.1f. =

---

[90] For the possible relationship of this detail to the comparison between cicada and king which follows it in the poem see Borthwick, *CQ* 16 (1966) p. 104 and n. 2.

[91] The dew is here referred to as 'liquid formed out of air' (cf. above p. 56 for dew as thus conceived). For passages which describe the cicada as 'feeding on air' see Borthwick ibid. pp. 107, 109 and 111).

[92] Note that cicadas and wine-drinking are mentioned in the same context as Hes. *Works and Days* 583ff. and Alcaeus fr. 347.1ff., though there, of course, the humans are the drinkers!

GP 81f., *Anacreonteum* 34.3f., Synesius *hymn* 9.45 Terzaghi. A letter of St Jerome (*epist.* 22.18) urging a female addressee to perpetual virginity bids her be a cicada of the night and bathe her bed and couch in tears. This metaphor is plausibly associated with the insect's honeydew by R.B. Egan, *Classical World* 77 (1984) 175f.

Immortality

Plato's myth conceives of the cicadas as dying, and this detail is at odds with another popular notion touched on by the author of *Anacreonteum* 34 when he says (l.15) that the cicada is not oppressed by old age. The Greeks used the same word for old age as for the skin or exuvia which insects such as the cicada slough off (*gêras*). Callimachus, in a memorable passage of his poem the *Aetia* (fr. 1.29ff. Pf.), expresses the wish that he could shed old age, in a context that mentions the cicada, dew and the Muses.[93] On this passage and others from Greek literature which refer to the cicada's shedding of its skin see Pfeiffer, *Hermes* 63 (1928) 324f. = *Ausgewählte Schriften* p. 118f. (adding Tzetzes on Lycophron 18 (2.19 Scheer)). Thus it is that *Anacreonteum* 34 ends by telling the cicada, 'You are like the gods.'[94]

Reproduction

According to Aristotle *HA* 556b6, 601a6f. → Pliny *NH* 11.93) the female puts her eggs in a hollow cane or twigs; upon emerging the larvae dig themselves into the earth and later emerge thence as fully-grown insects. (Hence the cicada is often said to be born of the earth: cf. Heraclides Ponticus fr. 55 Wehrli (7².22), Plato *Symp.* 191C,[95] *Anacreonteum* 34.16. Other references in E.K.

[93] And an ass (ll.31ff.), probably to remind us of the fable (see p. 123) of the ass and the cicadas (cf. M. Campbell, *Hermes* 102 (1974) 46). And the earthborn giant Enceladus (1.36), perhaps to remind us of the cicada-like insect (see below p. 130f.) of that name (see Borthwick *CQ* 16 (1966) p. 112 n.1).

[94] Rather wittily, this compliment is immediately preceded by an epithet meaning 'bloodless', a quality that applied both to Greek insects and to Greek gods (in whose veins ran *ichôr*, not blood). Cf. Onians, *Origins of European Thought* p. 506f.

[95] What Plato actually makes the comic poet Aristophanes say here is that cicadas beget and bear 'into the ground' (cf. Plutarch *Amator* (*moral.* 767C): male cicadas deposit their sperm in squills). This may either be an attempt at compromise between the alternatives of spontaneous and sexual generation (so Guthrie, *In the Beginning* (1957) p. 114f. comparing the Athenian myth of the

7. Cicada

28. Cicada and owl on a silver tetradrachm (obverse) from Athens, c. 196-187 B.C. (*Brit. Mus. Cat. of Coins Attica etc.* (1888) no.439 (p.62)).

Borthwick, *CQ* 16 (1966) 107ff., 111). According to Eustathius *Il.* 395.33 (1.622 Van der Valk) and Schol. Hermogenes (Waltz, *Rhet. Gr.* 4.79 n.40) it is for this reason that the cicada became the traditional badge of the autochthonous Athenian (and, indeed, Ionian) people. (On the relevant sources and the vexed issue of the exact nature of these badges see Cook, *Zeus* 3.250ff., A. Rumpf ap. *Symbola Coloniensia* (J. Kroll Festschrift) pp.85ff.).[96] They therefore appear on Athenian tetradrachms

---

birth of Erichthonius from the seed which Hephaestus spilled on the ground) or a mere confusing of cicada and grasshopper (some species of which lay eggs into the ground) and of the grasshopper's large ovipositor with a penis (so Dover's commentary on the Platonic passage).

[96] Rumpf argues that the reference is to the metal fastening or brooch at the front of a type of hair band shown on numerous Attic vases of the first half of the fifth century.

together with the national symbol the owl (see Cook, *Zeus* 3.254ff.; cf. Leonidas *AP* 6.120 = *HE* 2521ff. on a cicada (real or sculpted is unclear) on the spear of Athena's statue). When the cicadas emerge from the ground (continues Aristotle) they sit upon the branches of an olive tree (or on a reed) until their husk bursts. They then come forth (leaving behind a little liquid) and soon begin flying and singing. This account is largely accurate. In fact the female cicada places her eggs in slits which she has cut in branches and twigs with her saw-like ovipostor. The young do burrow into the soil with their forelegs, which are modified for digging. Their entire nymphal existence is spent under the soil and may last for several years (e.g. the seventeen-year cicada of North America). The nymphal exuviae left behind on tree trunks by emerging adults doubtless contributed to the myth of their immortality.

Myth of Tithonus

Many readers will be familiar with the story of how Eos the goddess of the dawn fell in love with the mortal Tithonus, carried him off to be her paramour, and successfully obtained immortality from him for the gods. But, having forgotten to obtain eternal youth to accompany it, she was forced to see her lover dwindling into decrepitude and senility until finally she transformed the withered old man into a cicada (for sources and interpretation see Cook, *Zeus* 3.247ff., Nisbet and Hubbard on Horace *Odes* 1.28.8 (1.326f.) and 2.16.30 (2.267), S. Kaempf-Dimitriadou, *Die Liebe d. Götter in d. attischen Kunst des 5 Jhdt. v. Chr.* (1979) p. 17f.). But when was the sad entomological climax of the tale conceived? Homer mentions Tithonus (*Il.* 11.1, 19.237; *Od.* 5.1) but not the story of his immortality. The *Homeric Hymn to Aphrodite* (and Mimnermus fr. 4 W) mention Tithonus' perpetual decline into old age but do not relate[97] the

---

[97] Kakridis may be right, however, to suggest that the hymn knows of (and even presupposes) the transformation, but purposely keeps quiet about it (*Wiener Studien* 48 (1930) 463ff.). Pfeiffer (*Hermes* 63 (1928) p. 325 n. 1 = *Ausgewählte Schriften* p. 118 n. 63) forbids us to connect the story of Tithonus' transformation with Callim. fr. 1.33ff. Pf., where the poet wishes he could be like a cicada and cast off his years. In a very memorable simile (see above p. 8) Homer (*Il.* 3.149ff.) compares the Trojan elders to cicadas. The picture is copied by Timon of Phlius fr. 804 *Suppl. Hell.* which compares the philosophers of the Athenian Academy to the same insects.

7. Cicada

metamorphosis into a cicada. (Eos merely concludes the hymn's account by locking away her former lover in a room in her palace). The historian Hellanicus (fifth century B.C.) is named as source, at the end of a narrative which includes the cicada, by a scholion on *Il.* 3.151 (*Fr.Gr.Hist.* 4.F140) but it is not clear that he is being credited with this particular detail (Jacoby in his note ad loc. (1B p. 446) suggests he is being quoted only for the genealogy of Tithonus, and Pfeiffer (*Hermes* 63 (1928) p. 325 n.1 = *Ausgewählte Schriften* p. 118 n. 63) agrees). Two peripatetic philosophers of the school of Aristotle, Clearchus (*c.* 340-250 B.C.) in fr. 56 Wehrli (3.26) and Hieronymus (*c.* 290-230 B.C.) in fr. 15 Wehrli (10.13) are said to have employed the detail, the latter charmingly motivating the metamorphosis in terms of Eos' desire perpetually to enjoy the sound of the cicada's voice.

For other references to the metamorphosis in scholia and proverbs see E. Wüst in *RE* s.v. Tithonus (6A (1937)) 1518.20ff.

Source of food to others

According to several authors, the swallow for its young (Aelian *NA* 8.6, Euenus *AP* 9.122 = *GP* 2318ff., Plutarch *moralia* 727E, Longus, *Daphnis and Chloe* 1.25) though Douglas, *Birds and Beasts of the Greek Anthology* p.194 says 'no swallow in its senses would dream of doing' this and finds Plutarch's version with the sparrow 'more probable'. In the world of fable the owl (Phaedrus 3.16) and the fox (Perry's Appendix 241). Among other insects the ant (Archias *AP* 7.213.5f. = *GP* 3720f.). Similarly Tiberius Ilus *AP* 9.372 = *FGE* 2062ff. envisages a cicada entangled in a spider's web. Douglas again finds this 'a strain on the imagination of anyone who has experienced the bullet-like impact of a flying cicada in his face' but adds that southern spiders' webs are sticky enough to have detained titmouse and lizard.

A source of food also to man, who hunted them with a *kalamos* (a limed reed rod)[98] as may be inferred from Aristophanes fr. 53

---

[98] Modern accounts of the luring of cicadas onto bamboo sticks or walking-canes to the accompaniment of rhythmical whistling or hand-clapping are collected by Peck in his translation of Aristotle's *HA* (2 p. 373f.). Compare the statement that cicadas will settle on a finger bent back and then stretched out again because their poor eyesight makes them think it a moving leaf (Aristotle *HA* 556b17ff. → Pliny *NH* 11.94 and 140).

K-A (*PCG* 3.2.57), Apollonides (?) *AP* 9.264 = *GP* 1223ff., and Bianor *AP* 9.273 = *GP* 1707ff. (cf. *AP* 9.373 (anon.); also perhaps[99] Theocritus *Id.* 5.110f.). On all these passages see the remarks of E.K. Borthwick, *CQ* 17 (1967) 110f. (whose findings were anticipated by K. Zacher, *Hermes* 19 (1884) 432ff.). They were hunted not as *pets* (cf. Gow, *CR* 6 (1956) p. 93 n.4, who observes[100] that they would silently starve if they were ever kept in caged captivity (which there is no evidence they were))[101] but as *food*. This is explicitly stated in the Aristophanic fragment cited above (see Kassel-Austin ad loc. for other literary references to eating cicadas) and has analogies the world over: see, for instance, F.S. Bodenheimer, *Insects as Human Food* (The Hague 1951) pp. 62f., 259, 267, 277f., 285f. etc. Aristotle (*HA* 556b7 and 15ff.; cf. Pliny *NH* 11.92 (who strangely refers the eating to orientals)) states that at first the males are the tastier, but after copulation the females, because of their eggs. Pliny *NH* 30.68 talks of roasting cicadas in a shallow pan. Douglas, *Birds and Beasts of the Greek Anthology* p.195 finds this 'a disgusting banquet', but modern experiments by American entomologists have reported no 'gastronomical success as far as soups and stews were concerned, but when fried in butter the pupae were very palatable, and not unlike shrimps'.[102] But so tender-hearted were

---

[99] But not certainly: cf. A.D. Pagliaro, *CR* 24 (1974) 176f. for a summary of interpretations of this passage and a new emendation which removes the bearers of the reed rod (*kalameutas*) and replaces them with frogs (*kalamitas*).

[100] Silently correcting his own notes on Theocritus *Id.* 1.52 (1.12) and 5.108 (2.110).

[101] Anyte *AP* 7.190 = *HE* 742ff. is an epigram for an *akris* (see below p. 137f.) and a cicada who were once the pets of a girl called Myro. Gow and Page ad loc. (2.101) suggest that the girl tied a thread to the cicada: compare Greek children's treatment of beetles (above p. 90). Alternatively, it may be the case that treatment appropriate to an *akris* has been transferred to a *tettix*, just as elsewhere the reverse happens (cf. Borthwick *CQ* 16 (1966) p. 103 n. 2). This motif-transference may also explain the picture of a captive cicada singing which underlies the story of Tithonus as presented by Hieronymus fr. 15 (above p. 127). However, for more recent evidence as to the keeping of the *Tettigonia viridissima* as a home pet in eighteenth-century Hamburg see E. Schmitschek, *Handbuch der Zoologie* 4.2.1 (Berlin 1968) p. 29. Myro is ludicrously confused with Myron the sculptor (*Myronem ... fecisse et cicadae monumentum* etc.) by Pliny *NH* 34.57: see Herrlinger (above p. 14 n. 45) and Gow-Page ad loc.

[102] Froggatt, *Agricultural Gazette of New South Wales* (April 1903) p. 334. Similarly the later experiment by Fabre (*Souvenirs entomologiques* 5.262ff., 10.103ff.) who agreed as to the resemblance to shrimps (compare the reported taste of locusts (below p. 142 n.115)) but found the consistency too like chewing parchment.

7. Cicada

some Greeks towards the cicada that Bianor and Apollonides (?) as cited above, relate that the cicada-hunters in their epigrams were punished by failure henceforward to snare any birds. Epigrams for dead cicadas killed by young boys are to be found in Pamphilus *AP* 7.201 = *HE* 2839ff. and (probably: see Gow-Page ad loc. (2.431)) Nicias *AP* 7.200 = *HE* 2767ff. See above p. 14. An Aesopic fable (no. 397 in Perry's Appendix) tells the tale of a fowler deceived into expecting a large catch by the very loudness of the cicada's song.

Miscellaneous

Cicadas are black according to Aristotle (*HA* 556b10 → Pliny *NH* 11.93), and poets tell the same story [Hesiod] *Shield* 393f., Martial 1.115.4f., Pliny *NH* 11.93, Meleager *AP* 7.196.4 = *HE* 4069 ('Ethiop'), Gow on Theocritus *Id.* 7.138 (2.165)). They are usually light-green or brown, but in fact the Greek word for 'black' (*melas*) covers a surprisingly wide range of tones (cf. H. Dürbeck, *Zur Charakteristik der gr. Farbenbezeichnungen* (Bonn 1977) pp. 142ff.). Hence Hesychius s.v. *killos* (2.478 Latte), an adjective conveying a darkish grey, glosses as '*tettix*': cf. Gil Fernández p. 100 and below p. 132f.

Lucian *Pseudologistes* states that the poet Archilochus (fr. 223 W) said of an enemy that he had caught a cicada (meaning himself) by the wing. Apostolius 16.32 (2.666 Leutsch-Schneidewin) and several other paroemiographers cite the saying without reference to Archilochus. The sources and meaning of the proverb-like phrase are discussed by Bodson, *L'Antiquité classique* 45 (1976) 81ff. who explains it in the light of the remark of Tzetzes (*Chil.* 9.998f.; cf. 8.66ff.) that if one takes hold of a cicada by the wings its singing becomes shriller (for the comparison of cicadas and poets see above p. 122). If true this would indicate (cf. Bodson p. 92) Archilochus' awareness that the cicada's chirruping is not produced by means of its wings. In a tradition concerning Archilochus' death, the Delphic Oracle elliptically refers to an individual as the Cicada (see Plutarch *de sera num. vind.* 17 (*moralia* 560E) = Archil. T 141 Tarditi, and *Suda* s.v. Archil. (1.376 Adler) = T 170 Tarditi).

There is a charming tale of a cicada taking refuge in a sleeping girl's bosom in Longus *Daphnis and Chloe* 1.25.

Finally, after so much praise of the creature, a few negative remarks: A large number of cicadas presages a year of sickness according to Theophrastus *de sign. temp.* 54. The constant song of the cicada could be seen in a way that presents the insect as a type of the improvident and impractical: this is most obviously so in the immortal fable of the ant[103] and the cicada (see above p. 4 and Borthwick, *CQ* 16 (1966) p. 111 and n. 6) but the theme also underlies Eubulus fr. 10 Hunter (as interpreted by Borthwick pp. 107ff.) where the musical Amphion is contrasted with his down-to-earth brother Zethus and assimilated to the cicada. That creature 'lives from day to day' as St. Ambrose (*epist.* 28.5) complained, and is a symbol of concupiscence (cf. R.B. Egan, *Classical World* 77 (1984) 176). On the useless and idle cicada see further Borthwick, *CQ* 17 (1967) 41ff., 18 (1968) 198.

For a selection of modern folk-tales concerning the cicada see Cook, *Zeus* 3 p. 257 n.1. For a list of representations of the cicada in the plastic art of antiquity see P.F. Davidson and A. Oliver Jr., *Ancient Greek and Roman Gold Jewelry in the Brooklyn Museum* (1984) p.13f.

Akanthios

An epithet applied to a cicada by Aelian *NA* 10.44; cf. *Suda* s.v. *akanthias* (1.76 Adler); according to Hesychius s.v. *akanthos* (1.82 Latte) the name of an insect. Zenobius *cent.* 1.51 (1.20 Leutsch-Schneidewin) and Stephanus of Byzantium s.v. *akanthos* claim the epithet is used proverbially of a silent cicada (cf. Simonides 610 P, above p. 118 n. 81); its name ('the prickly one') presumably refers to its regular habitat. Compare the epithet *akantho-batês* ('a.-climbing') applied to an *akris* by Leonidas of Tarentum *AP* 7.198.4 = *HE* 2087.

Enceladus

A stridulating insect similar to the cicada according to a scholion on Aristophanes *Clouds* 158 (*Ar. Schol.* I.III.1 p.45 Holwerda).

---

[103] The inaccuracy of the fable (since ants often attack cicadas in summer and cicadas do not survive the winter) was observed by Fabre, *The Life of the Grasshopper* pp. 4ff. On its afterlife in Byzantine literature see J. Vaio ap. *La Fable* p. 218f.; for more recent echoes see D.C. Allen, *Modern Language Quarterly* 18 (1957) p. 39 ≃ *Image and Meaning: Metaphoric Traditions in Renaissance Poetry*² (1968) p. 160 n.15.

7. Cicada

The Greek noun *kelados* means 'noise, din' and is used of the sound produced by both *tettix* and *akris* (see Borthwick, *CQ* 16 (1966) p. 112 n.1; cf. Strömberg p. 18).

Herpyllis

A *tettix* says Hesychius s.v. (2.198 Latte). The name derives from the plant *herpyllos*, a type of *Thymus sibthorpii* (cf. Strömberg p. 17).

Kalamaion

Mentioned by Pausanias Atticistes and Hesychius s.v. *kerkôpê*: see the following entry.

Kerkôpê

An important source of information is Athenaeus 133B who quotes such earlier references as Aristophanes fr. 53 K-A (*PCG* 3.2.57), Alexis fr. 92.2 (2.326 K), Epilycus fr. 4 (1.804 K), Speusippus fr. 10 Tarán (cf. Tarán's commentary ad loc. (p. 248f.) for the apparent differences between Aristotle's and Speusippus' classification of animals revealed by this fragment). The creature is also referred to in Aelian *NA* 10.44. It is stated to be female of sex by a scholion on Aristophanes *Birds* 1095 (p.205 White). Pausanias Atticistes s.v. (Erbse, *Untersuchungen zu den Attizistischen Lexika* p. 189) and Hesychius s.v. (2.465 Latte) stress its smallness (and that it is also called *kalamaion*). The latter records an alternative identification with the silent female cicada. Exact identification is rendered complex by the issue of the word's etymology, on which see Gil Fernández p. 45f. The most popular and obvious derivation is from the noun *kerkos* meaning 'tail', with a reference to the conspicuous ovipositor of the female (see above p. 126). But apart from the difficulty of explaining the second element *-ôpê* (connected with *ôps* ('face')) there is a further obstacle: Hesychius does, indeed, claim that some say the term is used of the silent female cicada (see above p. 120); but the fragment of Alexis cited above mentions it in the same breath as a male cicada and the *trygôn* (turtle-dove: see D'Arcy Thompson, *Greek Birds* s.v. (p. 291)) as a paradigm of loquacious chattering.

Gil Fernández himself hazards an onomatopoeic derivation from an original *kerka* (see below p. 146) on top of which has been laid a folk-etymology connecting it with *kerkos* (and perhaps also with the *kerkôpes* ('naughty boys who interfere with all passers-by' and were 'warned by their mother ... to mind they do not have to do with a "black rump" and so get what they deserve' (Fraenkel, *Aeschylus' Agamemnon* (Oxford 1950) 2.69)) since an isolated tradition preserved by *Etym. Magn.* names a *Kerkôpê* as mother of the *kerkôpes*: this would explain the puzzle of the second element, which, however, Chantraine s.v. *Kerkôpes* (2.520) thinks not so very problematical: 'qui présente une queue dans son aspect, qui a une queue.'

Kikous

A young cicada according to Hesychius s.v. (2.477 Latte). The name is another instance of onomatopoeia (compare the very word cicada and cf. above p. 114, Gil Fernández p.127).

Killos

See above p. 129

Kixios

A cicada says Hesychius s.v. (2.481 Latte). Cf. Gil Fernández p. 127 (more onomatopoeia).

Kôbax

A large cicada (Hesychius s.v. (2.555 Latte)). On the etymology see Gil Fernández p. 122f. detecting further onomatopoeia. Compare *kauax*, the name of a sea-bird (cf. D'Arcy Thompson, *Greek Birds* s.v. (p. 133)).

Lacetas

A type of cicada according to Aelian *NA* 10.44. On the etymology see Gil Fernández p. 122. The verb *lakein* meaning 'shout, cry' (for a full treatment of its range of significations see G. Björck, *Das alpha impurum und die tragische Kunstsprache* (Uppsala

7. Cicada

1950) pp. 280ff.) alludes to its characteristically shrill sound (above p. 116f.).

Ligantôr

Another type of cicada according to Hesychius s.v.: see above p. 117.

Membrax

A cicada according to Aelian *NA* 10.44 who confesses bafflement as to how it got the name. Gil Fernández p. 234 suggests another onomatopoeic derivation, from an original **bher-bhr-* variously developed or corrupted (compare his explanation of *pemphrêdôn* (see above p. 81)). With the final element compare *korax* ('crow') etc. (cf. p.149 below).

Sigalphos

A sort of wild cicada says Hesychius s.v. Further popular etymology (the Greek noun *sigê* means 'silence': on silent cicadas see above p. 120). Or have we here an instance of humorously incongruous etymology on a popular level (compare in the opposite direction the name Cerberus (the noisy hound of Hades) applied to the mute toad (Schol. Nicand. *Alex* 578 (p.198 Geymonat)) or the name 'lavender-bug' applied to noisesome insects?

Sigion

A silent type of cicada according to a scholion on Aristophanes *Birds* 1095 (p. 205 White). Another piece of popular etymology (see previous entry). Strömberg p. 18 connects with the verb *sizein* ('to hiss'), however.

Tephras

'The ashen one': a type of cicada mentioned by Aelian *NA* 10.44 who observes that the name is self-explanatory (see above p. 129).

29. Grasshopper (with two eagles tearing a hare) on a silver decadrachm from Acragas, c. 411 B.C., now in Munich (cf. Fraenkel, *Aeschylus Agamemnon* (Oxford 1950) 2.70).

8. CRICKET/GRASSHOPPER/LOCUST

These three insects are grouped together here because, as A.S.F. Gow observes of them (*CR* 6 (1956) p. 92 n.6),[104] they 'are superficially much alike. It may be doubted whether Greek laymen distinguished between locusts and grasshoppers.' The problem of nomenclature therefore becomes even more vexing than usual, especially since some poets seem to go out of their way to transfer to the grasshopper details appropriate only to the cicada (cf. Borthwick, *CQ* 16 (1966) p. 103 n.2).

[104] Compare the remarks of Hans Gossen in *RE* s.v. Heuschrecke 8² (1913) 1382.1ff.

8. Cricket/grasshopper/locust

One mode of distinguishing between these insects resides in their sound-production. Male[105] crickets (Gryllidae) and long-horned grasshoppers (Tettigoniidae) stridulate by rubbing their wings together: the sound constitutes a sexual signal intended (among other things) to attract females and facilitate mating (cf. Matthews, *Insect Behaviour* pp. 279ff. and 295ff.). Grasshoppers and locusts (Acrididae) scrape the hind femur against their tegmen (leathery forewings). This phenomenon is alluded to more or less accurately by several writers in antiquity: Aristotle *HA* 535b12 says that *akrides* produce their sound by rubbing with their 'paddles'; Pliny *NH* 11.267: (cf. 107) specifically mentions the thigh as rubbed by the wing in the case of *locustae* (*pennarum et feminum attritu*); Meleager *AP* 7.195.4 = *HE* 4061 talks of an *akris* beating its wings with its feet. (Inaccurately, therefore, the picture presented in Kaibel *Epigr.* 546.12 portraying an *akris* pouring its song from its *chest*.)

Akris

Etymology: scholia on the earliest literary evidence for this insect (*Iliad* 21.12ff. (5.126 Erbse)) reveal popular but impossible derivations from the verb *kran* ('to eat': cf. Callim. fr. 551 Pf.) or from the verb *akrizein* (= *ta akra esthiein*: 'to eat the tops'). Strömberg pp. 15ff. rejects these and more recent etymologies in favour of an interpretation of the word (p.19) as initial intensive *a-* + *-krizein* ('to cry, to pipe') referring to the insect's sound (cf. *hypokrizein* of the *parnops* in Aelian *NA* 6.19). This interpretation is approved by Gil Fernández p. 123f.

A.S.F. Gow summarises the facts compendiously when he states that this term is regularly used 'for orthopterous insects of the cricket-grasshopper-locust kind' and 'in one place or another[106] to explain *attelabos* [1], *broukhos* [2], *brukos* [3], *kornops* [4], *mantis* [5], *mastax* [6], *parnôps* [7]' (*CQ* 29 (1935)

---

[105] As with cicadas (see above p. 120) the females are silent. For further details as to sound production see Howard Ensign Evans, *Life on a Little-Known Planet*² (1984) pp. 85ff.

[106] To be a little more detailed (with the aid of the numbers interpolated in Gow's text within square brackets) *akris* is used in defining the relevant insect by *Etym. Magn.* s. vv. [2], [3], and [6], Hesychius s. vv. [3], [6] and [7], Photius, Galen 248.18 and Eustathius *Od.* 1496.53 on the question of [6], Artemidorus 2.22 on [7]. On Aristotle's use of *akris* and *attelabos* [1] (the two are treated separately at *HA* 555b18ff., listed together at 550b32) see p. 136 n.107 below.

67). A few authors (as Gow himself observes) depart from this general rule by *distinguishing* between *akris* and one of the seven names just listed. Thus Aristotle (*HA* 550b32; cf. 556a8) differentiates *akrides* from *atteleboi* (some such distinction[107] also underlies Theophrastus fr. 174 (4) (the *akris* troublesome, the *atteleboi* more so, especially the variety known as *broukoi*), Hesychius (2.749 Latte) and Photius s.v. *okornos*. And Aelian *NA* 6.19 differentiates between a buzzing *akris* and a lightly strumming *parnops* (Scholfield's translation (2.35) renders the participles thus and suggests that *akris* here signifies the 'field-cricket' (*Acheta* or *Gryllus campestris*)).

Akris: the problem

Our helplessness is indicated by passages like Leonidas of Tarentum *AP* 7.198 = *HE* 2084ff., an epitaph for an *akris* kept in captivity for two years: 'grasshopper, locust, or cricket must be meant' say Gow-Page ad loc. (2.331). Gow notes (*CR* 6 (1956) 93) that incidental details as to the circumstances in which the particular *akris* produces its sound may help us on the road towards a more specific identification. Thus in Meleager *AP* 7.195.4 = *HE* 4061 the *akris* is pictured as beating its wings with its feet: this detail suggests a locust or grasshopper, since these insects stridulate by scraping the hind femur on the wing (or rather the tegmen: see above p. 135).[108] Mnasalces *AP* 7.192.1 and 4 = *HE* 2647 and 2650, Mnasalces *AP* 7.194.1 = *HE* 2651 and Phaennus *AP* 7.197.2 = *HE* 2932 state that their *akris* makes

---

[107] Sturtevant, *Class. Phil.* 7 (1912) 235f. argues for a fairly clear-cut distinction between the *akris* and the *attelabos* (the former being the normal locust which poses no threat because sparse in numbers, the latter the destructive swarm) on the basis of Theophrastus fr. 174 (4) as cited, id. fr. 174 (3) (where the two are partly distinguished and may have been more so in the original unepitomised form of Theophrastus' remarks), and Aristotle *HA* 555b18ff. and 556a8ff., where *akrides* and *atteleboi* are certainly distinguished respectively and the statement that the former do not occur in mountainous areas reminds Sturtevant by contrast of Theophrastus' claim (fr. 174(3)) that the *atteleboi* swoop down onto tilled ground from mountains. Against all this it must be said that the *akris* of the first of the two Aristotelian passages may be a *grasshopper* rather than any kind of locust (so e.g. Peck ad loc.; similarly at *HA* 550b32); that their fragmentary nature makes all Theophrastean testimony on the two names extremely uncertain; and that other authors (see p. 135 n.106 above) do not distinguish them invariably on the lines laid down by Sturtevant.

[108] Simias *AP* 7.193.4 = *HE* 3275 refers to the 'tongueless mouth' of the *akris*.

8. Cricket/grasshopper/locust

music with its wings. This points towards the cricket (Gryllidae) or long-horned grasshopper (Tettigoniidae) since these stridulate by rubbing their wings together. Mnasalces' reference to evenings in *AP* 7.194.3 = *HE* 2653 and Phaennus' to sleep in *AP* 7.197.2 = *HE* 2932 would seem to narrow the identification down to that nocturnal stridulator the cricket. But Meleager *AP* 7.195.1 = *HE* 4058 calls his *akris* (which seemed likely to be a locust or grasshopper) an 'encouragement to' (or 'consolation of': see Gow-Page ad loc. (2.615)) 'sleep', and it has features (in particular a dew-diet) appropriate to a cicada (cf. Borthwick, *CQ* 16 (1966) 103ff.).

Akris = cricket or grasshopper

Pliny dates the song of the *akris* to the period between March 21 and September 23. Aristotle *de aud.* 804a23ff. links *akrides* with cicadas and nightingales as possessors of voices that are *liguros* (see above p. 117). Aristodicus of Rhodes *AP* 7.189.1f. = *HE* 772 uses the synonymous adjective *ligeia*. Compare Meleager *AP* 7.195.2 = *HE* 4059 who calls his *akris* a *ligupterugos* ('shrill-winged') Muse of the countryside; cf. Mnasalces *AP* 7.192.1 = *HE* 2647, Kaibel *Epigr.* 546.11f. Anyte *AP* 7.190.1 = *HE* 742 calls her *akris* a nightingale of the countryside and Leonidas of Tarentum his a songstress (*AP* 7.198.3 = *HE* 2086). Such passages remind us of the attitude displayed towards cicadas (perhaps there is motif-transference here: see above) and it is not surprising that Anyte (*AP* 7.190 = *HE* 742ff.) composed an epitaph on an *akris* and a cicada buried (by the girl whose pets they were) in a single tomb. Other epigrams reveal the practice of keeping the *akris* as a pet because of its pleasant sound: Argentarius *AP* 7.364 = *GP* 1407ff. (a close copy of Anyte's poem), Aristodicus of Rhodes *AP* 7.189.1f., Simias *AP* 7.193, Mnasalces *AP* 7.194, Phaennus *AP* 7.197, Leonidas of Tarentum *AP* 7.198: see C. Herrlinger, *Totenklage um Tiere in der Antiken Dichtung* (Stuttgart 1930) pp. 22ff. A grasshopper cage[109] is mentioned at Theocritus *Id.* 1.52: it is constructed from

---

[109] = *akridothēka*: some MSS have *akridothēra* (i.e. grasshopper *trap*) but the inferiority of this from the viewpoint of sense is exposed by Dover's note ad loc. A reference to a locust would be impossible here, as Douglas, *Birds and Beasts in the Greek Anthology* pp. 186ff. explained. World-wide parallels for such insect-cages in E. Estyn Evans, *Irish Folk Ways* (London 1957) p. 210.

rush and asphodel. Note also Simias *AP* 7.193.3 = *HE* 3274 which refers to a 'well-fenced house' (cf. Borthwick, *CQ* 16 (1966) p. 105 n.2). Chloe in Longus' *Daphnis and Chloe* plaits one (1.10.2) with the specific intention (1.14.4) of getting its inhabitant to lull her love-sick mind to sleep. Similar is Meleager *AP* 7.195 = *HE* 4058ff. as explained by Borthwick pp. 103ff. where the creature is promised a leek to cleanse its larynx (see Borthwick p. 104) as well as a refreshing spray of liquid[110] blown over it from its owner's mouth to encourage it to lull that love-lorn individual to sleep.

A pleasant analogy from Tokyo, Japan, at the end of the nineteenth century, where D'Arcy Thompson observed 'a barrow-load of cricket-cages, each with its tiny singer and the tiny slice of cucumber for his food. There are many kinds. Some sing by night and some by day; some are sold in little fairy birdcages made of the slenderest leafstalks of bamboo, and others in gloomy little tents of blackened gauze; and they have their several well-known songs or tunes, just as singing birds have. For in Japan men listen to the chirp of cricket and cicada as Vergil and as Theocritus did; it is the woodland music of the Old World and of the East, a song that to the ears of the older peoples is far better than the nightingale's.'[111] See further B. Laufer, *Insect and Cricket Musician-Champions of China* (Chicago 1927).[112]

Akris/parnops = locust

Another name for the locust is *parnops* (described as a type of *akris* by Suda s.v. *parnops* (4.60 Adler), scholion on Aristophanes *Acharnians* 150 (*Schol. Ar.* I.IB p.29 Wilson), scholion on Aristophanes *Birds* 185 (p.51 White) etc.) which has the variant form *kornops* (see below p.141). Sturtevant, *Class. Phil.* 7 (1912) 237ff. made an ambitious attempt to link the two forms and other allegedly related words (e.g. *akarnos* (see below p. 144), *karnos* (see below p. 146) etc.) and explain them as 'loan words'

---

[110] Actually dew, because the creature is being credited with some characteristics more appropriate to the cicada: see Borthwick p. 103 n.2.

[111] Thompson in an article entitled 'Goldfish' (*Country Life* (1923)) quoted by Ruth Thompson in the biography of her father (Oxford 1958) p. 118. Thompson visited Japan in June 1897.

[112] This rather inaccessible pamphlet is summarised by Ensign Evans, *Life on a Little-Known Planet*² p. 97f.

8. Cricket/grasshopper/locust

30. Locust on a corn stalk (with moth above) on a carnelian scarab, first half of the sixth century B.C. (*Brit. Mus. Cat.* no.512).

of external origin connected with mountains (where locusts were thought to breed) and conveying the appropriate notion of destruction. More recent discussion (see e.g. Gil Fernández p. 166f.) reveals greater reluctance to derive all such forms from a single root and a more modest derivation of *kornops* from *kornos*, a Sicilian word for tree. It will be convenient to treat the two names together here, carefully distinguishing them.

Food

Locusts normally eat the green parts of higher flowering plants, nibbling at the leaf-stalks for moisture; a particular threat to vines (Aristophanes *Birds* 588 (*parnopes*), Theocritus *Id.* 5.108f. (*akrides*)) therefore; cf. Simias *AP* 7.193.1 = *HE* 3272 where the poet finds an *akris* on a vine leaf, Agathias *AP* 11.365.14 where it is very strongly hinted that the *akris* is destructive to the harvest; Hesychius s.v. *brukedanos* (1.351 Latte) a word used of a locust's greed: cf. Thompson, *CQ* 40 (1946) 44. A Greek vase now in Oxford (*CVA* 2 p.88 and pl. IIDX; cf. Boardman, *JHS* 78 (1958) 4f. fig.1 and pl.1[a] (*c.* 550-540 B.C.): it is too fragmentary for its reproduction to be helpful here) shows a boy about to catch or crush one in a vineyard, and a black-figure cup now in the Louvre (F68 (*c.* 550 B.C.)) shows a locust similarly placed (Fig. 31).

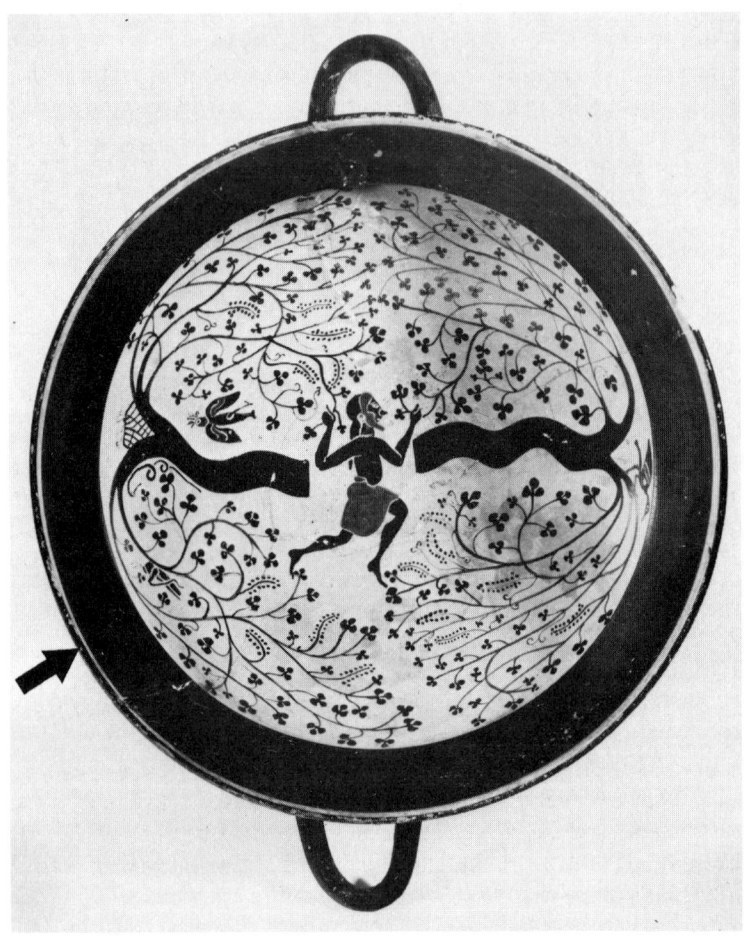

31. Locust (indicated by arrow) on a vine on a black-figure cup, c.550 B.C. (Louvre F68).

A simile of Homer's (*Iliad* 21.12ff.) merely refers to their numbers when it compares the Trojans plunging into the river Xanthus before Achilles' onslaught to *akrides* fleeing to a river before the onset of fire. But why should the locusts be fleeing fire? Presumably this is a device employed by farmers to keep them from the crops (so various ancient commentators ad loc., some of whom connect the practice with Cyprus and the Libyan

8. Cricket/grasshopper/locust 141

cities of Cyrene and Barca in particular: see 5.125 Erbse with note). The same point about numbers is combined with a specific mention of the great harm to crops in a simile used by Quintus of Smyrna (2.197ff.): here there is an explicit reference to the way in which locusts bring famine upon mankind. Plagues of locusts are familiar from the Bible (see e.g. J. Cloudsley-Thompson, *Insects and History* (London 1976) pp. 187ff.). 'The term "locust" is correctly given to a few species of Acridids which are capable under certain conditions not fully understood of forming large swarms which move over wide areas causing great devastation of natural and cultivated vegetation where they feed' (Imms, *Textbook of Entomology*³ p. 331). Classical authors tell of catastrophic swarms of locusts (Pliny *NH* 11.104ff.; 8.104, 10.75; cf. W. Warde Fowler, *CR* 18 (1904) 394f.). According to Pliny *NH* 11.106 and Aelian *NA* 3.12 the inhabitants of Thessaly, Illyria and Lemnos feed jackdaws at public expense for destroying young *akrides*; Aelian also quotes at ib. 17.19 Eudoxus (of Rhodes: *F.Gr.Hist.* 79 F4; cf. Lasserre, *Die Fragmente des Eudoxus von Knidos* p. 127) for the statement that in Galatia prayers are addressed to a species of highly-esteemed *parnops*-destroying birds. For ridding Mt. Oeta of locusts Heracles was called *Kornopiôn* (*kornops* = local dialect for *parnops*) if Strabo 13.613.64 is to be believed, and Apollo and Zeus were called *Parnopios* in Attica for rendering the same service (Pausanias 1.24.8f.; cf. Pliny *NH* 10.75). It seems likeliest that an originally independent deity invoked for help against locusts was later brought into line with the Olympian pantheon by means of identification with the aforenamed gods: see further Sturtevant, *Class. Phil.* 7 (1912) 236f., Bodson, *Hiera Zôia* p. 14f.

Akris = grasshopper or locust

Source of food to others

An Aetolian mole eats locusts according to [Aristotle] *Marvels Heard* 176 (847b). As for humans, the notion is familiar to us from the Bible and other sources (see Bodenheimer, *Insects as Human Food* pp. 40ff, esp. p.58f. and pp. 160ff. and 202ff., 210ff., 232ff, for evidence gathered world-wide concerning locusts as edible, and pp. 265, 173, 275f. etc. for similar information on

142 *Greek Insects*

grasshoppers) and several ancient authors mention locusts as eaten by an Ethiopian tribe who were therefore known as *akridophagoi* (Diod. Sic. 3.29;[113] Strabo 16.772.12; Pliny *NH* 6.195, 7.29; Agatharchides of Cnidus (*F.Gr.Hist.* 86 F22) is cited as source in the last of these passages. The idea that the Greeks (or at least the poor in ancient Greece) ate them is less securely founded. Of the passages usually cited to prove this (see e.g. Gossen, *RE* 8² (1913) 1386.18ff.) Theocritus *Id.* 1.52 in fact refers to the keeping of an *akris* as a tame singing pet (see p.137f.) while Aristophanes *Acharnians* 1116 is a comic passage in which one speaker offers the other an obviously ludicrous choice of menu between thrushes (regarded in antiquity as the greatest of delicacies)[114] and *akrides*, and then preposterously misunderstands the reply as expressing a preference for the *akrides*. (The reference to 'four-winged game' at l. 871 of the same play is generally taken as a humorous allusion to grasshoppers or locusts.) Nevertheless, an American experiment quoted by Bodenheimer (*Insects as Human Food* p. 58f.) ends with the verdict that 'John the Baptist ... had not fared badly on his diet in the wilderness', and the Greek palate may have agreed.[115] Aristotle *HA* 532b10 claims that the gut of the *akris* is convoluted: in fact it is simple in locusts and grasshoppers: the error is presumably to be explained in terms of a confusion with cicadas or textual corruption.

Medicine against scorpions' poison and other ailments

According to [Aristotle] *Marvels Heard* 139 (844b), because it eats scorpions. Accepted by Pliny *NH* 30.30, 111, 123 and Dioscorides *de mat. med.* 2.52, for instance. Odder is to follow. Our texts of Aristotle *HA* 612a34 present the bizarre picture of the locust fighting the snake and getting a tight hold of it by the neck. It is not surprising that various scholars have wished to emend the word *akrida* here to one of similar appearance (so *iktida* (the yellow-breasted marten) Aubert and Wimmer, *aspida* (the Egyptian cobra) the Aldine edition, *asida* (the stork)

---

[113] Who hardly encourages belief by adding that the *akridophagoi* are subject to attacks of chronic *phthiriasis* (on which fabulous disease see below pp. 173ff.).
[114] See D'Arcy Thompson, *Greek Birds* p. 149.
[115] The taste of fried or roasted locusts is variously compared in Bodenheimer's book to spinach, roast chestnuts, hazelnuts, shrimps, prawns and crayfish!

8. Cricket/grasshopper/locust

32. Locust and an ear of corn on a stater (obverse) from the Achaean colony of Metapontum in Southern Italy, c. 520-510 B.C., now in Berlin. 'The locust ... is, according to Lenormant (*Grande Grèce* 1 p.128) intended as a sort of propitiation of the destroying influences in nature ... It seems more probable, however, that it is merely a touch of local colour, like the beetle on the famous tetradrachm of Aetna' (Fig.19): Head, *Historia Numorum* (Oxford 1911) p.75. See S.P. Noe, *The Coinage of Metapontum: Parts 1 and 2* (with additions and corrections by A. Johnstone (New York 1984)) p.20f. (cf. p.9) for this and similar coins.

Thompson ad loc. (n.1)).

That several ancient writers seem to support the picture of the serpent-fighting locust (Pliny *NH* 11.103, Philo *de opificio mundi* 154 (1.250 Arnaldez), Hesychius (2.801 Latte) and *Suda* (3.596 Adler) s.v. *ophiomachês*, [Aristotle] *Marvels Heard* 30 (844b)) merely indicates that Aristotle's text was corrupt by their time.

In Aristophanes *Wasps* 1311f. an individual is compared to a locust (*parnops*) without its fig-leaves (? = its wings). Absurdly misunderstood by a scholion ad loc. (*Schol. Ar.* II.1 p. 209 Koster) which states that locusts sometimes change their colour like leaves! (For a locust's wings compared to leaves see e.g. Doughty, *Travels in Arabia Deserta* 1.351).

A proverb positing the *akris* as the type of senselessness and folly seems implied by Lucian *Iup. Trag.* 31 (1.233 Macleod): see R. Strömberg, *Greek Proverbs* (Göteborg 1954) p. 57.

Akarnos

Identified with the *attelabos* by Hesychius (1.89 Latte) and Photius s.v. (1.288 Theodoridis). See Theodoridis' note ad loc. for other late authors who make this identification.

A variant form of the word is *okornos*, glossed as *attelabos* by Hesychius s.v. (2.749 Latte), as a *parnops* by Photius, used in Aeschylus' lost tragedy *Philoctetes* (see above p. 10f.). Strömberg p.17 connects with the word *akorna* (fish thistle, *Cnicus acarna*: compare *akanthios* as used of the cicada (above p. 130; on Sturtevant's incompatible view see above p. 138f.).

[Astakos]

A type of locust according to Isidore 12.8.9. Probably confused (so Gil Fernández p. 51f) with the next entry.

Attakos

A kind of locust according to various Jewish authors writing in Greek (see *LSJ* s.v.).

Attelabos

Etymology unknown (for a brief bibliography of our ignorance see Chantraine s.v. (1.136)). MSS of the relevant authors present this word in a variety of spellings: see, for instance, Hunter's note on Eubulus fr. 107.10.

The word probably refers to a locust: Aristotle glosses it by *akris*, but also distinguishes the two (see above p. 135 and n.108). The evidence of Modern Greek *attelabos* points in the same direction (see Shipp, *Modern Greek Evidence for the Ancient*

8. Cricket/grasshopper/locust

Greek Vocabulary (1979) p. 112f.).[116] Herodotus states that a certain Libyan tribe in Cyrene dry the insect, mix the powder with milk, and drink it (4.172.1): both locale and diet are suggestive of the locust. Note also the more recent report by Doughty, on the Bedouin women of Arabia, who mingle locust meat 'brayed small, with their often only liquid diet of sour buttermilk' (*Travels in Arabia Deserta* (1936) 1.244 (cf. Index (2.641) s.v. 'Locusts')).

Our most explicit source of information is the admittedly late St. Jerome (*c.* 340-420 A.D.) who defines the creature in his commentary on Nahum as a small locust with little underdeveloped wings which consequently crawls rather than flies. Pliny too had already described it as wingless and the smallest of the locusts (hence *LSJ* Supplement's entry under this word: 'before *"locust"* insert *"wingless* or *larval"* '). Plutarch, *Isis and Osiris* 74 (*moralia* 380E) states that the Lemnians honour those crested larks which detect and crush the eggs of this creature (cf. Aelian *NA* 3.12 quoted above p. 141 and J. Gwyn Griffiths' note on Plutarch's passage (p. 555) for an emendation that would bring Plutarch into line with Aelian). Eubulus the comic poet used the word *attelabophthalmos* ('*attelabos*-eyed') in a now obscure riddle (fr. 107.10 Hunter). The point made presumably referred to the relative largeness of this part of the insect (compare English 'bug-eyed' and cf. Hesychius s.v. *triopis* 'three-eyed ... an animal like a locust'; cf. Strömberg p. 17).

Br(o)ukos, br(o)ukhos etc.

For a list of the numerous other variant forms of the word see Gil Fernández p. 149. A type of *akris* according to Hesychius (1.349 Latte), *Etym. Magn.* s. vv.

The name's derivation (cf. Strömberg p.17) from *brukein, brukhein* ('to eat noisily or greedily') would imply the locust, though, in view of the discrepancy in quantity between *brûk(h)ein* and such variant forms as *brĕker* or *brŏkos*, some (cf. Gil Fernández p. 149f.) prefer an etymology in terms of 'jump, leap' (cf. Slav *br̂knem, br̂kati* etc.): compare the next entry.

---

[116] Though the movement from Latin *bruchus* (locust) to Italian *bruco* ('caterpillar'), reminds us, as Douglas, *Birds and Beasts of the Greek Anthology* p. 189 says, 'how the meanings of these words shift about'.

Karnos

A large *akris* says Hesychius s.v. (2.415 Latte). Ambitiously, Sturtevant, *Class. Phil.* 7 (1912) 239 associated the name with such similar seeming words as *parnops*, *kornops* (see above p. 138), *karnê* (glossed as 'loss' by Hesychius s.v. (2.415 Latte) and s.v. *autokarnos* (1.284 Latte)) and *karos* (glossed as 'destruction' by Hesychius s.v. (2.415 Latte)) and reconstructed a large group of loan words of considerable antiquity sharing a basic notion of 'injure'. The *akris* would then be equivalent to the locust. But Sturtevant's theory is extremely speculative and there is much to be said for an alternative approach (cf. Gil Fernández p. 148) that links the word with the verb *akairein* meaning 'to hop, jump'. Compare such words as English *grasshopper*, French *sauterelle*, German *Heuschrecke*, *Heuhüpfer* etc.

Kerka

Glossed by Hesychius s.v. (2.464 Latte) as *akris*. The name is interpreted by Gil Fernández p. 128 as an example of expressive reduplication (see above p. 114).

Kynakris

Mentioned by *Corpus Glossorum Latinorum* 7.567 with the gloss *gillus* (= *gryllus*). The initial *kyn*- is presumably (as Strömberg p. 19 took it) diminutive-pejorative: cf. *kynamuia* (see below p. 155).

Mantis

See below p. 176 and n.163.

Mastax

Stated to be a type of *akris* by Photius s.v., Eustathius *Od.* 1469.53. The derivation from *mastasthai* 'to chew' (or from *mastazein* 'chew, eat': see Strömberg p. 17f.) indicates a locust; this is how the word is used by Nicander *Ther.* 802 who calls it

8. Cricket/grasshopper/locust

'corn-devouring', and perhaps by Sophocles (see above p. 10). Claimed as an Ambracian word by Clitarchus the glossographer.

Okornos

See above p. 10.

Petêlis or petênis

According to Hesychius s.v. a type of *akris*. From the adjective *petênos* (*petêlos*) meaning 'winged'.

Pranô

A type of *akris* says Hesychius s.v. The word is a short form of *parnops* (see above p. 138) according to Sturtevant, *Class. Phil.* 7 (1912) 237f. (cf. Strömberg p. 17 who sees it as an instance of metathesis (or transposition) of that word).

Stitthon

A type of *akris* according to Hesychius s.v. One is reminded of the onomatopoeic nature of the word *tettix* (cf. Gil Fernández p. 131).

Trôxallis

Name: first element from the verb *trôgein* ('eat'); second element diminutive suffix (cf. *pyr-allis*, *chrys-allis* etc.; compare Chantraine, *La Formation des noms en grec ancien* (Paris 1933) p. 252). This etymology would suggest a locust. Note, however, that Hesychius glosses the verb *trôzein* by *psithyrizein* ('to make a light chirruping sound'). The ambiguity persists on other levels. *Trôxallis* was tentatively suggested as a Greek word for the cricket by Gow, *CR* 6 (1956) p. 92 n. 6 (cf. before him Keller, *Antike Tierwelt* 2.460: *Grillus domesticus*). This is consistent with references in Aelian *NA* 6.19 (where, in the company of various sound-producing insects, it is 'not silent'; taken to be a grasshopper by Scholfield's translation (2.35)) and Pliny *NH* 30.49 (*esse animal locustae simile sine pennis, quod troxallis Graece vocetur, Latinum nomen non habeat, aliqui arbitrantur, nec pauci auctores, hoc esse quod grylli vocentur*), but is perhaps incompatible with Alexis fr. 15.12 (2.302 K) where their connection with a vegetable shortage would seem to indicate locusts. Gil Fernández p. 104 would resolve the issue by suggesting that Alexis has in mind an insect like the *trôx* (the weevil: cf. Strattis fr. 80 (1.733 K)), Aelian one like the *trôxallis*.[117]

A special case

He odotus 2.75 and 3.107 mentions flying snakes of Arabia which invade Egypt from the East but are killed en route by ibises.[118] In South Arabia itself they guard incense-bearing trees from which they can only be driven by smoke. They are small in size and elaborate (or many-coloured) and have wings which resemble those of bats. Numerous identifications of these creatures have been advanced (see the list and critique by Lloyd in his commentary on the first passage (2.326f.)). Some scholars (most notably R.W. Hutchinson, *CQ* 8 (1958) 100f.) have suggested the locust, but as Lloyd says this interpretation 'seems least likely'. That an Anacreontic ode (35.10) can make the bee-stung Eros complain he has been injured by a winged snake is perfectly irrelevant since the point of the faux-naïf comparison resides in the insect's sting (see above p. 63). Hutchinson also argues that Herodotus' story of the winged snake eating its way out of its mother's womb[119] 'is a countryman's explanation of the sloughed-off skins of snakes and of the exuviae of the last pupal stage of the locust before it emerged as the perfect imago.' Both, he thinks, 'give the impression that something has eaten away the body inside'.[120] But the Greeks knew about exuviae and had their own tales about them (see above p. 124). It is unlikely that either they or the Egyptians would feel obliged to explain them

---

[117] MSS of Photius refer s.v. *mulabrides* to a word *trixalides* (emended to *trôxallides* by Naber). The MSS of Pliny *NH* 30.49 have *trixallis* which has been similarly emended away. Gil Fernández p. 124 takes the form *trixallis* seriously and derives from the Greek verb *trizein* meaning 'to produce a shrill sound'.

[118] Hence, claims Herodotus, the Egyptians' reverence and respect for the ibis (with this motif compare pp. 141 and 145 above).

[119] At 3.109 Herodotus has a similar story about the young of the echidna: see Gow-Scholfield on Nicander *Ther.* 128ff.

[120] For a bibliography of scholars who have (unbeknown to Hutchinson) anticipated this identification see D. Fehling, *Die Quellenangaben bei Herodot* (1971) p.22 n.6.

9. Flea 149

in the terms of Herodotus' account. For flying serpents as a folk-tale motif see e.g. Gaster, *Myth, Legend and Custom in the Old Testament* p. 573. D. Fehling, *Quellenangaben bei Herodot* (1971) pp. 20ff. argues plausibly that Herodotus has invented the flying-serpents to explain the Egyptians' reverence for the ibis (see above n. 118).

9. FLEA (psylla/pulex)

On the etymology of the word see Gil Fernández p.21f., Chantraine s.v. (4.1294). To be associated with such forms as Sanskrit *plúṣiḥ* (whence, ultimately, the English word 'flea') and in particular Baltic **blus-* whose transposition (or metathesis) will provide Greek **psul-* (a rearrangement possibly influenced by such words as *psallein* ('leap'), *psauein* ('touch'), *psên* (see above p. 81f.) and Latin **pusl* ($\rightarrow$ *pulex*)). A variant form *psyllax* mentioned by Hesychius s.v. is explicable on analogy with *myrmêx* (see above p. 37), *sphêx* (see above p. 75), *membrax* (p. 133) etc.

Object of a joke in Aristophanes' *Clouds* 145 where, a flea having leaped from the eyebrow of Chaerephon to the head of his associate Socrates,[121] the latter worthy arranges an experiment to measure the length of the leap: the creature's feet are dipped in wax which cools to form slippers which are then removed and used for measurement.[122] The comic poet Epicharmus (fr. 199 Kaibel) also used the word, but we are ignorant as to the context in which he did so. In *AP* 11.432.1f. a fool being bitten by fleas extinguishes the lamp and cries triumphantly 'you can't see me any more!' For Aristotle's views on fleas' generation see above p. 22.

Psyllitês in Theophrastus *HP* 7.5.4 is the diminutive form (cf. G. Redard, *Les noms grecs en -TÊS / -TIS* (Paris 1949) p. 85). Against the notion that the plague which devastated Athens during the Peloponnesian War was the bubonic variety (usually spread by rat fleas) see A.J. Holladay and J.C.F. Poole, *CQ* 29 (1979) 287ff. (cf. p. 299 n. 57) and ib. 34 (1984) 483.

---

[121] For the close connexion in popular thought between philosophers and vermin see below p. 174. For another joke about insects from this part of the play see below p. 166f.

[122] Measuring a flea's jump occurs as a proverbial instance of wasting one's time in [Lucian] *Philopatris* 12.

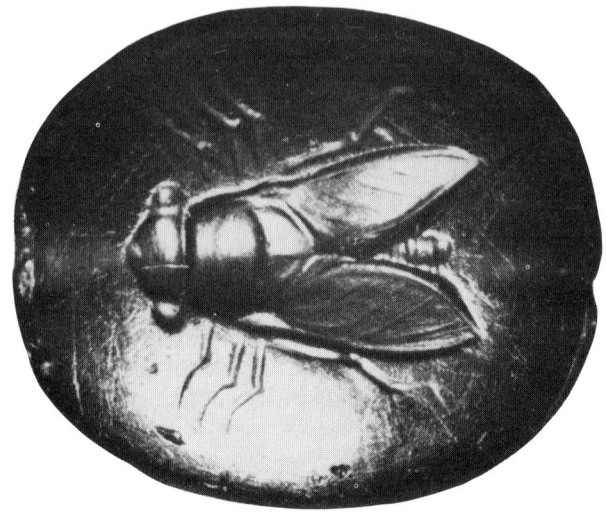

33. Fly on a carnelian scaraboid, fifth century B.C. (Leningrad, Hermitage Museum, 584): Boardman, *Greek Gems and Finger Rings* (1970) no.582.

10. FLY

Muia/musca

Name: an onomatopoeic imitation of the insect's buzz (mu-mu-mu: for similar onomatopoeic words of animal and insect sounds see Thompson, *CQ* 40 (1946) 44; see further Gil Fernández p. 20f. who explains how an -s- comes to intrude in the Latin and other forms of the word) which Aristotle recognised as produced by the friction of air between wings opened and closed in flight (*HA* 535b10 → Pliny *NH* 11.266).

The most notable description of the creature is Lucian's famous *The Fly* where, to quote Christopher Robinson in his book on this author (p. 90), we find 'an ingenious description of the physical qualities and life-style of the fly, in which an essentially trivial subject is raised in status by as many comparisons made to its advantage as the rhetorician can manage'. Lucian praises the fly's peacock-coloured wings, musical flight, intelligence, courage (called impudence by others: see below p. 155f.), the precedence over kings allowed it

10. Fly

in feasting and so on. The notion was common in antiquity that this insect could fly around even after its head had been cut off (taken seriously by Tertullian[123] *de anima* 15.2 (p. 19 Waszink)) and can be brought back to life if ashes are sprinkled on its corpse (so too Aelian *NA* 2.29, Pliny *NH* 11.120). He concludes the whole with an ingenious aetiological myth (compare Plato on cicadas: see above p. 122) that the fly was once a girl called Muia turned into an insect by the angry goddess of the moon Selene because her chatter kept waking Endymion, Selene's beloved. But she still wakes sleepers in her insect form by her buzzing.

Aristotle (*HA* 490a20) says the fly's sting is in front, draws blood by a touch (*HA* 532a13); its proboscis is tongue-shaped (*HA* 528b29), and it feeds on every kind of juice (*HA* 596b14).

Says Pliny *NH* 11.258 house-flies have longer front legs the better to rub their eyes.

Aristotle says their copulation lasts a long time (*HA* 542a12 followed by Lucian *The Fly* 7)[124] and results in grubs (*HA* 539b13 → Pliny *NH* 10.190) found in dung heaped up by farmers (*HA* 552a20ff.). The grubs are small at first, of reddish colour, originally motionless, then moving but relapsing into motionlessness. It then emerges as a perfect fly. For analogous traditions see H.J. Uther ap. *Enzyclopädie des Märchens* 4.1277.

'Flies are a nuisance, flies are a pest ... '

Muisobai or fly-swatters, are mentioned as a Persian luxury in a fragment of Menander (fr. 437 Koerte (2.154); cf. also Anaxippus fr. 7 (3.301 K); Aelian *NA* 15.14 (an Indian practice)). There is mention of three (with handles of ivory, gold and onyx) in a temple inventory on Delos: see *Inscr. Délos* 298A 26-7. The association with a religious centre is not fortuitous: flies were a particular pest and nuisance at festivals and sacrifices, being attracted by the unusually large amount of meat and blood exposed (cf. Aelian *NA* 5.17). Various gods were credited with the power to disperse these unwelcome hordes.[125] (A supposed

---

[123] He quotes the physician Asclepiades as his source. Insects can, of course, continue to exist for some time after decapitation.

[124] Cf. Ensign Evans, *Life on a Little-Known Planet*² pp. 153ff.

[125] Contrast the Oriental picture of gods swarming like flies around the sacrifice, as presented in the *Epic of Gilgamesh* (XI 159-61): cf. p.40 of the Penguin translation and *Atra-Ḫasīs: the Babylonian Story of the Flood* III v 34f. (p. 98f. in the edition with translation by W.G. Lambert and A.R. Millard (Oxford 1969)).

analogy has often been detected in Beelzebub, 'Lord of the Flies' (2 Kings 1:2: see e.g. Cloudsley-Thompson, *Insects and History* p. 21; but specialist studies (e.g. J. Gray's commentary on the passage (London 1970) p. 463, Gaster, *Myth, Legend and Custom in the Old Testament* p. 514) make this less likely). Various divinities were supposed to be useful in such emergencies by virtue of their apotropaic powers. Note especially:

(a) *Zeus Apomuios* ('Zeus the averter of flies'), successfully prayed to by Heracles when sacrificing at Olympia (Pausanias 5.14.1; cf. Eust. *Od.* 1454.25f. etc.) and by the Eleans there in imitation of the great hero: hence flies avoid the Olympic Games (Aelian *NA* 5.17). The same deity was also given the analogous titles *Muiagros* and *Muiodês* there (Pliny *NH* 10.75, 29.106).

(b) *Apollo*: according to Heraclides of Pontus fr. 153 Wehrli (7.45) an ox is sacrificed to the flies in the Acarnanian temple of Apollo at Cape Actium. Similarly Aelian *NA* 11.8, who adds the sequel that the flies, replete with blood, disappear (bribery he calls it, comparing the flies unfavourably to those who shun the Olympic Games voluntarily). For Apollo's general rôle as averter of threatening dangers see Burkert, *Griechische Religion* p. 398 ≃ *Greek Religion* p. 265.

(c) *Muiagros* ('fly-catcher'): an unspecified deity to whom the inhabitants of the small Arcadian town of Aliphera sacrifice first at the start of a festival according to Pausanias 8.26.7, with the result that the flies cease to be a nuisance.

For further examples of these practices see Cook, *Zeus* 2 (1).781ff. Compare the treatment of locusts (above p. 140f.). If prayers failed, fumigations were resorted to, and other devices (e.g. the sprinkling of a decoction of elder leaves mentioned by Pliny *NH* 24.52). On these practices in general see M. Wellmann in *RE* s.v. *Fliege* 6^2 (1909) 2746.32ff.; cf. Bodson, *Hiera Zôia* pp. 10ff.

Aelian (*NA* 15.1) preserves some interesting information about a type of fly that haunts a river in Macedonia. It is unlike all other flies and resembles the *anthrêdôn* (see above p. 79) in size, the honey-bee in buzz, and the wasp in colour. The natives call it the *hippouros*. It settles on the surface of the water in search of

10. Fly

34. Fly (to the left of Apollo, who is naked and holding a branch; on the right, a stag) on a stater from the Achaean colony of Caulonia in South Italy, *c.* 420-410 B.C., now in Berlin.

food and thus becomes the prey of fishes; unfortunately for fishermen, these fish can detect and shun flies that have been caught by human hands, so there is no question of using flies as bait; instead judicious use of wool and feathers (cf. *NA* 12.43) lures the fish on to the hook, our earliest mention of an artificial 'fly' unless the *musca* in Martial 5.18.8f. is not a genuine one. Scholfield ad loc. (3. p. 203 n.b) identifies it with the species *Stratiomys* ('soldier fly').

Symbolism and metaphor

In a memorable metaphor, Simonides (fr. 521.3f. P) says that the change of man's fortune (*sc.* from good to bad) is swifter than the *metastasis* (change of position) of a long-winged fly (*tanup-*

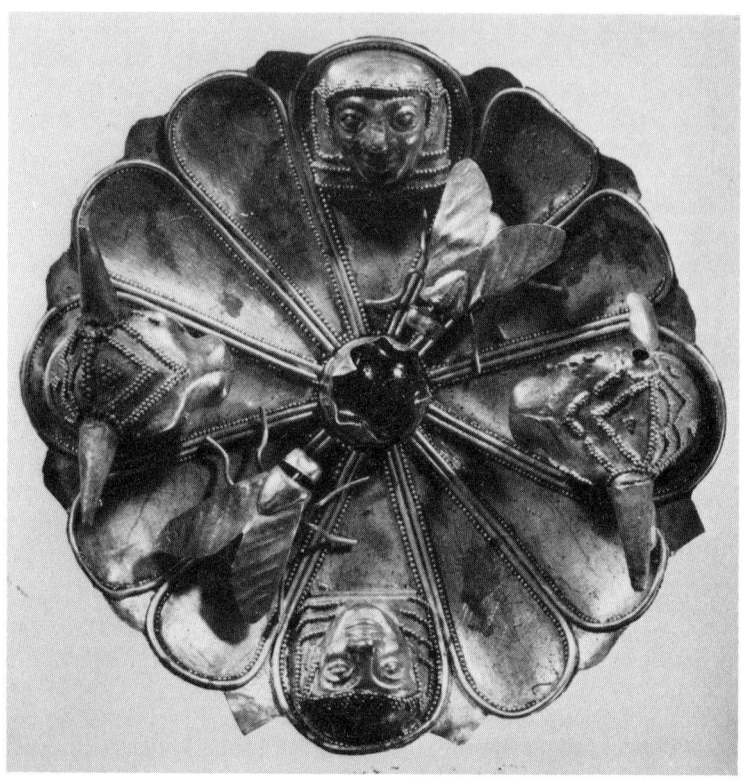

35. Two flies (with two bulls' heads and two human heads) on a rosette from Melos, third quarter of the seventh century B.C. (Paris, Cabinet des Médailles): see Jacobsthal, *Greek Pins* (Oxford 1956) p.75 ('the flies have four wire legs and no proboscis') and p.218.

terugou muias). This is usually taken to refer to a dragon-fly[126] but it is hard to see what is so 'miraculously apt and right'[127] about the application of the image to this particular insect. The adjective *tanusipteros* which means the same as *tanupterugos* is used generically in Homer of any bird, regardless of its size, and seems similarly used here of the unpredictable flitting of a fly from one place to another.

---

[126] So e.g. Bowra, *Greek Lyric Poetry*[2] (Oxford 1961) p. 325, Campbell in his note ad loc. Gerber's note ad loc. (in *Euterpe* p. 313) is better.
[127] To quote Bowra.

10. Fly

For the fly's rôle in ancient proverbs see in general Köhler p.52. As in English (see Tilley, *Dictionary of Proverbs* F 396, 398), it features in proverbial expressions as a small, insignificant, or weak creature: see Headlam's note on Herodas 1.15; the Greek for 'make a mountain out of a mole-hill' is 'make an elephant out of a fly' (Lucian *The Fly* (ad fin.), L. Cohn, *Philol. Suppl.* 6 (1892) = *Corp. Paroem. Graec. Suppl.* (IV) p. 244 (264)). It is a paradigm of daring or impudence (*Tr.G.F.* 2 (adesp.) F295, Aelian *NA* 2.29, Xenophon *Mem.* 3.11.5). Likewise in Egyptian hieroglyphs. Antiphanes fr. 195.7 (2.94K) compares an uninvited dinner guest to a fly, which reminds us that a fly is included in some gruel as a practical joke at Aristophanes *Banqueters* fr. 6 Cassio = fr. 208 K-A (*PCG* 3.2.127): see Kassel and Austin ad loc. for the point of the joke. Eurynomus the demon of decay and putrefaction was portrayed as a fly (Pausanias 10.28.7). For parallels see Gaster, *Myth, Legend and Custom in the Old Testament* p.515, A. Lopasic ap. *Animals in Folklore* (ed. J.R. Porter and W.M.S. Russell, 1978) p. 63.

Fable of flies attracted to and perishing in honey: Perry's Appendix 80 (cf. Karadagli, *Fabel und Ainos* p. 123). Ill-attested proverbial reference to 'a fly's tear': C. Theodoridis, *Glotta* 52 (1974) 61ff.

Kynamuia

[This is probably the original form and the variant *kynomuia*, recorded in some late authors, an incorrect development of a kind not without parallel – see e.g. Schwyzer, *Gr. Gr.* 1.440]. 'Dog-fly': This term of abuse is used by Ares of Athena in Homer *Il.* 21.394f., by Hera of Aphrodite in the same book of the *Iliad* 1.421. At first sight it is a little difficult to explain, and some scholars in antiquity seem to have felt the same, since at least one of them (Neoptolemus of Parion) insisted on spelling the word *kinamuia* and interpreting it as a reference to the motion of the eye's muscle: see fragment 9 of Neoptolemus as edited by H.J. Mette, *Rh. Mus.* 123 (1980) 5; cf. p. 21. Most ancient critics, however, preferred the more obvious reading of the word as an amalgam of two animal names, dog and fly, the former being a symbol of shamelessness, the latter of impudence (for ancient interpretations along these lines see the scholia on the first of the two Iliadic passages (5.219 Erbse) and Erbse's note ad loc.: add Suetonius *peri blasphêmiôn* 5 (p. 48 Taillardat)). Modern scholars too have, by and large, accepted this view:[128] the combination of two abusive animal names is seen as emphatic (compare German 'Schweinehund'). Dogs certainly were a by-word for lack of shame as early as Homer,[129] and the impudence of the fly is presupposed by Homeric simile (see above p. 7f.). Lucian in *The Fly* 12 claims that a certain variety of this insect is sometimes called the dog (cf. Gil Fernández p. 48f.). Athena's boldness[130] is specifically mentioned by Ares in *Il.* 21.395. The word recurs in Athen. 4.157A (of an *hetaera* or courtesan: for animal and insect names applied to such see Headlam on Herodas 2.73 (p. 96f.)) and Athen. 3.126A (of the philosopher Cyn-ulcus as a pun on his name and his sect (he belonged to the school of *cynics*).

Initially, then, the word *kynamuia*, as Gil Fernández says, 'no es nombre de insecto, sino un insulto' (p. 168). But usage changed with time. In two passages of Aelian (*NA* 4.51 and 6.37) the horse-fly is said to be like the dog-fly. Similarly Lucilius *AP* 11.265.1 mentions 'dog-flies' in the company of fleas, frogs, mice and locusts (?), and there are indications in other late writers that the Homeric 'dog-fly' was sometimes taken to be an actual insect that afflicted dogs. Thus some of the scholia on the first Iliadic passage mentioned above (5.220 Erbse) refer to blood-sucking and ticks. Similarly Eustathius' commentary ad loc.[131] (1243.24) and one of the scholia on *Od.* 17.300 observe that some critics, diverging from the great Alexandrian scholar Aristarchus, supposed that Odysseus' dog Argus (see above p.8) was suffering from the attention of these animals. The 'dog-fly'

---

[128] See, for instance, E. Risch, *Indogermanische Forschungen* 59 (1944) 59 = *Kl. Schr.* p.59 and M. Faust, ibid. 74 (1969) 112f.

[129] See the article by M. Faust mentioned in n. 128 above, p. 109f. n. 204 and his remarks in *Glotta* 48 (1970) 8ff. esp. 25. Also S. Lilja, *Dogs in Ancient Greek Poetry* (Helsinki 1976) pp. 21ff. Bees that have stung a child in search of honey are called 'dogs' in Antipater of Thessalonica *AP* 9.302.2 = *GP* 452 and a caterpillar that has eaten an apple is called 'dog' in Antiphanes *AP* 9.256.3f. = *GP* 743f. Faust remarks on p. 112 of the first article that it is unlikely *muia* was ever an independent term of abuse. For the running together of two words to form an abusive compound cf. S. Koster, *Die Invektive in der griechischen und römischen Literatur* (Beitr. zur. kl. Phil. 99 (1980)) Index (p. 365) s.v. 'ad hoc - Bildungen'.

[130] An anonymous epigram in the Planudean Appendix (9) to the *Greek Anthology* calls a hungry belly *kynamuia* (i.e. 'shameless').

[131] Another section of Eustathius' commentary (1243.29) says that the game of blind-man's buff known as 'bronze fly' (*chalkê muia*: see p. 160) was once called 'dog-fly'.

10. Fly

thus defined was identified with the *muôps* in *Corpus Glossorum Latinorum* II 259 10 and 37. A modern scholar, D. Moutsos, in *Zeitschrift für Vergleichende Sprachforschung* 94 (1980) 156f., has accepted this interpretation of 'dog-fly', comparing the way in which modern Greek calls the gadfly the 'horse-fly', the 'ox-fly' etc.

On dog-fleas see Aristotle *HA* 557a18 → Pliny *NH* 11.116. The Greek word is *kynoraistês* (the word used by the poet of the *Odyssey* (17.300: see above p. 8) and in an Aesopic fable reported by Aristotle (see p. 6), glossed by Hesychius s.v. (2.549 Latte) with *krotôn* and meaning (cf. Gil Fernández p. 137) 'dog-devouring', the common tick *Ixodes ricinus*). *Kynamuia* is the Greek translation in the Septuagint for the flies that formed one of the plagues of Egypt in Exodus (8.21).

Ephêmeron

The 'day-fly': mentioned by Aristotle *HA* 552b18ff.: on the river Hypanis (in the Cimmerian Bosphorus) there appear about the time of the summer solstice certain objects bigger than grapes and the shape of wallets. These objects break and a winged four-footed creature emerges to fly forth and live until sunset, whence the name (cf. *HA* 490a34: it has four feet (see above p. 19) and four wings for flight: cf. *PA* 682a5f.: insects with relatively few feet have the compensation of wings). Aristotle's description is cited by Aelian *NA* 5.43, and a very similar one[132] by Pliny *NH* 11.120. Thompson ad loc., following the lead of Sundevall, *Die Tierarten des Aristoteles* p. 199, took this to be a type of may-fly, probably the *Ephemera longicauda* Oliv. still common in the south of Russia (which fits Aristotle's location of it).

Aelian also applies this name to an insect supposedly generated in wine, which will fly out if the wine-cask is opened, see the light, and die (*NA* 2.4 with a moralising tag on the good fortune of creatures prevented so quickly from learning their own and others' misfortunes). This has been identified with the

---

[132] The only significant difference being that Pliny states that the objects or membranes from which the insect emerges look like grapes (thus slightly misrepresenting Aristotle) and says it is called the *hêmerobios* (which means the same as *ephêmeron*), a word used by Theophrastus *Metaph.* 29. Aelian calls it *monhêmeron* (*NA* 5.43), another synonym.

158 Greek Insects

'vinegar-fly' of the genus *Drosophila* by several scholars (e.g. Scholfield ad loc. (p. 91 n.b)).

Pyrolampis, lampyris

'Fire-fly' or 'glow-worm'. *Pyrolampis* is the usual term, though *lampyris* occurs at Aristotle *PA* 642b3ff. and has given rise to various modern European names for the creature (e.g. *lamburída* from Reggio in South Italy; see further Gil Fernández p. 84). The variant spelling *lampouris* at *Suda* s.v. (4.275 Adler) probably represents etymological connection on a popular level with the noun *ourá* ('tail'). For the inversion of compounds represented by the two forms see Strömberg p.2 (compare such alternatives as *leontomyrmêx* and *myrmêkoleôn* (above p. 45)).

Strömberg p.13 argues that *lampyris* is the older form and derives it from the verb *lampyrizô* ('shine brightly'). Gil Fernández p. 85 derives noun from verb, alleging that in the latter's first attested appearance (Theophrastus *On Stones* 58-9) the meaning is specifically 'shine like a fire-fly'. As for priority between the nouns, note the various forms of *pyrolampis* ('shining with fire') which is what we find in *HA* 523b21 with the variant reading *pygo-lampis* (which would have to mean 'shining out of the anus'). *Pyrolampis* is also attested by Hesychius and Photius s.v., the latter with the trivial variation *pyri-lampis*. The natural impulse to reject *pygo-* as a slip may, however, be checked when we find the analogous *kyso-lampis* ('shining out of the (female) genitalia') in Hesychius s.v. (2.554 Latte). Gil Fernández p. 85f. argues that *pygo-* and *kyso-* were the original primitive forms, the product of coarse but anatomically accurate folk-etymology.[133] The former, he suggests, was decorously modified in the course of time into *pyro-*, just as the latter has become the pretentious euphemism *chryso-lampis* ('golden-shining') at Phrynichus *Praep. Soph.* 126.8 (p. 126 de Borries).

Pliny *NH* 11.98 says they shine like fire at night-time because of the colour of their sides and loins, producing flashes of light by opening their wings and then growing dark when they close them

---

[133] Cf. 'the briskly anatomical nature' of much terminology for plants and animals in seventeenth-century England as analysed by Thomas, *Man and the Natural World* p.85. They include 'open-arse' for the medlar fruit and 'twitch-ballock' for the black beetle, and were, of course, later bowdlerised out of existence.

(cf. *NH* 18.252f.) and adds that they generally appear when the crops are ripe (cf. *NH* 18.253). Pliny's explanation of the production of light was accepted until 1885, when the French physiologist Raphael Dubois proved by experiment that two substances, luciferin and luciferase, are responsible: for details see Matthews, *Insect Behaviour* p. 236 who provide an interesting survey of the whole question of insect biolumine- scence.[134] The poetic statement that these creatures are the offspring of the Pleiades (Pliny *NH* 18.253) refers to their time of appearance at the end of cold weather when that star-cluster is first visible. On their actual generation Aristotle (*HA* 551b23ff.) states that they emerge wingless from a small black and hairy caterpillar and endure further metamorphosis into the winged *bostrychus* ('hair-curl'). Elsewhere, he claims (*HA* 523b20) that the glow-worm can be both winged and wingless. This refers to the fact that in some species the female lacks wings but is much more the brilliant while in others (e.g. *Luciola italica*) the winged male is brighter and the female very rare.

To be distinguished from the creature anonymously mentioned by Aristotle (*HA* 552b10ff. → Pliny *NH* 11.119 (who calls it *pyrallis* or *pyrotocon* (= 'fire-born')), Aelian *NA* 2.2. (who calls it *pyrigonos* (= 'fire-engendered')) which is allegedly produced in the fire of copper ore smelting furnaces at Cyprus, is slightly larger than a big fly but winged, jumps and crawls through the fire, and dies when kept from fire. It is usually assumed that Aristotle showed more discernment when he wrote (*GA* 737a1; cf. *meteor.* 382a8) that fire generates no animal, and that the insect in question is totally fabulous; but the entomologist Em. Janssens in *Latomus* 9 (1950) 285f. identified it with the *Melanophila acuminata* de Geer mentioned by the English entomologist W.E. Sharp as found on the calcined trunks of *Pinus sylvestris* in the immediate aftermath of fire (see his remarks in the *Ent. Month. Mag.* 54 (1918) 244f.)

Horse fly and gad fly

Talking of both *muôps* and *oistros* Aristotle calls them bloodsuckers (*HA* 596b15) which pierce the skins of quadrupeds

---

[134] On the general question see E. Newton Harvey, *A History of Luminescence from the Earliest Times to until 1900* (1957).

(*HA* 528b32). Their sting is in front (*HA* 490a21) and takes the form of a hard tongue (*HA* 532a10; cf. Pliny *NH* 11.100). So much for their common characteristics. But ancient authors variously distinguish them. Let us see.

Muôps

Name: the etymology is much disputed: see the recent study by D. Moutsos in *Zeitschrift für Vergleichende Sprachforschung* 94 (1980) 147ff. Attempts to derive it from the word for fly (*muia*: see above p. 150) and the word for *face* (*ôps*) or from an onomatopoeic representation of the insect's buzz (mu-mu-mu: cf. *muia* (p. 150), *tettix* (p. 114) etc.) leave the second element of the word unexplained. The idea that the name relates to *muôps*, the adjective meaning 'short-sighted', (cf. English '*myopic*' etc.) does at least account for both constituent parts but hardly seems to offer promising sense. However, Moutsos compares (pp. 147f. and 156f.) German *Blindfliege*, Modern Greek *tuphlomuga* (literally 'blind fly') and Lithuanian *aklỹs* (used of the gadfly but literally meaning 'blind'). He further notes that the game of blind-man's buff sometimes went, in antiquity, under the name of *muinda* or *chalkê muia* ('bronze fly': the game is described by e.g. Hesychius s.v. (2.682 Latte), Pollux 9.110, 113 (2.178 Bethe) and 9.123 (2.181 Bethe) = *carm. pop.* 876 P, and is presupposed by Herodas 12.1). For other references see J. Taillardat's edition of Suetonius' *peri paidiôn* (Paris 1967) p. 81. For a detailed explanation see D'Arcy Thompson, *Discovery* 4 (1923) 56 (the fly is the player blindfolded (because the insect was thought blind), called 'bronze' as a reference to the fly's yellow, wasp-like colour; the other players are the cattle. Whoever is caught becomes the fly). A similar (independently reached) explanation in Taillardat p. 172f. (arguing for *chalkê muia* as a secondary derivation from *muinda* (which he relates to the verb *muein* = 'shut one's eyes') in which *muia* has a 'sens tres large'). Further discussion and world-wide analogies to the game in Iona and Peter Opie, *Children's Games in Street and Playground* (Oxford 1969) pp. 117ff. (see esp. p. 119f. on Italian 'Mosca Cieca') and pp. 302ff. Ancient authors clearly accepted this etymology: thus Aristotle (*HA* 553a16 → Pliny *NH* 11.120) states that the insect dies when its eyes catch dropsy.

The *muôps* is identified with the *oistros* or gad-fly by

10. Fly

Aeschylus *Supplices* 307 and other poets (the references are assembled by R.F. Thomas in *HSCP* 86 (1982) 83f.), but the two are distinguished by Aristotle[135] *HA* 490a20, 528b31 who observes that the *muôps* is produced from wood (cf. *HA* 552a30 → Pliny *NH* 11.113: the *muôps* generated from wood). In fact, many Tabanid larvae live in decayed wood. Aristotle's point is repeated and a further distinction based on a different criterion is added by Aelian *NA* 4.51, 6.37 and other late authors who state that the buzz of the *muôps* is louder but its sting smaller relative to the *oistros*. It seems very likely that this particular distinction is post-Aristotelian and derives from the first-century B.C. Sostratus, who is actually cited as source by some of these late authors: see M. Wellman, *Hermes* 26 (1891) 344ff. for a useful collection of the passages concerned (he prints the relevant quotation of Sostratus as fr. 10 (p. 348) of this author).[136]

Greek literature frequently exploits the *topos* whereby the excellence of a work of art is proved by its ability to deceive animals: sparrows fed at the grapes painted by Zeuxis, a stallion tried to mate with a mare painted by Apelles and so on.[137] Within the framework of this theme falls the epigram on Myron's bronze statue of a heifer[138] (Julian the Egyptian *AP* 9.739) which deceived a *muôps* into trying to sting its brazen hide.

Metaphor

Plato *Apology* 30E has Socrates at his trial compare his provoking and irritating questioning of the Athenians to the effect of a *muôps* upon a horse. A certain type of goad for horses

---

[135] Aristotle *HA* 487b5 may state that the *oistros* develops from river worms but the text is uncertain: see Thompson and Peck ad loc.

[136] E.L. de Stefani, however, prefers (*Stud. It. Fil. Class.* 12 (1904) 441f.) to suppose that only 6.37 derives from Sostratus; that 4.51 (like 4.49 and 4.55) comes from Aristophanes of Byzantium (see above p. 27 n. 78); and that Sostratus himself actually drew on that source.

[137] See for instance, E. Kris and O. Kurz, *Die Legende vom Künstler: ein geschichtlicher Versuch* (Vienna 1934); cf. Sir Ernst Gombrich in *Illusion in Nature and Art* (ed. R.L. Gregory and E.H. Gombrich 1973) p. 194. The possibility of bees settling on *painted flowers* is raised by Philostratus, *Imagines* 1.23.2.

[138] For the popularity of this statue as a subject for Greek epigrams see Gow and Page, *The Garland of Philip* 2.86, *Hellenistic Epigrams* 2.63.

was known as the *muôps*: see J.K. Anderson, *Ancient Greek Horsemanship* (1961) p. 88.

Oistros

Name: cf. Gil Fernández p. 157 on the etymology. The word is cognate with the Greek nouns *oima* ('rush') and *oistos* ('arrow'). We may ignore the ancient derivation from the verb *oisein* exhibited by such late lexica and commentators as *Et. Gud.* 194.12, Eustathius *Il.* 1161.29, 1928.16.

Aelian *NA.* 4.51 ≃ 6.37, schol. *Od.* 22.229 tells us that it is like a very big fly, that in appearance it is tough and well-built, that it emits a loud buzzing sound, and that it is fitted with a powerful sting at the mouth. Elsewhere (*HA* 551b21ff.) Aristotle derives the gadfly from a flat-animalcule that skims the surface of rivers. But as Thompson observed ad loc. (n.2) this latter detail seems to be referring to small beetles (not larvae) of the genus *Cyrinus* and the insect erroneously derived from them is probably a species of *Syrphus* or *Stratiomys* whose larvae are aquatic.

Parasites that infest the tunny and the sword-fish are nicknamed the gadfly according to Aristotle *HA* 602a26ff., a grub beside their fins like a scorpion in shape, a spider in size. Identified with *Pennella filosa* L in the case of the sword-fish and *Brachiella thynni* Cuv. or *Crecops latreilli* Leach in the tunny's by Thompson ad loc. (n.3).

A notoriously difficult passage in the *Odyssey* (10.81ff.),[139] describes the land of the Laestrygonians, where the shepherd driving his flock home calls to the shepherd driving his flock forth, and where a man who never slept could earn double wages for tending cattle and pasturing sheep, since the paths of day and night are near. A scholion on 1.85 preserves one ancient interpretation of this puzzle in terms of a Sicilian custom: by this cattle were fed after sundown in order to avoid the torment of the *oistros*. That such a custom did obtain in Sicily is shown to be highly likely by L.G. Pocock, *CR* 8 (1958) 109ff., who cites several analogies from different parts of the world. One's acceptance of this as a probable practice is quite independent of any verdict on its plausibility as an explanation of the Odyssean lines (approved by Pocock because consistent with his view that

---

[139] See on it, for instance, Page, *Folk Tales in Homer's Odyssey* pp. 39ff.

10. Fly

Odysseus' wanderings are to be located in Sicily).

Metaphor and myth

Io, one of Zeus' numerous amours, was transformed into a cow by that deity in the hope of avoiding the attention of Hera, his jealous wife. In vain, for she demanded the cow as a gift and then subjected it to several indignities including the attentions of a gadfly which hounded the cow from Greece to Egypt (see Aeschylus *Supplices* 306ff. with Johansen and Whittle's note on 308 (2.249)) and for a brief survey of the myth as it appears in ancient literature D.F. Sutton, *Sophocles' Inachus (Beitr. zur kl*

36. Gad-fly pestering a bull on a rock crystal scaraboid (Boston Museum of Fine Arts 01.7545): Boardman, *Archaic Greek Gems* (1968) no.525.

Phil. 97 (1979) pp. 1ff.).[140] Several gems show a bull being attacked by a gadfly. We reproduce here one instance, a rock crystal scaraboid now in Boston (01.7545) which depicts a kneeling bull[141] with the insect perched on its hindquarters.

---

[140] Sophocles *Tr.G.F.* 4 F 279 Radt, a mysterious quotation from this play, is interpreted as a 'comparison of the afflicted animal's hide ... swollen and uneven, to the carapace of a tortoise' by S. West, *CQ* 34 (1984) 300ff.

[141] On the significance of this pose see J. Boardman, *Archaic Greek Gems* (1968) p. 143.

Since some Cretan coins[142] show Europa on obverse, a bull being worried by a gadfly on reverse, it has been argued[143] that the bull there and here is Zeus, and the gadfly Hera's agent, as in the story of Io. This certainly seems preferable to Cook's notion (*Zeus* 1.532 and n.12) that the fly 'was an emanation of Zeus himself' who may be speculated to have turned himself into a fly in Crete as he became an ant in Thessaly (see above p. 42). We should also bear in mind the metaphor, common in Greek literature, whereby *oistros* is used of the sting of erotic passion (see Headlam's note on Herodas 1.57, Kost's on Musaeus' *Hero and Leander* 134).[144]

Another myth involving the *oistros* concerns the hero Bellerophon who tried to ride up to heaven on his winged steed Pegasus; he was, however, thrown off when an indignant Zeus sent an *oistros* that bit Pegasus and made him rear: see Asclepiades *F.Gr.Hist.* 12 F.13, scholion on Pindar *Ol.* 13.130A (1.382 Drachmann) etc. The tale was told in Euripides' lost tragedy *Bellerophon*.

The term *oistros* also occurs in the context of apiculture, where it is used of an insect that is unlikely to be the gadfly. For a detailed discussion see B.G. Whitfield, *CR* 5 (1955) 12f., who concludes that some sort of drone is the likeliest object of the reference (a similar conclusion was independently reached by Gil Fernández p. 62f.; cf. n.34).

11. GNAT/MOSQUITO

Antiquity did not clearly distinguish the two (or even segregate them strictly from the fly). Both English words were also used of what we now call mosquitos until *c.* 1900: see S.R. Christophers, *Aedes Aegypti: the Yellow Fever Mosquito* (Cambridge 1960) p.1.

---

[142] Boardman (above, n.141), p. 158 n. 23 gives references.
[143] Boardman, p. 151.
[144] Compare the more general use of *oistros* as a metaphor for madness (on which see J. Mattes, *Der Wahnsinn im gr. Mythos und in der Dichtung bis zum Drama des 5. Jahrhunderts* (1970) p. 110).

11. Gnat/mosquito

Empis and kônôps

Etymology: the former word is plausibly derived from the verb *empinein* ('drink one's fill') by Strömberg p. 14f. (approved by Gil Fernández p. 28). That is to say it means 'bloodsucker'. (Ancient derivations from the verb *empneô* = 'to sing' (so e.g. schol. Aristophanes *Clouds* 157 (*Schol. Ar.* I.3.2. pp. 32 and 233 Koster)) may safely be dismissed. For the form *empis* (rather than *empotês*) from *empinein* cf. *engklis* ('couch') from *engklinein* (cited by *Etym. Magn.* s.v)). For *kônôps* the etymological derivation is quite unclear: see the discussion by Gil Fernández p. 75f., Chantraine s.v. (2.607), the latter declaring that the frequent invocation of *kônos* (pointed object → sting) is 'ruineuse'. The identity of *empis* and *kônôps* is sometimes alleged in antiquity (e.g. Bachmann, *An. Gr.* 2.320, Hesychius s.v. *empides* (2.81 Latte), scholion on Lucian's *The Fly* (p.10 Rabe), schol. Aristophanes *Clouds* 157 (*Schol. Ar.* I.3.1 p. 32 Koster): on these passages see R. Kassel, *ZPE* 52 (1983) 53; see too *Suda* s.v. *pênion* cited above p. 112), sometimes denied (e.g. *Schol. Ar.* ibid., Hesychius s.v. *empis* (2.81 Latte) alleging the *empis* to be bigger). *Empis* also seems to be used in a variety of ways by Aristotle (of a mosquito or gnat at *HA* 490a21, 551b27, but of a may fly at 601a4 and at 487b5 of the larva of an *oistros*). Likewise *kônôps* at HA 552b5 seems to refer to an *oinopota cellaris* since it emerges from larvae engendered out of vinegar-slime (cf. *HA* 535a3f. → Pliny *NH* 10.195 (it will only settle on acid objects)).

Nuisance value

Greek authors were aware that these insects constituted a plague in more southerly climates. Herodotus 2.95 says that the *kônôps* is without number in Egypt and that the inhabitants evade the insect either by sleeping in 'towers' on the top of their roofs, which the insects are prevented from reaching by winds (R. Carrington ap. *Animals in Archaeology* ed. A.H. Brodrick (1972) p. 83 doubts this from personal experience); or by getting hold of fishing nets with a mesh so fine that when they sleep inside the creature cannot get at them (on the plausibility of these details see Lloyd's commentary (2.382ff.)). Diod. Sic. 3.2f. → Aelian *NA* 17.40 describes how in India the rising of Sirius the dog-star heralds a swarm of *kônôpes*, far stronger than those of Greece, which terrorise lions by their sting and buzz, while the human inhabitants seek refuge in marshes. Pliny *NH* 11.61 says they even attack bees. According to Pausanias 7.2.11, the inhabitants of Myus (see on *muia* above p. 150) were compelled by *kônôpes* to desert their home and move to Miletus.

Their status as pest is recognised (and comically exaggerated) by Aristophanes (*Birds* 244ff., *Lysistrata* 1032, *Wealth* 537; also Meleager *AP* 5.151 = *HE* 4166ff. (for whose mock-heroic touches see Gow and Page ad loc. (2.626)) in terms of their painful bite (for brief references to which see Aristotle *HA* 490a21 (*empis*), 523a9f. (*kônôps*) → Pliny *NH* 11.100)). For a modern account of the process see Christophers, *Aedes Aegypti* pp. 484ff.) This earned them the humorous nickname *toxotês* ('bow-man'): Achilles Tatius 2.22.3 (cf. G. Giangrande, *Mnemos.* 25 (1972) 300). Mosquito-nets were not imported from Egypt (cf. Herodot. 2.95) to the West until Augustus' time (see Steier's article s.v. Mücke in *RE* (16[1] (1933)) 454.24ff.). They earned the Latin name *conopium* (because they kept off the *kônôps*) whence the English word 'canopy', French 'canapé'. Three epigrams by Paulus and Agathias (*AP* 9.764-6) make these nets sing their own praises. Generally the worst[145] that is said of these insects is that they produce a high-pitched whine or buzz or hum which can keep a restless individual awake for hours. Aeschylus' Clytemnestra speaks feelingly of this (see *Agamemnon* 892 as explained by W.S. Barrett in Fraenkel's commentary on that play (3.830)). For the possibility that such a sound may wake a sleeper see Meleager *AP* 5.152 = *HE* 4174ff. Several writers hyperbolically compare the sound to that produced by a trumpet (see Fraenkel's note on *Ag.* 892 (2.404)) in which context one is reminded of the sublime line 'so the arse is the trumpet of *empides*' (Aristophanes *Clouds* 165). This represents the grand climax of an unlikely piece of Socratic ratiocination reported

---

[145] While acquainted with the disease (see W.H.S. Jones, *Malaria and Greek History* (Manchester 1909)), Antiquity was perfectly ignorant of the mosquito's rôle in the transmission of malaria (first discovered in the course of the 1880s: see the classic treatment of this topic by Christophers, *Aedes Aegypti* esp. pp. 10ff. and 77ff.) but knew that the insect was associated with rivers and marshes (*empis*: schol. Aristoph. *Birds* 244 (p. 58 White); *kônôps*: schol. Aristoph. *Clouds* 157C (*Schol. Ar.* 1 III.1 p.44 Koster); Babrius *fab.* 84.4 (quoted above p. 2), Pausan. 7.2.11) and that its larvae were bred there (Aristotle *HA* 487b5).

12. Leekbane

very much tongue-in-cheek in that play: the philosopher is asked whether the gnat's distinctive noise is produced through its mouth or its anus and in reply ludicrously plumps for the latter.[146] In the case of the yellow-fever mosquito, morphological studies have established the presence of a stridulating organ at the base of the female's wing (cf. Matthews, *Insect Behaviour* pp. 289ff. esp. p. 292).

The creature is produced from moisture turning sour, according to Pliny *NH* 11.118. This rather lapidary statement represents a crude summary of Aristotle *HA* 551b27ff. (cf. *HA* 487b5,[147] *GA* 721a10) where the insects grow from ascarids which in turn are engendered in the slime of wells or other water deposits. The decaying of the water produces red weed[148] which at first wriggles about together, then breaks up to form the aforesaid ascarids. These, after a few days, become hard and motionless until their husk breaks and the gnat emerges. Thompson ad loc. (n. 5) refers to the 'blood-worm' or larva of *Chironomus*, a common gnat.

12. LEEKBANE (prasocuris)

Etymology: the word literally means 'leek-slasher' from *prason* ('leek') and *keirein* ('cut'): cf. J. André, *Rev. Phil.* 34 (1960) 55. Gèze and Thomas in *Comptes Rendus de l'Académie des Inscriptions et Belles-Lettres* (1931) 47ff. cite comparable names from the Languedoc and Provence: *coupo-cabo, taio-cabo, copo-porri* etc. Mentioned by Aristotle *HA* 551b19f. in a textually corrupt passage which can be healed by reference to the derivative account in Aelian *NA* 9.39. See also Theophrastus *HP* 7.5.4, *de lapidibus* 37 on the stone called *prastis*, and Photius and Hesychius s.v. *Prima facie* Strattis fr. 66.1 (1.730 K) suggests a myriapod, but this seems inconsistent with Aristotle, who gives them wings: cf. E.K. Borthwick, *Hermes* 96 (1968) 72.

André identifies this animal with *Acrolepia assectella* Zell.

---

[146] As Dover sagely observes in his commentary on l. 157f.: 'We do not know whether anyone seriously believed that a gnat's hum was produced through its anus ... but the idea suits the comic preoccupation with excretion.' It also exploits the similarity between the sound of a trumpet and a fart: see Dante's *Inferno* Canto 21.139. On the gnat's trumpet see too Achilles Tatius 2.22.3.

[147] A textually faulty passage which probably refers to the same process: see Peck ad loc. (1 p. 10f. n.a).

[148] Or 'little worms' (conjectured by Aubert and Wimmer).

13. LOUSE (phtheir/pediculus)

Etymology: from the verb *phtheirô* ('destroy': cf. Gil Fernández p. 118f.; compare Hesychius s.v. *sathrax* (from *sathros* meaning 'rotting, rotten'): 'a type of louse'). For details as to word-forms see Gossen s.v. Laus in *RE* 12 (1925) 1034. Plutarch (*How to tell flatterer from friend* 2 (*moralia* 49C)) compares flatterers that shrink from the individual who is no longer successful to the lice that abandon the dying, a grim reminder of one aspect of the co-existence of insect and man.[149] There is an excellent study of the operation of the louse throughout history, in many differing environments, by Busvine, *Insects, Hygiene and History*. We are indebted to this for much of the comparative detail cited below. H. Keil, 'The louse in Ancient Greece' (*Bull. Hist. Medicine* 25 (1951) 305ff.) collects some useful material. What follows assumes the conventional and convenient division into hair louse and body louse (though see Busvine p. 42f. on the incomplete separation of the head and body forms of the *pediculus*. Aristotle did not distinguish the two (*HA* 557a4ff.)).

Hair louse
(medical term *pediculus humani capitis*)

Boys' heads (according to Aristotle *HA* 557a7ff.) are more prone to lousiness than men's, and women more subject to lice than men. A small consolation (presumably) was the notion (recorded by Aristotle ib.) that people with lousy heads are freer from headaches than usual. That the young have proportionately more head lice is true, though Aristotle's explanation of this at *Problemata* 2.16 (860b) as due to the greater moistness of their brains (as witness their runny noses) is unfortunate.

The existence of a proverbial phrase 'to be shorn to the louse' meaning to have one's hair cut very close is significant (see Pollux *Onomasticon* 2.29 (1.89 Bethe) citing Eubulus fr. 32 Hunter) as to the extreme familiarity of the phenomenon.

---

[149] Aristotle fr. 288 Rose (from his work on *zôika*) as quoted by Apollonius Dyscolus (*Historia Mirabilium* 27) stated that lice leave the head of the dying. For the related notion that lice are a sign of health see A. Wirth ap. Bächtold-Stäubli, *Handwörterbuch des deutschen Aberglaubens* 5.935.

13. Louse

Likewise, in telling the story of the founding of Tarentum by the Spartan Phalanthus, Pausanias (10.10.7) casually mentions that Phalanthus' wife 'among other endearments placed his head on her knees and began to pick out the lice'. There is no implication that this state of affairs was out of the ordinary. J.G. Frazer's note ad loc. (5.269f.) observes that 'this is a service which savages very commonly render each other' and that 'in fairy tales the same operation is performed by princesses on the heads of kings, ogres etc.' and copiously exemplifies both statements. Cf. Stith Thompson, *Motif-Index of Folk-Literature*² Index Volume s.v. 'Lousing' (p. 476). Busvine (p. 92) quotes Swift's *Pastoral Dialogue* (an exchange between two bucolic sweethearts): 'When you saw Tady at long bullets play, You sat and lous'd him all the sunshine day' etc.

The Roman emperor Julian the Apostate's jocose reference to his own beard wherein the lice run free as if in a thicket for wild beasts (*Misopôgon* ('The Beard Hater') 228C: cf. Ammianus *AP* 11.156, Martial 12.59.8, John of Carpathos *epist.* 95) is suggestive of the widespread reign of the louse through all classes of society, though for Julian's ostentatious aping of the unkempt manners and appearance of pagan philosophers such as Socrates (cf. p. 174) see Bowersock, *Julian the Apostate* (1978) pp. 14, 60, 71f. (cf. p. 103f. on *Misopôgon*).

Body louse
(medical term *pediculus humani vestimenti* or *corporis*)

Arguing against the notion that the Athenian Plague could have been spread by this creature, D.L. Page stated (*CQ* 3 (1953) p. 114 n.2) that it was a 'very improbable assumption that the Athenians had already in the spring of 430 B.C. sunk to such a state of filth that the disease might be generated and the infection universally transmitted in this way'. Replying to this, W.P. MacArthur (*CQ* 4 (1954) 171) cited the evidence of Aristophanes[150] and added that 'even if the mixed population of Athens were clean in normal times, this would profit them little in the vicissitudes of war and siege', the reference being to the

---

[150] See above p. 12 n.38 for the element of bias inherent in this type of evidence. Against the notion that the Athenian Plague is to be identified with typhus fever (spread by the body louse and occasionally by the rat flea) see A.J. Holladay and J.C.F. Poole, *CQ* 29 (1979) 291 and ib. 34 (1984) 483.

Peloponnesian War (on Aeschylus' imaginative extension of this principle back to the Trojan War see above p. 10). Compare H. Zinsser, *Rats, Lice and History* (London 1935) p. 184: 'As everyone who has really been to war knows, let the water supply fail, or soap become scarce, or a change of clothing be delayed – it takes no time at all before the louse comes back into its own. It was not so long ago, indeed, that its prevalence extended to the highest orders of society and was accepted as an inevitable part of existence.' See further A.E. Shipley, *The Minor Horrors of War* (London 1915) pp. 7ff. Herodotus' account (2.37) of Egyptian priests who shave their entire body every other day in order to avoid contact with lice or any other impure objects while they are serving the gods is an index of extreme religious purity (see A.C. Lloyd's commentary ad loc. (1.166). Apollodorus of Athens in his work on the *hetaerae* or prostitutes of that city (*F.Gr.Hist.* 244 F209) mentions one such woman who was called 'louse-gate' (*phtheiro-pylê*) because she picked the lice off herself as she stood at her door.[151] According to MacArthur, 'the Hippocratic Collection contains an unmistakable description of louse-borne relapsing fever in Thasos', to wit *Epidemics* 1.20ff. In general the Hippocratic Corpus has surprisingly little to say of infestation by lice, though the reported case of a victim of mania in *Internal Affections* where the patient imagines the threads of his bedclothes to be lice, proves acquaintance with the phenomenon.

Anecdotes involving lice

Plutarch (*Apophthegmata Laconica* 8 (*moralia* 208E)) relates how the Spartan king Agesilaus was bitten by a louse while sacrificing. He killed it on the spot, declaring that it was a pleasure to kill the plotter even at the altar. Appian in his history of the civil wars at Rome (*Bell. Civ.* 1.101 = Aesop *fab.* Appendix no. 471 Perry (p. 519f.)) records the telling to the plebs of the fable of the ploughman and the lice by the ruthless politician Sulla, in which the farmer, failing to shake the insects from his shirt, resorts to the more drastic remedy of burning shirt and lice. The sinister moral to be drawn is clear. Archilochus

---

[151] One is reminded (perhaps without cause) of the young women of Northern Siberia who threw their lice at whoever won their affections as a token of their love.

apparently used the phrase 'afflicted with lice' (fr. 236 W). A famous story, known to the pre-Socratic philosopher Heraclitus (fr. B56 DK), links Homer's death with his failure to explain a riddle posed him by a few fisher boys who had killed some lice, which action they then described with the enigma 'what we saw and caught we left behind (= fish), what we didn't see and catch we bring (= lice)'. On this tradition see Lefkowitz, *Lives of the Greek Poets* p. 17f., G.L. Koniaris, *Wiener Studien* 5 (1971) 29ff.; cf. A.-H. Chroust, *Modern Schoolman* 44 (1967) 177≃ *Aristotle* 1.178ff. For the folk-tale motif see Stith Thompson, *Motif-Index of Folk-Literature*² H 583.3.

Aristotle on human lice

HA 556b21ff.[152] For a critique of this interesting section see Busvine pp. 125ff. The idea here mentioned that fleas are generated from (dry) excrement (see above p. 22) is as erroneous as the statement that lice are spontaneously generated (see above p. 21f.) from the flesh. Much of the passage is very difficult to evaluate, e.g. the description of small eruptions on the skin whence a louse will jump if the eruption is pricked: some (e.g. D'Arcy Thompson) have identified this with the minute itch mite *Sarcoptes scabiei* which produces scabies. As described by A.C. Chandler and C.P. Reid, *Introduction to Parasitology with Special Reference to the Parasites of Man*[10] (New York 1966) pp. 544ff., this insect's 'impregnated females excavate their tortuous tunnels in the epidermis, especially where the skin is delicate and thin. The tunnels measure a few millimetres to over an inch in length'. Such a phenomenon might indeed be compatible with Aristotle's account and his easily explicable failure to detect that the female laid her eggs within the flesh would encourage a belief in 'spontaneous generation'. On scabies and alleged remedies for it in antiquity see Busvine pp. 204ff. The 'wild' lice of *HA* 557a5 have been identified with 'crab' lice by Busvine and others.

Aristotle on animal lice

Animals victimised (*HA* 557a10ff.) include birds, especially pheasants (for whom they can prove fatal unless frequent

---

[152] On the first proper scientific evaluation of this section (by Aldrovandi, *de Animalibus Insectis* (1602)) see Busvine pp. 139ff.

dust-baths are resorted to: cf. *HA* 633a29ff. on such dust-bathing) cattle, dogs (but see above p. 157), pigs (plagued by especially large, hard lice), fish (*HA* 537a5, 557a22ff., 602b28) especially the red mullet (? reading uncertain: see Peck ad loc. (2.212 n.a)). A certain fish which lives off the dolphin is therefore nicknamed 'louse' (cf. Thompson, *A Glossary of Greek Fishes* p. 276). Asses, Aristotle insists, do not suffer from lice (*HA* 557a15 → Pliny *NH* 11.115), an erroneous statement that went uncorrected until Francesco Redi's refutation in 1668 (cf. Busvine p. 127): *Haematopinus asini* is the correct term for this creature, whose existence Aristotle denied. According to Plutarch *Quaest. Conv.* 2.9 (*moralia* 642Bf.) sheep bitten by wolves have a sweeter flesh but a wool which breeds lice.

Alleged phthirophagy

The idea that the Greeks were acquainted with the custom of eating lice seems to rest on very fragile grounds. Herodotus 4.109 mentions a tribe in the middle Volga who eat the *phtheir*, but in this context the word could mean 'fir-cone' and this is how most scholars have taken it.[153] Such an interpretation is by no means refuted by a later passage of Herodotus (4.168) which recounts how women of the Adyrmachidae in Libya, when they catch lice on themselves, bite them before throwing them away.

Lice-eating has been reported in Scythia, for instance, and also among the Budini, the Hottentots (as described by P. Kolben, *The Present State of the Cape of Good Hope* (London 1738) 2.179), American Indians and those of the Amazon (A.R. Wallace, *Transactions of the Ent. Soc. London* 2 (1852/3) 244); also monkeys – accidentally, in the course of grooming. See in general Busvine pp. 86ff. who lists other alleged instances but cautiously concludes that what is actually involved is the disposing of the lice by cracking them between the teeth, a practice 'by no means uncommon among primitive peoples (which) when observed by divers imaginative travellers ... gave rise to stories of the use of lice as food'. In fact, such a diet might

---

[153] So first C. Ritter, *Die Vorhalle Europaischer Volkergeschichten vor Herodotos* (Berlin 1820) p. 154. Also e.g. Stein in his commentary on the Herodotean passage (2.(2)102), A. Herrmann, *RE* s.v. *Phtheirophagoi* (20[1] (1941)) 947f. For those scholars who prefer a reference to lice see Macan's note on the passage in Herodotus (1.79); and cf. K. Meuli, *Ges. Schr.* 2 p. 773f. n.3 and Busvine p. 86.

13. Louse

prove seriously dangerous, louse-borne relapsing fever being a risk; also, in a Chinese tale cited by Busvine p. 89, the eater dies of accumulated lice. 'There is much more danger involved when man bites louse then when louse bites man' as Chandler and Read, *Introduction to Parasitology* p.631 remind us. The biting of the lice was probably a convenient way of killing them[154] (alternative to bursting them between the finger nails) though an element of satisfaction and revenge cannot be ruled out.[155]

According to Aelian *NA* 9.19 a gecko that falls into oil and dies will make the oil taste nasty (not surprisingly). Further, anyone who eats the gecko will break out in lice (for antiquity's attitude to the gecko as an uncanny creature see A.D. Nock, *PBA* 17 (1931) 276 = *Essays on Religion and the Ancient World* 1.273f.).

How to be rid of lice

Various remedies are recommended in Pliny's *NH*, mostly apropos of *pthiriasis* (see below) and including viper broth applied all over the body; details in Gossen's article s.v. 'Laus' (*RE* 12 (1925) 1036 29ff.; cf. Busvine pp. 187ff.). A miraculous recovery from pediculosis is recorded on votive tablets from Epidaurus (the centre of the worship of Asclepius god of medicine) dating from the second half of the fourth century B.C. (*IG* 4²1.121 B 28 = E.J. and L. Edelstein, *Asclepius: a collection and interpretation of the testimonies* T423 (1.226); cf. R. Herzog, *Die Wunderheilungen von Epidauros* (Leipzig 1931) p. 108) following a dream by the patient that Asclepius stripped him naked, set him upright, and brushed the lice from him with a broom. Interpreted as referring to *pediculosis vestimenti* by Keil p.310.

Phthiriasis

An alleged disease whereby body lice are produced spontan-

---

[154] One is sad to have to deny credence to this from Wallace: 'Head lice of men are probably more a delicacy than an article of food and they are caught exactly in the same way the monkeys catch them in the zoo. A couple of Indian belles will often devote a spare half hour to entomological researches in each other's glossy tresses, every capture being immediately transferred with much gusto to the mouth of the operator.'

[155] Kolben's Hottentots are quoted as stating: 'They suck our blood and we devour them in revenge.'

eously in such quantities that the body's tissues decompose. On this question the fullest and most recent treatment is by A. Keaveney and J.A. Madden, *Symbolae Osloenses* 57 (1982) 87ff. See also Thomas Africa, *Classical Antiquity* (1982) 1ff. Several ancient authors attribute such a death to Sulla (especially Plutarch in his *Life of Sulla* (36.3f.); also Pliny *NH* 11.114, 26.138, Pausanias 1.20.7, anon. *de vir. illustr.* 75.11) and other famous figures of antiquity are also said to have perished in this way. (Plutarch in the passage just cited mentions Acastus son of Pelias from the world of myth, Alcman the lyric poet (T 15-18 Calame), Pherecydes[156] the theologian (these two are also named in this context by Aristotle *HA* 557a2 → Pliny *NH* 11.114[157]), Callisthenes of Olynthus (Aristotle's nephew), Mucius Scaevola (the Roman jurist)[158] and Eunus the slave who began the servile uprising in Sicily (these are also mentioned as suffering from the disease by other authors: full details in Keaveney and Madden pp. 90ff.).) Further supposed victims include Socrates and a number of philosophers (cf. Keil pp. 309 and 316f.) and individuals noted for impiety: again see Keaveney and Madden for details; cf. Busvine p. 103.

Not surprisingly, learned opinion in modern times has by and large denounced the disease as imaginary: 'It is medically impossible to die of lice alone' (Keaveney and Madden p. 89). The fact that such a large proportion of alleged victims can be described as either philosophers or impious wrongdoers is in itself suspicious. Popular opinion often associated philosophers with vermin and filth (see e.g. K.J. Dover, *Aristophanes Clouds* (Oxford 1968) pp. xxxiii and xxxixf.; cf. Keaveney and Madden p. 93)[159] and passages such as Pausanias 1.20.7 and Aelian *VH* 4.28 (on Sulla and Pherecydes respectively) reveal a view of the disease as a punishment for impious or tyrannical behaviour. Keaveny and Madden themselves argue for 'a compromise view'

---

[156] On the identity of Pherecydes see Jacoby, *Mnemos.* 13 (1947) 15ff. esp. 21ff. = *Abhandl. z. gr. Geschichtschr.* pp. 101ff. esp. pp. 106ff.

[157] Who confusingly refers to lice in the *hair*.

[158] On the likely identity of this individual see Keaveney and Madden p. 99 n. 56.

[159] For philosophers and lice see further Stith Thompson, *Motif-Index of Folk-Literature*² J 1452. The followers of Pythagoras enjoyed a similar reputation in the popular mind, so that an attack on them by the comic poet Aristophon (fr. 12.9 K-A (*PCG* 4.10)) mentions their unwashed state and infestation by lice: for Antiquity's view as to the Pythagoreans see e.g. Lloyd-Jones, *CR* 24 (1974) 5.

13. Louse

(p.88) whereby Sulla[160] and some of the more reliably attested victims did actually suffer from the genuine disease of scabies (see above p. 171) but died from other, independent causes.[161] However, this compromise seems to end up with the worst of all worlds, since none of the relevant individuals is actually recorded as suffering from scabies but from a fatal disease which falls within a recognised framework of popular belief.

Busvine pp. 103ff. and 195ff. provides a useful list of this and similar diseases[162] from all portions of the world (including China, Portugal and Spain (Philip II was reported to have died at the Escorial covered in masses of lice)) and from all periods of history (supposed cases continued to be described until well into the nineteenth century). In attempting to explain the sheer persistence of the myth, he considers (pp. 202ff.) the possibility that the activities of some sort of parasite mite were involved ('some Hyrpyrynchus species tend to make pouch-like burrows in animals' and some such temporary infestation may have coincided with an independent infection by lice) but agnostically concludes that 'the ancient curse of the lousy disease remains a mystery'. He had earlier remarked that antiquity displays 'a morbid fascination with this gruesome subject' (p. 104) and the tales do indeed seem to appeal to something deep-rooted in the human soul (replaced now by the grand guignol of Edgar Allan

---

[160] Some scholars have, reasonably enough, associated the tradition of Sulla's death from phthiriasis with that of his fable of the ploughman and the lice (see above p. 170): see Keaveney and Madden p. 98 n. 52 who claim, however, that this overlooks 'the fact that the story was told to a Roman audience' while 'the notion that Sulla's illness was divinely inspired clearly had its origins among Greeks who were outraged at his behaviour in their country' (p. 94). But the fable of the ploughman could be Greek in origin, like the ostensibly Roman fable told by Menenius Agrippa in Livy 2.32 (see Ogilvie's commentary ad loc. (p. 312), Karadagli, *Fabel und Ainos* p. 24f.). Cf. Thomas Africa, *Classical Antiquity* 1 (1982) p. 6 and n.36.

[161] T.F. Carney, *Acta Classica* 4 (1961) 64ff., to maintain his implausible hypothesis that Sulla died of a venereal disease, has to interpret the symptoms described by Plutarch as some stage of this, and consequently argue that in accounts of pthiriasis the word '*ptheir*' has developed from meaning 'louse' to meaning 'a sore caused by a louse', 'a louse-like sore', and finally the simple 'sore'. Adequate refutation in Keaveney and Madden p. 99 n. 55.

[162] Including *skôlêkôsis* (being eaten up by worms): Keaveney and Madden (pp. 90 and 95) are at pains to distinguish this from *pthiriasis* as an Eastern phenomenon of Judaeo-Christian origin, but the similarities from the point of view of story patterns (not least the idea of punishment for impiety) are at least as informative as the obvious zoological differences between louse and worm. See Thomas Africa, *Classical Antiquity* 1 (1982) 4ff. and 7ff.

Poe (consider the climax of *The Facts in the Case of M. Valdemar*) or the Hammer horror film and 'video nasty').

From a fabulous lousy disease to a fabulous louse: Agatharchides erroneously alleges the existence of a winged variety.

Kar and karnos

Glossed as louse by Hesychius s. vv. (2.411 and 415 (D43) Latte); cf. p. 146 above.

Sathrax

See above p. 168.

Konis (nit) is given as the name of the young of the louse by Aristotle *HA* 539b11 (*HA* 556b23 more comprehensively makes them the young of fleas and (bed-) bugs as well). On the etymology of the word see Gil Fernández p. 22f. Analogous forms such as Anglo-Saxon *hnith* or Russian *gnída* suggest an original Greek **knis*, expanded to *konis* under the influence of the differently accented *konis* meaning 'dust' (for the popular association of small creatures and dust see above p. 110).

14. PRAYING MANTIS (Mantis religiosa)

Known in Greek as *mantis* or *akris*[163] with or (in the case of the former sometimes without) the addition of the adjectives *arouraia* ('of the field') or *kalamaia* ('of the cornstalk') which adjectives can also stand *tout court* for the insect itself.

Why the insect was called *mantis* ('priest, seer') is a question given some unsatisfactory answers by scholion *i* on Theocritus *Id.* 10.18 (p. 229f. Wendel): because its appearance foretells famine; because it is of a bad (?) and green colour and bodes ill to whatever it stares at; and by the *Suda* s.v. *mantis* (3.320 Adler): because people make prophecies in the light of its movements. The notion that the creature's stare does harm recurs in several other of the scholia on the aforementioned Theocritean passage:

---

[163] Hesychius s.v. *mantis* (2.628 Latte: cf. *Suda* s.v. *mantis* (3.320 Adler)) says the insect is a type of *akris*; Dioscorides *de Simpl.* 1.149 (2.208 Wellman) that it resembles the Indian *akris*.

14. Praying mantis

note especially scholion *e* (p. 229 Wendel) which traces the belief back to the Alexandrian scholar Aristarchus and mysteriously associates it with a proverbial 'old woman of Seriphos'. This link also occurs in the *Suda* s.v. *Seriphos* (4.343 Adler) and Hesychius s.v. *kraugê* (2.527 Latte), the latter stating that 'the old woman of Seriphos is an *akris*, the so-called "Evil Eye" '. The connection receives final explication from Zenobius *cent.* 2.94 (1.56 Leutsch-Schneidewin) where after quoting Apollodorus (*F.Gr.Hist.* 244 F301) the paroemiographer tells us that in Sicily the creature is named after the old woman of Seriphos and brings evil to whatever creature it stares on, a clear reference to the concept of the 'Evil Eye' (Greek *baskania*, Latin *fascinum*: for a general study of this see S. Seligmann, *Die Zauberkraft des Auges und das Berufen* (Hamburg 1922); for further bibliography of discussions of this superstition see Bömer on Ovid *Metamorphoses* 7.365 (291)), the conspicuous eye of the *mantis* fastened upon its victim (see Seligmann p. 174f.).

Nevertheless, the notion of the old woman of Seriphos is probably (as seen by Gil Fernández p. 191f.) a misunderstanding of a Sicilian joke which compared old women (*seriphon* a kind of wormwood (cf. *LSJ* s.v.)) to these insects, either because of the effect of the creature's stare ('if looks could kill ... '), or because of a supposed resemblance between old woman and insect (the latter being described by scholion *a* on Theocritus *Id.* 10.18 (p. 228 Wendel) as 'dry, withered and wasted').[164] A similarly insulting use of the term *mantis* ... *kalamaia* to describe a thin and scrawny girl occurs in Theocritus *Id.* 10.18: see Gow ad loc. (2.197f.).[165] For insulting and abusive insect names in general see above p. 111.

We have still not explained the significance of *mantis* as

---

[164] An aging spinster who frequents the church is called 'cucaracha del templo' ('church cockroach') in Mexico (*Women in Ritual and Symbolic Rôles* (ed. J. Hoch-Smith and A. Spring (1978)) pp. 50ff.).
[165] M. Strano, *Helikon* 16 (1976) 457f. implausibly interprets the passage of Theocritus in the light of a contemporary Sicilian superstition ('una credenza molto diffusa tra i contadini etnei') to the effect that the *mantis* is a lucky animal. Gow as cited thinks it unlikely that Antiquity knew of the female mantis' habit of devouring the male during mating. E.K. Borthwick, in an unpublished paper whose findings he has kindly discussed with us, shows that there are stronger reasons than hitherto supposed for concluding that some ancient authors *did* know of this habit and that the Theocritean passage may presuppose it, as may some other of the passages here cited (cf. *CR* 17 (1967) 254).

37. Two types of praying mantis. *Above*: *CVA* Brit. Mus. 3 1 c pl. 48, 3a.b: Phineus (see above p.10) on a fifth-century Attic red-figure neck amphora from Nola (Brit. Mus. E291: ARV^2 662) by the Painter of the Yale lecythos (see further P. Blome, *Antike Kunst* 21 (1978) p.74 and n.38). *Right*: the insect.

14. Praying mantis

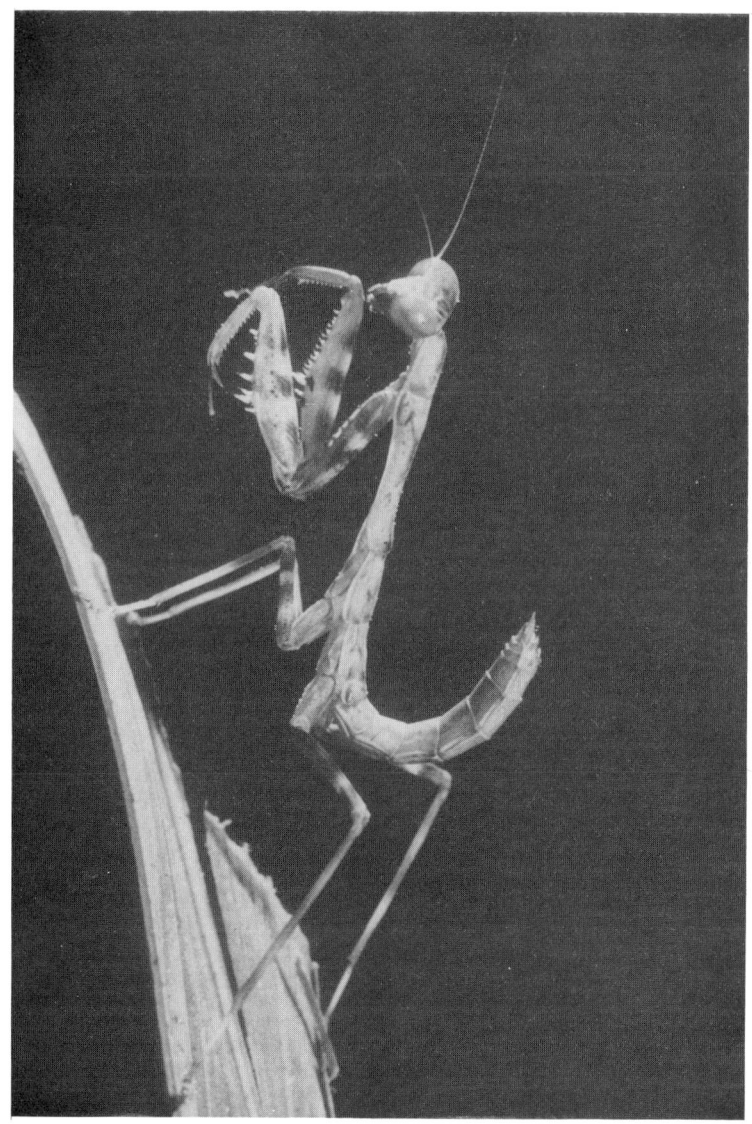

meaning priest or seer: compare the modern English term for it[166] 'soothsayer'; French 'prie-Dieu', German 'Gottesanbeterin' (cf. Gil Fernández p. 189f. for Spanish versions). The praying motion of its front legs (described to perfection by scholion *f* on Theocritus *Id.* 10.18: 'Its front feet are long and kept in constant motion') seems indicated; in the ancient world people prayed with both hands uplifted to the sky (cf. *Il.* 7.177f.; Kannicht on Eur. *Hel.* 1095f. (2.273f.); G. Neumann, *Gesten und Gebärden in der gr. Kunst* (Berlin 1965) pp. 78f. and 191; H. Demisch, *Erhobene Hände: Geschichte einer Gebärde in der bildenden Kunst* (Stuttgart 1984) pp. 121ff.): compare our Fig. 37.

> The tiller of the soil is not particular about analogies: where points of resemblance are not too clear, he will make up for their deficiencies. He saw on the sun-scorched herbage an insect of imposing appearance, drawn up majestically in a half-erect posture. He noticed its gossamer wings, broad and green, trailing like long veils of finest lawn; he saw its fore-legs, its arms so to speak, raised to the sky in a gesture of invocation. That was enough; popular imagination did the rest; and behold the bushes from ancient times stocked with Delphic priestesses, with nuns in orison.
>
> (Henri Fabre, *The Life of the Grasshopper*, p. 78)

---

[166] Cf. *O.E.D.* s.v. *mantis*: Thomas Moffet in 1658 referred to 'Insects ... called Mantes, foretellers' (*Theat. Insects* 984).

Index of modern works

References to pages in this book are in **bold** type.

Africa, Thomas. *Classical Antiquity* 1 (1982): **174, 175nn**
Aldine Press. Aristotle, *Historia Animalium*: **142**
Aldrovandi. *de Animalibus Insectis* (1602): **171n**
Allen, D.C. *Image and Meaning: Metaphoric Traditions in Renaissance Poetry*[2] (1968): **100, 115n, 130n**
Modern Language Quarterly 18 (1957): **130n**
Anderson, J.K. *Ancient Greek Horsemanship* (1961): **162**
Andre, J. *Rev. Phil.* 34 (1960): **167**
Rev. Phil. 36 (1962): **100**
Annual of the British School at Athens 12 (1905/6): **71**
Ansell Robin, P. *Animal Lore in English Literature* (1932): **viii, 21n, 85, 109**
Ardener, E. ap. *Social Anthropology and Language (ASA Monograph* 10 (1971)): **18n**
Arnott, W.G. ap. Daris, S. *Actes du XVe Congrès International de Papyrologie* 2 (1979): **97**
Aubert and Wimmer. Aristotle, *Historia Animalium*: **142, 167**
Bachmann. *Anthologia Graeca*: **165**
Bächtold-Stäubli. *Handwörterbuch des deutschen Aberglaubens*: **xiin, 22n**; see also Hoffmann-Krayer, Karle, Riegler, Wirth
Balme, D.M. *Generation of Animals* and *Parts of Animals* (trans.) (1972): **22n, 27**

Journal of the Soc. for the Bibliography of Natural History (1970): **5n**
Phronesis 7 (1962): **21n**
Barnes, J. *Aristotle* (1982): **16, 25n**
CR 33 (1983): **17n**
Barrett, W.S. ap. Fraenkel, *Aeschylus' Agamemnon*: **166**
Bazin, Gilles Augustin. *The Natural History of the Bees* (1744) (Eng. trans.): **62n**
Beattie, A.J. *CQ* 6 (1956): **10**
Beazley, J.D. *Attic Black-Figure Vases* (1956): **32**
Attic Red-Figure Vases[2] (1963): **ii, 5, 31, 33, 114, 178**
Benét, Stephen Vincent. *The Devil and Daniel Webster*: **xii**
Bennett, E.T. (ed.) *Natural History of Selbourne*: **54**
Benton, S. *CR* 18 (1968): **95**
Bergk, *Poetae Lyrici Graeci*: **92**
Björck, G. *Das alpha impurum und die tragische Kunstsprache* (1950): **132-3**
Blome, P. *Antike Kunst* 21 (1978): **178**
Boardman, John. *Archaic Greek Gems* (1968): **163, 164nn**
Greek Gems and Finger Rings: Early Bronze Age to Late Classical (1970): **35, 74, 150**
JHS 76 (1956): **139**
JRS 48 (1958): **35n**
and Vollenweider, M.-L. *Engraved Gems and Finger Rings in the Ashmolean Museum, Oxford I: Greek and Etruscan* (1978): **37,**

182 Index of modern works

44
Bodenheimer, F.S. *Animal and Man*: **95**
Insects as Human Food (1951): **128, 141, 142**
Bodson, Liliane. *The Classical Outlook* (Oct/Nov 1983): **ii, vi, 18n, 19, 23n, 29**
Hiera Zoia: contribution à l'étude de la place de l'animal dans la réligion grecque ancienne (1978): **47, 64, 70, 141, 152**
L'Antiquité classique 44 (1975): **120n**
L'Antiquité classique 45 (1976): **117, 121, 129**
Böhme, R. *Jhb. d. Deutsch. Arch. Inst.* 69 (1954): **8, 122n**
Boisacq. *Dictionnaire étymologique*: **110**
Bolton, J.D.P. *Aristaeus of Proconnesus* (1962): **45**
Bomer (ed.). Ovid *Metamorphoses*: **177**
Borthwick, E.K. *CQ* 16 (1966): **4n, 118, 123, 124-5, 128n, 130, 131, 134, 137, 138**
CQ 17 (1967): **128, 130**
CQ 18 (1968): **130**
CR 15 (1965): **113, 117, 118**
CR 17 (1967): **115, 177n**
CR 18 (1968): **95**
Hermes 96 (1968): **42, 167**
Bowersock, G. *Julian the Apostate* (1978): **169**
Bowra, Sir M. *Greek Lyric Poetry* (1961): **154n**
Boyde, P. *Dante Philomythes and Philosopher* (1981): **100**
Brandt, E. *Antike Gemmen in Deutschen Sammlungen I.2: Munchen* (1970): **104**
Bremmer. *The Early Greek Concept of the Soul* (1983): **100n, 104n**
Brendel, O. *Mitteilungen des Deutsch. Arch. Inst. (Röm. Abt.)* 49 (1934): **104**
Brian, M.V. *Social Insects: ecology and behavioural biology* (1983): **38, 40, 44, 55, 58**
Brit. Mus. Cat.: **78, 139**
Brit. Mus. Cat. of Coins Attica etc. (1888): **125**
Brit. Mus. Cat. of Greek Coins: **57**
Brit. Mus. Cat. of Greek Coins: Ionia (1892): **60**
Bronn. *Allgemeine Zoologie* (1850): **19**
Brunn. *Geschichte des griechischen Künstler*: **31n**

Bühler (ed.). Zenobius *cent.*: **27, 55, 74**
Burkert, W. *Griechische Religion (Greek Religion)*: **152**
Sitzb. d. Heidelberg. Akad. d. Wiss. phil.-hist. Kl. 1 (1984): **1n**
Bury, G.W. *The Land of Uz* (1911): **70n**
Busvine, J.R. *Insects, Hygiene and History* (1976): **6n, 46, 47, 168, 171-5 passim**
Byl, Simon. *Recherches sur les grands traités biologiques d'Aristote: sources écrites et préjugés* (1980): **16-25 passim, 27, 48, 59, 61, 63**
L'Antiquité classique (1976): **19**
Ludus Magistralis 16/17 (1968): **48, 56**
Calame, C. *Alcman* (1983): **97**
Caley and Richards (ed.). Theophrastus *de lapidibus*: **97**
Campbell (ed.). Simonides: **154n**
Capelle, W. *Rh. Mus.* 98 (1955): **21n, 102n**
Rh. Mus. 105 (1962): **102, 107, 108, 112n, 113**
Carney, T.F. *Acta Classica* 4 (1961): **175n**
Carrington, R. ap. *Animals in Archaeology* (ed. A. Brodrick (1972)): **165**
Chadwick, H. *Journal of Theological Studies* 48 (1947): **60**
Chandler, A.C. and Reid, C.P. *Introduction to Parasitology with Special Reference to the Parasites of Man* (1966): **171, 173**
Chantraine, Pierre. *Dictionnaire Etymologique de la Langue Grecque*: **ix, 37, 73, 75, 81, 95, 99, 108, 110, 132, 144, 149, 165**
La Formation des noms en grec ancien (1933): **147**
Charteris, *Life of Gosse*: **111**
Chernetsov, V.N. ap. *Studies in Siberian Shamanism* (ed. H.N. Michael (1963)): **xiii**
Christophers, S.R. *Aedes Aegypti: the Yellow Fever Mosquito* (1960): **164, 166**
Chroust, A.-H. *Aristotle*: **49n, 171**
Classical Folia 18 (1966): **25n**
Modern Schoolman 44 (1967): **49n, 171**
Clagett, M. ap. *Dictionary of Scientific Biography* 8 (1973): **26**
Clodd, E. *Magic in Names and in Other Things* (1920): **101n**
Cloudsley-Thompson, J. *Insects and*

Index of modern works

History (1976): 141, 152
Cohn, L. Corp. Paroem. Graec. Suppl. (IV): 44, 155
Philol. Suppl. 6 (1892): 44, 155
Cook, A.B. Zeus: 43, 65-8 passim, 70, 102-7 passim, 113, 117, 125, 126, 130, 152, 164
JHS 15 (1895): 65, 69, 72
Crane, E. The Archaeology of Beekeeping (1983): 30, 47, 50, 52
Crusius, O. Märchenreminiszenen im antiken Sprichwort (Versamml. Deutsch Philol. und Schulmänner (1889)): 16n
Cunningham (ed.). Herodas: 90n
Currie, H. MacL. Hermes 96 (1968): 10
Corpus Vasorum Atticorum[2]: 139
Brit. Mus.: 178
Los Angeles 1: 33
Louvre 9: 32
Al-Damīrī, Kamāl al-Dīn. Hayāt al-hayawan (ed. Bulag (1868)): 49
Daris, S. Actes du XVe Congrès International de Papyrologie[2] (1979): 97
Darling Buck. Selected Synonyms: 47
Darwin, C. Journal of the Linnaean Society 6 21: 43n
Davidson, P.F. and Oliver, A., Jnr. Ancient Greek and Roman Gold Jewelry in the Brooklyn Museum (1984): 130
Davies, M. (ed.). Stesichorus (forthcoming): 117
Hermes 109 (1981): 1n
de Stefani, E.L. (ed.). Et. Gud.: 79n
Stud. It. Fil. Class. 12 (1904): 27n, 161n
Dechelette, F. L'Argot des poilus (1918): 46
Delatta, A. and Derchain, Ph. Les Intailles Magiques Greco-Egyptiennes (1964): 36n
Demisch, H. Erhobene Hände: Geschichte einer Gebärde in der bildenden Kunst (1984): 180
Detienne, M. Les Jardins d'Adonis (1972): 70
QUCC 12 (1971): 69, 70
Dickie, M. HSCP 82 (1978): 8
Dictionary of Scientific Biography: 21n
Diels-Kranz. Vorsokratiker: 47
Dierauer, U. Tier u. Mensch im Denken der Antike (1977): 28, 30, 100n
Dietrich, B.C. The Origins of Greek Religion (1974): 65, 95, 107
Dietz, A., ap. Social Insects 3 (1982): ed. H.R. Hermann): 63
Dihle, A. HSCP 71 (1966): 114
Dodwell. A Classical and Topographical Tour through Greece (1819): 116
Dohm, H. Mageiros (Zetemata 32 (1964)): 119n
Dorsey, D.F. CR 20 (1970): 117n, 119n, 122
Doughty. Travels in Arabia Deserta (1936): 144, 145
Douglas, N. Birds and Beasts of the Greek Anthology (1928): 13, 16, 48, 117n, 118n, 127, 128, 137n, 145n
Dover, K.J. Aristophanes Clouds (1968): 88, 167n, 174
Aristophanic Comedy (1972): 11-12
ap. Fifty Years (and Twelve) of Classical Scholarship: 13n
Greek Homosexuality (1978): 108
(ed.) Plato Symposium (1980): 125n
(ed.) Theocritus (1971): 13n,. 14n, 137n
JHS 86 (1966): 42, 122n
Dumpert, K. Das Sozialleben der Ameisen (1978) = The Social Biology of Ants (1981): 38, 39, 41, 43
Dürbeck, H. Zur Charakteristik der gr. Farbenbezeichnungen (1977): 129
Düring, I. Acta Univ. Gotob. 56 (1950): 27n
Ebeling, E. Die babylonische Fabel und ihre Bedeutung für die Literaturgeschichte (Mitteilung der altorientalischen Gesellschaft 2.2 (1927)): 2n
Edelstein, E.J. and L. Asclepius: a collection and interpretation of the testimonies: 173
Egan, R.B. Classical World 77 (1984): 115, 124, 130
Ehrenberg, V. The People of Aristophanes (1951): 12n
Eicholz (ed.). Theophrastus de lapidibus: 97
Ensign Evans, Howard. Life on a Little-Known Planet (1984): ix, 19, 66n, 135n, 138n, 151n
Erbse (ed.). Iliad, scholia to, see Index Locorum
Untersuchungen zu den Attizistischen Lexika (1950): 76, 96, 118, 131
Estyn Evans, E. Irish Folk Ways (1957): 137n
Fabre, Jean Henri. The Life of the

Grasshopper: **130n**, **180**
Souvenirs Entomologiques: **x**, **79**, **85**, **128n**
Farley, J. *The Spontaneous Generation Controversy from Descartes to Oparin* (1977); **21n**
Faust, M. *Glotta* 48 (1970): **156n**
Indogermanische Forschungen 74 (1969): **156n**
Fehling, D. *Die Quellenangaben bei Herodot* (1971): **148n**, **149**
Fernández, Gil. *Nombres de Insectos en Griego Antiguo* (1959): **ix** and **passim** under Greek insect names
Flannigan, J.T. and Hudson, A.P. (ed.). *Folklore in American Literature* (1958): **xii**
Fleischer, R. *Artemis von Ephesos* (1973): **70**
Forbes, W.T.M. *Classical Philology* 25 (1930): **112n**
Fössing, P. *The Thorvaldsen Museum: Catalogue of the antique engraved gems and cameos* no. 504 (1929): **104**, **105**, **106**
Fraenkel, E. *Aeschylus' Agamemnon* (1950): **10n**, **132**, **134**, **166**
Beobachtungen zu Aristophanes (1962): **71**, **86-7**
Fraser, H. Malcolm. *Beekeeping in Antiquity*² (1951): **47-51 passim**, **66n**
Frazer, J.G. (ed.). *Apollodorus*: **42**
The Golden Bough: **xiii**, **101n**, **103**
(ed.) Ovid *Fast*.: **54n**
(ed.) *Pausanias*: **169**
Totemism and Exogamy: **103**
Totemism and Monogamy: **70n**
Frazer, P. *Ptolemaic Alexandria* (1972): **27n**
Froggatt, W.W. *Agricultural Gazette of New South Wales* (April 1903): **122**, **128n**
Gardner, Martin. *The Sacred Beetle and other great essays in science* (1985): **x**
Gaster, T.H. *Myth, Legend and Custom in the Old Testament* (1969): **42n**, **56**, **67**, **100n**, **109**, **149**, **152**, **155**
Gauthiot, R. *Mémoires de la Société de Linguistique de Paris* 16 (1925): **101n**
Georgi, Laura. *Class. Phil.* 77 (1982): **82**
Gerber. *Euterpe*: **154**
Gerhardt, Mia I. *Vivarium* 3 (1965): **45**
Gezé and Thomas. ap. *Comptes Rendus de l'Académie des Inscriptions et Belles-Lettres* (1931): **167**
Giangrande, G. *Mnemosyne* 25 (1972): **166**
Gibbon, E. *Decline and Fall of the Roman Empire*: **7n**
Gilmour, D. ap. *The Insects of Australia* (1970): **121**
Gombrich, Sir Ernst. *Art and Illusion*: **viii**
and R.L. Gregory (ed.) *Illusion in Nature and Art* (1973): **161**
Goossens, R. *L'Antiquité classique* 18 (1948): **94**
Gordon, E.I. *Sumerian Proverbs: glimpses of everyday life in ancient Mesopotamia* (Philadelphia 1959): **2n**
Gossen, Hans. *RE* (1913): **134n**
RE 2A (1923): **101n**
RE 12 (1925): **168**, **173**
RE Suppl. 8 (1956): **91**, **92**
Sudhoffs Archiv für Geschichte der Medizin und der Naturwissenschaften 30 (1938): **90**
Gow, A.S.F. (ed.). Theocritus: **44**, **90n**, **115n**, **116**, **119**, **123**, **177**
CQ 29 (1935): **116**, **135-6**
CR 6 (1956): **121**, **122**, **128**, **134**, **136**, **147**
CR 58 (1944): **65**
and Page. *The Garland of Philip*: **161n**
Hellenistic Epigrams: **13-14;** see also Index Locorum, under names of poets
and Scholfield, A.F. *Nicander: The Poems and Poetical Fragments* (Cambridge 1953): **15n**, **46**, **48**, **73**, **77-8**, **91**, **109**, **148n**
Grant, J.A. *Countryside: the Journal of the British Naturalists' Association* 21 (Summer 1970): **122**
Graves, Robert. *I, Claudius*, **43**
Gray, J. (ed.) *2 Kings*: **152**
Grensemann, H. *Knidische Medizin* 1 (1975): **93**
Griffin, J. *Homer on Life and Death*: **9**
Latin Poets and Roman Life = *Greece and Rome* 26 (1979): **60**
Griffiths, J. Gwyn (ed.). Plutarch *Isis and Osiris*: **84**, **96**, **145**
Guntert, H. *Kalypso* 2: **104n**
Guthrie, W.K.C. *In the Beginning: some Greek views on the origins of life and the early state of man* (1957): **xii**, **124-5n**

Hafner, G. *Wiener Jahreshefte* 32 (1940): **35**
Haldane, J.B.S. *JHS* 75 (1955): **23-4, 55-6**
Halffter, G. and Matthews, E.G. *The Natural History of Dung Beetles of the Subfamily Scarabaeinae (Coleoptera, Scarabeidae)* in *Folio Entomologica Mexicana* 12/14 (1966): **88, 89**
Halliday, W.R. *Folklore Studies, Ancient and Modern* (1924): **92**
Harpaz, I. ap. *History of Entomology* (ed. R.F. Smith et al.): **18n, 95**
Hartung, J.A. *Sophokles Fragmente* (1851): **10n**
Harvey, F.D. *Echos du monde classique/Classical Views* 3 (1984): **59n**
Harvey, Sir William. *Exercitationes de generatione animalium* (1650/1) = *Anatomical Exercitations concerning the generation of living creatures* (tr. M. Llewelyn(?) 1653): **28n**
Hatch, M.H. 'Theophrastus of Eresus as an economic entomologist', *Journal of the New York Entomological Society* 46 (1938): **29**
Hatzfield, H. *Leitfaden der vergleichenden Bedeutungslehre* (1927): **46**
Hauser, A. *Bauernregeln* (1973): **43, 55**
Head. *Historia Numorum* (1911): **87, 143**
Headlam (ed.). *Herodas*: **7n, 111, 155, 156, 164**
Hemmerdinger. *Glotta* 46 (1968): **97**
Herber, H. *Rheinische Jahrbuch für Volkskunde* 1 (1950): **110n**
Herington, C.J. *JHS* 87 (1967): **86n**
Herrlinger, G. *Totenklage um Tiere in der antiken Dichtung (mit einem anhang Byzantinischer, Mittellateinischer und Neuhochdeutscher Tierepikedien)* (1930): **14n, 128n, 137**
Herrmann, A. *RE* 20[1] (1941): **172n**
Herter, H. *Rh. Mus.* 119 (1976): **104, 105**
Herzog, R. *Die Wunderheilung von Epidaurus* (1931): **173**
Higgins, R.A. *Catalogue of Terracottas in the British Museum 1* (1954): **31**
Hobley, C.W. *Bantu Beliefs and Magic* (1922): **xii**
Hoch-Smith, J. and Spring, A. (ed.). *Women in Ritual and Symbolic Roles* (1978): **177n**
Hoffmann, H. and Davidson, P.F. *Greek Gold: jewelry from the age of Alexander* (1966): **34**
Hoffmann-Krayer, E. ap. *Bächtold-Stäubli* (q.v.): **55, 70n**
Holladay, A.J. and Poole, J.C.F. *CQ* 29 (1979) and 34 (1984): **149, 169**
Hopkinson (ed.). *Callimachus Hymn to Demeter*: **8**
Hopper, R.J. *JHS* 73 (1953): **12n**
Horowitz, M.C. *Journ. Hist. Biol.* 9 (1976): **63n**
Hudson-Williams, T. *CR* 49 (1935): **62**
Hunter (ed.) *Eubulus*: **144**
Hutchinson, R.W. *CQ* 8 (1958): **148**
Hutton, J.H. *The Angami Nagas* (1921): **70n**
The Sama Nagas (1924): **70n**
Immisch, O. *Glotta* 6 (1915): **104n, 106n, 107, 108, 109**
Imms *Text-book of Entomology*: **45, 94, 141**
Ingrams, H. *Arabia and the Isles* (1924): **63n**
Jacobsthal, P. *Greek Pins* (1956): **31n, 32, 33, 34-5, 66n, 72, 154**
Jacoby. *Abhandl. z. gr. Geschichtschr.*: **174n**
Fr. Gr. Hist.: **69, 127**
Mnemos. 13 (1947): **174n**
Jacques, J.-M. *Nicandre de Colophon: Contribution à l'étude des rapports entre la poésie et la science à l'époque hellénistique* (forthcoming): **15n**
Jaeger, Werner. *Aristoteles: Grundlegung einer Geschichte seiner Entwicklung* (1923): **24n**
Aristotle (1948): **24n**
Jahn, O. *Archäol. Beiträge* (1847): **104n**
Janssens, Em. *Latomus* 9 (1950): **159**
Jashemski, W.F. *The Gardens of Pompeii* (1979): **xi**
Jenkins, G.K. *Ancient Greek Coins* (1972): **35, 87**
Jennison, G. *Animals for Show and Pleasure in Ancient Rome* (1937): **45**
Johansen and Whittle (ed.). *Aeschylus Supplices*: **163**
Joly, R. *Récherches sur le traité pseudo-hippocratique Du Régime* (1960): **105-6**
Jones, W.H.S. *Malaria and Greek History* (1909): **166n**
Kádár, Z. *Survival of Greek Zoological Illuminations in Byzantine*

Manuscripts (1978): **35, 92, 93**
Acta Classica Universitatis Debreceniensis 3 (1967): **113**
Kaempf-Dimitriadou, S. *Die Liebe d. Götter in d. attischen Kunst des 5 Jhdt. v. Chr.* (1979): **126**
Kaiser-Minn, H. *Die Erschaffung des Menschen auf den spätantiken Monumenten des 3. und 4. Jahrhunderts (Jhb. für Antike und Christentum Ergänzungsband* 6 (1981)): **107**
Kakridis, J. Th. *Homer Revisited* (1971): **75-6**
Wiener Studien 48 (1930): **126n**
Kannicht (ed.). Euripides *Helen*: **180**
Karadagli, I. *Fabel und Ainos: Studien zur gr. Fabel (Beitr. zur kl. Phil.* 135 (1981)): **1n, 3nn, 4nn, 6nn, 122n, 155, 175n**
Karle, B. ap. *Bächtold-Stäubli* (q.v.): **93**
Kassel, R. *Winkelbrummer: Antike Kritik an Philologie und Philologen* (1973): **111**
ZPE 52 (1983): **165**
Kassel and Austin (ed.) Aristophanes fragments: **128, 155**
Keaveney, A. and Madden, J.A. *Symbolae Osloenses* 57 (1982): **174, 175n**
Keele, K.D. ap. *Dictionary of Scientific Biography* 8 (1973): **26**
Keil, H. 'The louse in Ancient Greece', *Bull. Hist. Medicine* 25 (1951): **168, 173, 174**
Keller, O. *Die Antike Tierwelt*: **39n, 41, 92, 94, 100, 108-9, 113, 147**
Kenna, V.E.G. *Cretan Seals: with a catalogue of the Minoan Gems in the Ashmolean Museum* (1960): **99**
Kenner, Hedwig. *Das Phänomen des verkehrten Welt in der griechisch-römischen Antike* (1970): **36**
Keynes, G. (ed.). Blake, *Songs of Innocence and Experience* (1970): **106n**
The Life of William Harvey (1966): **28n**
Klíma, J.R. ap. *Enzyklopädie des Märchens*: **42, 47-8, 64**
Knox, A.D. *CR* 39 (1925): **ix**
Koch, G. and Sichterman, H. *Römische Sarkophage* (1982): **107**
Köhler, C.S. *Das Tierleben im Sprichwort der Griechen und Römer* (Leipzig 1881): **16n, 86n, 155**

Kolben, P. *The Present State of the Cape of Good Hope* (1738): **172, 173n**
Koniaris, G.L. *Wiener Stud.* 5 (1971): **171**
Kost (ed.) Musaeus *Hero and Leander*: **164**
Koster, S. *Die Invektive in der griechischen und römischen Literatur (Beitr. zur kl. Phil.* 99 (1980)) Index: **156n**
Kris, E. and Kurz, O. *Die Legende vom Künstler: ein geschichtlicher Versuch* (1934): **161n**
La Fable (Entretiens sur l'Antiquité Classique 30 (1984)): **1n, 3n, 5**
Lambert, W.G. and Millard, A.R. (ed.). *Atra-Ḫasis: The Babylonian Story of the Flood* (1969): **7, 151n**
Lambros, S.P. *Suppl. Aristotelicum* 11 (1885): **27n**
Lasserre. *Die Fragmente des Eudoxus von Knidos*: **141**
Lattimore, R. *Themes in Greek and Latin Epitaphs* (1942): **100n**
Laubscher, H.P. *Archäologische Anzeiger* (1966): **79**
Laufer, B. *Insect and Cricket Musician-Champions of China* (Chicago 1927): **138**
Leaf (ed.) Homer *Iliad*: **8**
Lee, D.J.N. *The Similes of the Iliad and Odyssey Compared* (1964): **7n**
Lee, H.D.P. *CQ* 42 (1948): **24n**
Lefkowitz, M. *Lives of the Greek Poets* (1981): **72, 171**
Leigh Fermor, Patrick. *Mani* (1958): **116-17**
Leitner, H. *Zoologische Terminologie bei Älteren Plinius* (1972): **29, 98**
Lendrum, W.T. *CR* 20 (1906): **111**
Lenormant. *Grande Grèce* 1: **143**
Lentz. *Grammatici Graeci*: **80**
Leutsch-Schneidewin (ed.). *Zenobius, cent.*: **3n**
Liddell, Scott and Jones. *Greek Lexicon*: **viii, 8n, 38, 73n, 89, 97, 102, 108, 112n, 120n, 144, 177**; Supplement: **145**
Lienau (ed.). *Corp. Medic. Graec.*: **108n**
Lilja, S. *Dogs in Ancient Greek Poetry* (1976): **156n**
Arctos 10 (1976): **12n, 46**
Lindroth, S. ap. *Yearbook of the Swedish Linnaeus Soc. Com-*

Index of modern works

mem. Vol. (1978): **19n**
Linnaeus. *Systema Naturae* (1st ed. 1735; 10th 1758): **19**
Lippold. *RE* 10 and 16: **31**
Lloyd, A.C. (ed.). Herodotus: **80, 148, 165, 170**
Lloyd, G.E.R. *Aristotle: the growth and structure of his thought* (1968): **24n**
Magic, Reason and Experience (1979): **17n**
Science, Folklore and Ideology (1983): **17n, 19-20, 25n, 28, 29n**
ap. *The Legacy of Greece* (ed. M.I. Finley, 1981): **29n**
PCPS 10 (1964): **21**
Lloyd-Jones, H. (trans.). Aeschylus' *Agamemnon*: **10n**
Estudios sobre la Tragedia Griega (1966): **71**
Females of the Species (1975): **3n**
and Parsons. *Supplementum Hellenisticum*: **111n**
CR 24 (1974): **174n**
Stud. It. Fil. Class. 1 (1984): **13n, 14n**
Lopasic, A. ap. *Animals in Folklore* (ed. J.R. Porter and W.M.S. Russell, 1978): **155**
Lorch, J. *Isis* 69 (1978): **56n**
Macan (ed.) Herodotus: **172n**
MacArthur, W.P. *CQ* 4 (1954): **9, 169, 170**
MacDowell, D. Aristophanes, *Wasps* (1971): **75n, 76**
Mackay, W.P. and E.E. *Sociobiology* 9 (1984): **43**
Marriot, P.J. *Red Sky at Night Shepherd's Delight: weather lore of the English countryside* (1981): **43n**
Mattes, J. *Der Wahnsinn im gr. Mythos und in der Dichtung bis zum Drama des 5 Jahrhunderts* (1970): **164**
Matthews, R.W. and J.R. *Insect Behaviour* (1978): **39, 135, 159, 167**
Medawar, P.B. and J.S. *Aristotle to Zoos: a philosophical dictionary of biology* (London 1984): **17-18**
Merkelbach, R. *Roman und Mysterium in der Antike* (1962): **107**
Mette, H.J. *Rh. Mus.* 123 (1980): **155**
Meuli, K. *Ges Schr.* 2: **172n**
Odyssee und Argonautika (1921): **7n**
W.F. *Otto Festschrift (Schweizerisches Archiv für Volkskunde* 50 (1954)): **1n, 3n, 4n, 6n, 7n**
Meyer, J.B. *Aristoteles Thierkunde: ein Betrag zur Geschichte der Zoologie, Physiologie und alten Philosophie* (1855): **19**
Michelet, J. *L'Insecte* (1863): **60**
Michener, Charles D. *The Social Behaviour of the Bee: a comparative study* (1974): **47, 52-5 passim, 58, 60-1, 62**
Mills, J.P. *The Ao Nagas* (1926): **103**
Moffet, Thomas. *Theat. Insects* (1658): **180n**
Morge, G. ap. *History of Entomology* (ed. R.F. Smith et al., *Annual Reviews Inc.* (1973)): **13n, 18n**
Morin-Jean. *Le Dessin des animaux en Grèce d'après les vases peints* (1911): **32**
Morsink, J. *Journ. Hist. Biol.* 12 (1979): **63n**
Moutsos, D. *Zeitschrift für Vergleichende Sprachforschung* 94 (1980): **97, 157, 160**
Nails, D. *Echos du monde classique/ Classical Views* 4 (1985): **59n**
Naturphilosophie des Aristoteles (Wege der Forschung 225 (1975)): **24n**
Neumann, G. *Gesten und Gebärden in der gr. Kunst* (1965): **180**
Newton Harvey, E. *A History of Luminescence from the Earliest Times to until 1900* (1957): **159n**
Nicolaidis, N.J. [Beekeeping: modern intensive methods] (1959): **49-50**
Nilsson, M. *Geschichte der gr. Religion* 1[3]: **100n, 104n**
The Minoan-Mycenaean Religion and its Survival in Greek Religion (1950): **107**
Nisbet and Hubbard (ed.) Horace *Odes*: **52, 91, 126**
Nivaille, J. *Cercle d'Études Numismatiques* Bulletins 15.4 (Oct/Dec 1978) and 16.1 (Jan/March 1979): **72**
Nock, A.D. *Essays on Religion and the Ancient World*: **173**
Noe, S.P. *The Coinage of Metapontum: Parts 1 and 2* (with additions and corrections by A. Johnstone (1984)): **143**
Nussbaum, A.J. *Head and Horn in Indo-European* (1986): **94**
Ogilvie (ed.) Livy: **175n**
Olck. *RE* 3 (1899): **52n**
Onians. *Origins of European Thought*:

104, 105, 106, 124
Onions. *Dictionary of English Etymology*: 106n
Opie, Iona and Peter. *Children's Games in Street and Playground* (1969): 160
Osten-Sacken, C.K. *On the Oxen-born bees of the Ancients (Bugonia) and their relation to Eristalis tenax, a two-winged insect* (1894): 66
Otto, A. *Die Sprichwörter und Sprichwörtlichen Redensarten der Römer*: 44, 57
Overbeck, J. *Die antiken Schriftquellen zur Geschichte der bildenden Künste bei den Griechen* (1868): 31
Oxford English Dictionary: 106n, 180n
Page, D.L. *Folk Tales in Homer's Odyssey*: 74, 162n
Greek Literary Papyri: 51, 118n
CQ 3 (1953): 169
and Denniston. Aeschylus *Agamemnon* (1957): 10n
see also Gow
Parker, R.C.T. *Miasma* (1983): 103n
Phronesis 29 (1984): 16n, 17n, 25n, 27n, 45
Partridge, E. *A Dictionary of Slang and Unconventional English* (ed. P. Beale): 46
Slang Today and Yesterday (1950): 46
Pearson, A.C. (ed.). Sophocles *Fragments* (1917): 11, 76
Journ. Philol. 30 (1907): 102
Pearson, L. *The Lost Histories of Alexander the Great* (1960): 83
Pease, A.S. (ed.). Cicero *de divinatione*: 43, 72
(ed.). Cicero *de natura deorum*: 68
Peck, A.L. (ed.). Aristotle *de Generatione Animalium* (Loeb 1953): 27
(ed.). Aristotle *Historia Animalium* (Loeb: vol1. 1 1965; vol. 2 1970): 17n, 18, 23, 26, 54, 113, 122, 127n, 136n, 161n, 167, 172
(ed.). Aristotle *de Partibus Animalium* (Loeb 1955): 27
Pellegrin, P. *La Classification des animaux chez Aristote* (1982): 17n
Perrotti. Appendix to Phaedrus *fab.*: 4
Perry, B.E. (ed.). Babrius and Phaedrus (Loeb 1965): 1-4 passim, 100n; see also Index Locorum under Fables

Persson, A.W. *The Religion of Greece in Prehistoric Times* (1942): 68, 69
Peters, F.E. *Aristotle and the Arabs* (1968): 49n
Petersmann, H. ap. *Serta Indogermanica* (G. Neumann Festschrift (1982)): 7n, 10n
Pfeiffer. *Ausgewahlte Schriften*: 123, 124, 126n, 127
(ed.). Callimachus: 102
History of Classical Scholarship I: 111n
Hermes 63 (1928): 123, 124, 126n, 127
Platnauer (ed.). Aristophanes *Clouds* (1964): 88n
Platt, A. *CQ* 5 (1911): 22n
Pocock, L.G. *CR* 8 (1958): 162
Poliakoff, M. *Studies in the Terminology of the Greek Combat Sports (Beitr. zur kl. Phil.* 146 (1982)): 44
Pollard, J. *Seers, Shrines and Sirens* (1965): 74
Pope, M.H. (ed.). Book of Job (1965): 109
Porter, E. *Cambridgeshire Customs and Folklore* (1969): xii
Powell, J.U. *Collectanea Alexandrina*: 51
New Chapters in the History of Greek Literature First Series (1921) and Second Series (1929): 51
Preus, A. *CQ* 18 (1968): 120n
Journal of the History of Biology 3 (1970): 106
Pringle, J.W.S. 'The structure and evolution of the organs of sound production in cicadas' (*Proceedings of the Linnaean Soc.* 167 (1957)): 121
Radt, S.L. *Tragicorum Graecorum Fragmenta* (1971): 71, 109
Ranke, K. ap. *Enzyklopädie des Märchens*: 47-8, 64
Ransome, Hilda. *The Sacred Bee in Ancient Times and Folklore* (1937); 47, 49n, 64, 65, 66, 70n
Rau, P. *Paratragodia (Zetemata* 45 (1967)): 12n
Redard, G. *Les noms grecs en -TÉS/-TIS* (1949): 81, 149
Richmond, J. *Chapters on Greek Fish-Lore (Hermes Einzelschrift* 28 (1973)): 28n, 30n, 39n, 59n
Richter, G. *The Engraved Gems of the*

Index of modern works 189

Greeks and the Etruscans (1968): **9**
Richter, G.M.A. *AJA* 33 (1929): **112n**
Richter, W. ap. *RE* Suppl. 15 (1978): **77**
Riegler, R. ap. *Bächtold-Stäubli* (q.v.): **22n, 103, 106n, 109, 110n**
Risch, E. *Indogermanische Forschungen* 59 (1944): **156n**
Ritter, C. *Die Vorhalle Europaischer Volkergeschichten vor Herodotos* (1820): **172n**
Robinson, Christopher. *Lucian*: **150**
Rodgers, B.B. Aristophanes *Clouds* (1867): **88n**
Roscher, W.H. *Nektar und Ambrosia* (1883): **56**
Rose, H.J. *CR* 38 (1924): **103**
Rumpf, A. ap. *Symbola Coloniensia* (J. Kroll Festschrift): **125**
Ruschenbusch. *Historia Einzelschrift* 9 (1966): **52n**
Russell, D.A. *Plutarch* (1972): **30**
Russell-Wilson (ed.). Menander Rhetor *peri epideikt.*: **117**
Scarborough, J. *Class. Phil.* 75 (1980): **81**
Coleopterist's Bulletin 31 (1977): **92**
Journ. Hist. Biol. 11 (1978): **108**
Melsheimer Entomological Series no. 26 (1976): **xi, xii**
Pharmacy in History 19 (1977) onwards: **15n**
Pharmacy in History 21 (1979): **15n, 46, 81, 91, 92, 93, 109**
Schear, L. *Échos du monde classique/Classical Views* 3 (1984): **59n**
Scheinberg, S. *HSCP* 83 (1979): **69, 70, 71, 72**
Schmidt, J. ap. *RE* 14 (1933): **42**
Schmitschek, E. *Handbuch der Zoologie* (1968): **128n**
Schneider (ed.). Aristotle *Historia Animalium*: **110**
Scholfield, A.F. Aelian *de natura animalium (On the Characteristics of Animals)* (Loeb 1958-9): **29-30, 136, 147**
see also under Gow
Schwyzer. (ed.), *Griechische Grammatik*: **155**
Sedlar, J.W. *India and the Greeks:* **45**
Seeck, G.A. (ed.). *Die Naturphilosophie des Aristoteles (Wege der Forschung* 225 (1975): **17n**
Seligmann, S. *Die Zauberkraft des Auges und das Berufen* (1922): **177**
Seltman, C.T. *Athens, its History and Coinage before the Persian Invasion* (1924): **32-3**
Seminar Classics 609 (State Univ. of New York at Buffalo) *Arethusa Monographs* 1 (1969) (Porphyrius, *The Cave of the Nymphs in the Odyssey*, text & translation): **64**
Sharp, W.E. *Ent. Month. Mag.* 54 (1918): **159**
Shaw. *Travels (or Observations referring to several parts of Barbary and The Levant)* (1783): **116**
Shelley, P.B. *A Defence of Poetry* Part 1: **111**
Sherwin-White, S. *Ancient Cos (Hypomnemata* 51 (1978)): **112n, 113n**
Shipley, A.E. *The Minor Horrors of War* (1915): **170**
Journ. Phil. 34 (1918): **51, 65**
Shipp, G.P. *Modern Greek Evidence for the Ancient Greek Vocabulary* (1979): **80, 144-5**
Shrewsbury, J.F.D. *The Plague of the Philistines* (1964): **46**
Sichtermann, H. and Koch, G. *Griechische Mythen auf römischen Sarkophagen* (1975): **106**
Sifakis, G.M. *Parabasis and Animal Choruses* (1971): **76**
Silliti, G. *Tragelaphos: storia di una metafora e di un problema* (1984): **45-6**
Singer, C. *Greek Biology and Greek Medicine* (1922): **25**
A History of Biology to about the year 1900 (1959): **29n**
ap. *The Legacy of Greece* (1921): **17n, 29n**
ap. *A Short History of Scientific Ideas* (1959): **29n**
ap. *Studies in the History and Method of Science* 2 (1921): **48, 63**
Sittig. ap. *RE* 7 (1912): **10**
Skoda, F. *Le Redoublement éxpressif: un universal linguistique* (1982): **113**
Slater, W. *Aristophanis Byzantii Fragmenta* (1986): **27n**
Slings, S.R. *ZPE* 45 (1982): **44**
Smit, P. ap. *Yearbook of the Swedish Linnaeus Soc. Commem. Vol.* (1978): **19n**
Solmsen, F. *Hermes* 106 (1978) and 107 (1979) = *Kl. Schr.*: **24**
Sommerstein (ed.). Aristophanes *Peace* (1985): **88**
Sourvinou-Inwood, C. *CQ* 29 (1979):

190 Index of modern works

69, 70
Stählin (ed.). Clement of Alexandria *Strom*: 84
Stanford, W.B. *Phoenix* 23 (1969): 117n
Steier. *RE* 5A 1 (1934): 114, 116
RE 16¹ (1933): 166
Stein (ed.). Herodotus: 172n
Stemplinger, E. ap. *Bächtold-Stäubli* (q.v.): 43n
Stith Thompson. *Motif-Index of Folk-Literature*: 42, 64, 103, 169, 171, 174n
Strano, M. *Helikon* 16 (1976): 177n
Strömberg, R. *Greek Proverbs* (1954): 44, 85, 144
Griechische Wortstudien (1944): **ix, xii**, 81, 84, 89-90, 109, 110, 117, 131, 133, 135, 144-7 passim, 158, 165
(ed.). Plutarch: 145
Sturtevant. *Class. Phil.* 7 (1912): **46n**, **136n**, 138-9, 141, 144, 146, 147
Sudd, J.H. *An Introduction to the Behaviour of Ants* (1967): 40, 43
Sundevall. *Die Tierarten des Aristoteles*: 157
Sutton, D.F. *Sophocles' Inachus* (Beitr. zur kl. Phil. 97 (1979): 163
Taberner, P.V. *Aphrodisiacs: the science and the myth* (1985): 93
Taillardat, J. *Les Images d'Aristophane*² (1965): 62, 76, 112
(ed.). Suetonius *peri blasphemiôn* (1967): 98
(ed.). Suetonius *peri paidiôn* (1967): 89, 160
Tarán (ed.). Speusippus *On Similarities*: **112n**
Tarrant, D. *CQ* 40 (1946): 62
Theiler, W. ap. *RE* Suppl. 14 (1974): 47
Theodoridis, C. (ed.). Photius: 144
Glotta 52 (1974): 155
Thomas, K.V. *Man and the Natural World: changing attitudes in England 1500-1800* (1983): **21n**, **54n**, 60, **62n**, **70n**, **100n**, **158n**
Thomas, R.F. *HSCP* 86 (1982): 161
Thompson, D'Arcy Wentworth. *Aristotle as a Biologist* (1913): **24n**
A Glossary of Greek Birds (2nd ed. 1953): **vii**, 59, 85, 131, 132, **142n**
A Glossary of Greek Fishes (1947): **vii, 94, 172**
Die Naturphilosophie des Aristoteles: 79, 100, **101n**, 113
Oxford Translation of Aristotle

(1910): **vii, 24n**, 26
ap. *The Legacy of Greece* (1921): **24n**, 79, 100, 113
ap. *Revised Oxford Translation of Aristotle* (ed. J. Barnes) Princeton (Bollingen Series LXX1.2 vol. 1): 26
CQ 39 (1945): **38n**
CQ 40 (1946): 139, 150
CR 52 (1938): 45
Discovery 4 (1923): 160
'Goldfish' (*Country Life* 1923): 138
Thompson, H.A. *Hesperia* 24 91955): ii
Thompson, Ruth. *D'Arcy Wentworth Thompson, The Scholar Naturalist, 1860-1948* (1958): **138n**
Thorley, J. *Greece and Rome* 18 (1971): 113
Thorley, John. *Melisselogia or, The Female Monarchy* (1744): **62n**
Thorpe, W.H. ap. *Non-Verbal Communication* (ed. R.A. Hinde, 1972): **55n**
Thraede, K. *Reallexikon fur Antike und Christentum*: 68
Tilley, M.P. *Dictionary of Proverbs in England in the Sixteenth and Seventeenth Centuries* (1950): **2n, 44n**, 109, 155
Tzetzes. *Chil.*: 129
commentary on Hesiod *Works and Days*: 96
commentary on Lycophron: 124
Uther, H.J. ap. *Enzyklopädie des Märchens*: 151
Vaio, J. ap. *La Fable*: **130n**
van Thiel, H. *Antike und Abendland* 17 (1971): **3n**
Vartanian, A. ap. *Dictionary of the History of Ideas* 1973/4): **21n**
Verrall, M. de G. *CR* 24 (1910): 65
Vollenweider, M.-L. *Deliciae Leonis: Antike geschnittene Steine und Ringe aus einer Privatsammlung [Leo Merz]* (1984): 36, 50, 101, 107
von Bothmer, D. *The Amasis Painter and his World* (1985): 32
von Frisch, Karl. *The Dance Language and Orientation of Bees* (1967): **55n**
The Dancing Bees (1954): **55n**
Wallace, A.R. *Transactions of the Ent. Soc. London* 2 (1852/3): 172, 173
Wallace, W.A. ap. *Science in the Middle Ages* (ed. D.C. Linberg (1978)): **18n**
Walz. *Rhet. Gr.*: 118
Ward, W.A. *Studies on Scarab Seals* 1

(1978): **95**
Warde Fowler, W. *CR* 18 (1904): **141**
Waser ap. *Archiv für Religionswissenschaft* 16 (1913): **104n**
Roschers Ausführliches Lexikon d. gr. und röm. Mythologie: **100n, 104n**
Waszink, J.H. *Biene und Honig als Symbol des Dichters und der Dichtung in der griechisch-römischen Antike* (Rheinisch-Westfalische Akademie der Wissenschaften, Vorträge G (1974): **70-1, 72**
Weichers, A. *Aesop in Delphi (Beitr. zur kl. Phil.* 2 (1960)): **3n**
Wellman, M. ap. *RE* 6² (1909)): **152**
Hermes 26 (1891): **161**
Wenner, A.M. ap. *Advances in the Study of Communication and Effect* vol. 1 (*Non-Verbal Communication*) (1974): **55n**
West, M.L. (ed.). Hesiod, *Theogony* (1966): **8, 51, 52n**
(ed.). Hesiod *Works and Days* (1979): **51, 57, 117, 119**
Studies in Greek Elegy and Iambus (1974): **11n**
ap. *La Fable (Entretiens sur l'Antiquité Classique* 30 (1984)): **1n, 3n**
'Near Eastern material in Hellenistic and Roman literature', *HSCP* 73 (1969): **2n**
West, S. *CQ* 34 (1984): **163n**
Wheeler, Sir George. *A Journey into Greece* (1682): **49**
White, Gilbert. *The Natural History of Selbourne*: **54**
Whitfield, B.G. *CR* 5 (1955): **164**
Whitfield, G.B. *CR* 8 (1958): **56**
Wilamowitz. *Glaube d. Hellenen*: **107**
Willcock (ed.). Homer *Iliad*: **8**
Willetts, R.F. *Cretan Cults and Festivals* (1962): **66, 67, 68**
Williams, F. (ed.). Callimachus *Hymn to Apollo*: **58, 69, 70**
Williams, Gordon. *Tradition and Originality in Roman Poetry* (1968): **viii-ix**
Wirth, A. ap. *Bächtold-Stäubli* (q.v.): **168n**
Wöhrle, G. *Theophrasts Methode in seinem Botanischen Schriften* (1985): **29**
Wright, E.M. *Rustic Speech and Folk-lore* (1913): **100**
Wust, E. ap. *RE* 6A (1937): **127**
Younger, J.G. *Kadmos* 22 (1983): **30, 31**
Zacher, K. *Hermes* 19 (1884): **128**
Zazoff, P. *Die Antiken Gemmen* (1983): **68, 96**
Etruskische Skarabäen (1968): **68, 105**
Archäologische Anzeiger (1965): **69**
Zinsser, H. *Rats, Lice and History* (1935): **170**
Zwierlein-Diehl, E. *Die Antiken Gemmen des Kunsthistorischen Museums in Wien* 1 (1973): **83, 107**

Index locorum

References to pages in this book are in **bold** type

Abstemius
  16:**2n**
Achilles Tatius
  1.15.8: **117**; 2.7.2: **77**; 2.22.3: **166**
Acts of John (New Testament Apocrypha) 60-1: **47**
Aelian
  de Natura Animalium 1.10: **58**; 1.11: **55**; 1.20: **116, 117, 119, 120**; 1.22: **40**; 1.28: **77**; 1.38: **85**; 1.55: **81**; 1.58: **55, 64, 76, 78**; 1.60: **63**; 2.2: **159**; 2.4: **157**; 2.25: **38, 39**; 2.29: **151, 155**; 3.12: **141, 145**; 3.38: **122**; 4.18: **85**; 4.39: **78**; 4.43: **40, 42**; 4.49: **161n**; 4.51: **156, 161, 162**; 4.55: **161n**; 5.9: **119**; 5.11: **55, 58, 76**; 5.12: **59**; 5.13: **54, 59, 72**; 5.15f: **77**; 5.16: **77**; 5.17: **151, 152**; 5.42: **57, 58**; 5.43: **157**; 5.49: **41**; 6.19: **136, 147**; 6.36: **103**; 6.37: **156, 161, 162**; 6.43: **38, 40, 41**; 6.46: **85**; 6.50: **41**; 6.51: **81**; 8.6: **127**; 8.13: **95**; 9.11: **81**; 9.15: **77**; 9.19: **173**; 9.39: **93, 167**; 10.15: **84, 85**; 10.42: **44**; 10.44: **130, 131, 132, 133**; 10.47: **80**; 11.8: **152**; 11.28: **76**; 12.43: **153**; 15.1: **79n, 152**; 15.14: **151**; 16.14: **96**; 16.15: **40**; 17.19: **141**; 17.40: **165**; 17.42: **44**
  Varia Historia 4.28: **174**
Aelius Dionysius Atticist.
  Erbse p.143: **118**
Aeschylus
  Agamemnon 560-2: **10**; 892: **166**
  Lycurgus (*Tr.G.F.* 3 p.234f): **11**
  Philoctetes (*Tr.G.F.* 3 F256 Radt): **10-11, 144**
  Phineus (*Tr.G.F.* 4 F716 Radt): **10**
  Sisyphus the Stone-roller (*Tr.G.F.* 4 F233 Radt): **86**
  Supplices 306ff: **163**; 307: **161**
  Tr.G.F. 3 F288 Radt: **109**; 3 T112A Radt: **10**; 3 TK 88ff Radt: **86n**
Aesop
  see Fables
Agatharcides of Cnidus
  F.Gr.Hist. 86 F22: **142**
Agathias
  AP 9.764-6: **166**; 11.365.14: **139**
Agathon
  Tr.G.F. 1.39.T21: **42**
Alcaeus
  fr. 307C LP: **117**; 347 LP: **121, 123n, 115, 119**; 347B LP: **115, 121**
Alcman
  fr. 93 P: **97**; T15-18 Calame: **174**
Alexander
  3.373K: **120n**
Alexis
  fr. 15.12 (2.302 K): **148**; fr. 92.2 (2.326 K): **131**
Ambrose, St.
  epist. 28.5: **130**
Ammianus
  AP 11.156: **169**
Ammonius
  de adfinium vocabulorum differentia 244: **96**
Anacreontea
  34.1: **118, 120**; 34.2: **115**; 34.3: **123**; 34.3f: **124**; 34.11: **116**; 34.12f: **188, 122**; 34.15: **124**; 34.16: **124**; 35.10: **148**

Index locorum 193

Anaxippus
  fr.7 (3.301 K): **151**
Anon.
  AP 9.122: **117**; 9.373: **128**; 9.584.11: **116**; 11.432.1f: **149**
  Kaibel *Epigr.* 546.10: **117**; 546.11f: **118n, 137**
  de vir. illustr. 75.11: **174**
  see also Fables
Antigonus of Carystus
  mirab. 14 (p.4 Keller): **85**
Antimachus
  fr. 20.2 Wyss: **ix**
Antipater of Thessalonica
  AP 9.92.1f = *GP* 81f: **117, 123-4**; 9.302.2 = *GP* 452: **156n**
Antiphanes
  fr. 195.7 (2.94 K): **155**
  AP 11.322.2 = *GP* 722: **111**; 11.322.6 = *GP* 776: **46**; 9.256 = *GP* 741ff: **14, 156**
Antiphilus
  AP 9.71.1 = *GP* 985ff: **115**; 9.404.7 = *GP* 1049: **69**
Antisthenes
  fr. 139 Caizzi: **76**
Antonius Liberalis
  Metam. 13: **67**; 19: **66**; 22.5: **94**
Anyte
  AP 7.190 = *HE* 742ff: **14n, 115n, 128n, 137**
Apollodorus (historian)
  F.Gr.Hist. 244 F209: **170**; 244 F301: **177**
[Apollodorus] (mythographer)
  bibl. 3.12.6: **42**
  epitome 1.14f: **11**
[Apollonides]
  AP 9.26.4 = *GP* 1226: **117**; 9.264.1 = *GP* 1223: **115, 128, 129**; 9.264.2 = *GP* 1224: **116**; 9.264.3 = *GP* 1225: **115, 121**
Apollonius Dyscolus
  Historia Mirabilium 27: **168n**
Apollonius of Rhodes
  Argonautica 1.879ff: **15, 51**; 1.1265ff: **14**; 3.275ff: **14**; 4.1129ff: **67**; 4.1452ff: **14**
Apostolius
  16.32 (2.666 Leutsch-Schneidewin): **129**
Appian
  Bell. Civ. 1.101: **170**
Aratus
  Phaenomena 956: **43**; 1064ff: **78**
Archelaus
  FGE p.22: **77**
Archias
  AP 7.191.3 = *GP* 3712: **119**; 7.201.3 = *GP* 3718: **119**; 7.213 = *GP* 3716ff: **14n, 115n**; 7.213.3 = *GP* 3718: **120**; 7.213.4 = *GP* 3719: **118**; 7.213.5f = *GP* 3720f: **127**
Archilochus
  23.16W: **44**; 223W: **129**; 236W: **170-1**; T 141 Tarditi; **129**; T 170 Tarditi: **129**
Argentarius
  AP 7.364 = *GP* 1407ff: **14n, 137**
Aristophanes of Byzantium
  hist. an. ep. 1.36: **102**; 9.6: **102-3**
Aristodicus of Rhodes
  AP 7.189 = *HE* 772ff: **14n, 118n, 137**
Aristophanes
  Acharnians 150: **138**; 871: **142**; 1116: **142**
  Birds 1f: **115**; 39f: **115, 119**; 185: **138**; 244ff: **166**; 588: **139**; 590: **98**; 748ff: **71**; 1095: **116, 119, 133**
  Clouds 145: **88, 149**; 145: **131, 130**; 165: **166**; 634: **46**; 710: **46**; 742: **46**; 763: **83, 89, 90**
  Frogs 115: **46**; 443: **46**; 1679ff: **119**
  Lysistrata 475: **75**; 695: **3**; 1032: **166**
  Peace 1ff: **11-12**; 10f: **88**; 4ff: **88**; 6ff: **88-9**; 27f: **88**; 34ff: **88**; 82: **84n**; 722: **12**, 723f: **12**; 724: **88**; 72ff: **11n**; 73: **86**; 129ff: **3**; 1017: **95**; 1159: **119**; 1160: **117**
  Thesmophoriazusae 100: **42**; 1175: **98**
  Wasps 107: **73**; 222ff: **76**; 404ff: **76**; 420: **76**; 430: **76**; 457: **78**; 1101ff: **76**; 1116: **75**; 1311f: **143-4**; 1341: **89, 90**; 1341: **90**; 1446ff: **3**
  Wealth 537: **166**; 541: **46**
  Fragments 53 K-A (*PCG* 3.2.57): **127-8, 131**; fr. 208 K-A (*PCG* 3.2.127): **155**; fr. 393 K-A (*PCG* 3.2.217): **112**
Scholia
  Acharnians 150 (1I.IB p.29 Wilson): **138**
  Birds 185 (p.51 White): **138**; 244 (p.58 White): **166n**; 1095 (p.205 White): **131, 133**
  Clouds 157 (1.III.1 p.32 Koster): **165**, (1.III.2 p.32 K): **73, 165**, (1.III.2, p.233 K): **165**; 157C (1.III.1 p.44 Koster): **166n**; 158 (1.III.1 p.45 Holwerda): **121, 130**; 763 (1.III.1 p.158 K): **9**, (1.III.1 p.159 K): **83, 89**; (1.III.2 p.114 K): **83, 89, 90**
  Wasps 1311f (II.1 p.209 K): **144**; 1341 (II.1 p.212 K): **90**; 1341b (II.1 p.213 K): **90**
  Peace 73 (II.II p.20 Holwerda): **86**;

194 Index locorum

82 (II.II p.23 H): **84n**
Aristophon
 fr. 10.4 K-A (*PCG* 4.8): **103**; fr. 10.6f
  K-A (*PCG* 4.8): **116**; fr. 12.9
  K-A (*PCG* 4.10): **174n**
Aristotle
 de aud. 804a22: **117**; 804a23ff: **137**;
  1393b23ff: **6, 157**
 de generatione animalium 715b2ff:
  22; 720b32f: **25**; 721a2ff: **22**;
  721a6ff: **92**; 721a10: **20, 167**;
  721a21ff: **20**; 721a25: **20**; 737a1:
  159; 758b6ff: **22**; 759a1ff: **78**;
  760b27ff: **28**; 761a2ff: **78**; 761a5:
  69; 761b: **49**
 Historia Animalium 487a31: **23**;
  487a33ff: **18**; 487b5: **161n, 165,
  166n, 167**; 488a10: **38**; 489a20ff:
  23; 490a6: **54**; 490a20: **151, 161**;
  490a21: **160, 165, 166**; 490a34:
  157; 490b14f: **23**; 494b26ff: **22**;
  501b19f: **21**; 519a27ff: **54**;
  523a9f: **166**; 523b12ff: **18**;
  523b20: **38**; 523b21: **158**;
  528b29: **151**; 528b31: **161**;
  528b32: **160**; 531b20ff: **18**;
  531b23: **38n**; 531b25: **94**;
  531b26ff: **19**; 532a10: **160**;
  532a13: **151**; 532a15f: **77**;
  532a26: **103**; 532a27: **94**; 532b10:
  142; 532b11ff: **119**; 532b13: **123**;
  532b14: **123**; 532b16: **119, 120n**;
  532b17: **120**; 533a11f: **70**;
  533b5ff: **53**; 534b18: **55**; 534b19:
  98; 535a3: **69, 165**; 535b5: **23**;
  535b6: **119, 54**; 535b7: **120**;
  535b10: **53, 122, 150**; 535b12:
  135; 537a5: **172**; 537b: **53**;
  539b11: **176**; 539b12: **102n**;
  539b13: **151**; 542a11: **95**;
  542a9ff: **92**; 542a12: **151**;
  550b32: **135n, 136**; 551a14: **99,
  102**; 551a29ff: **77, 78**; 551b6ff:
  111; 551b10ff: **112**; 551b12: **102**;
  551b17ff: **94, 96**; 551b19f: **167**;
  551b21ff: **162**; 551b23ff: **159**;
  551b27: **165, 167**; 552a16ff: **90**;
  552a17ff: **85**; 552a20ff: **151**;
  552a30: **161**; 552b1ff: **92, 93**;
  552b5: **165**; 552b8ff: **21**;
  552b10ff: **159**; 552b18ff: **157**;
  552b26ff: **80**; 553a16: **160**;
  553a29: **62**; 553b14ff: **63**;
  553b29ff: **56**; 554a11ff: **57**;
  554a14ff: **58**; 554b6f: **62**; 554b22:
  63n, 79; 554b23ff: **80**; 554b25ff:
  77; 555a13ff: **73**; 555b18ff: **135n,
  136n**; 556a8: **136**; 556a10ff:
  136n; 556a17ff: **120n**; 556a20:
  119; 556a21: **120n**; 556a24f: **115**;
  556b6: **124**; 556b7: **128**; 556b10:
  129; 556b11f: **119**; 556b14ff: **123**;
  556b15ff: **128**; 556b16: **123**;
  556b17ff: **127n**; 556b21ff: **171**;
  556b23: **176**; 556b25ff: **46**;
  557a2: **174**; 557a4ff: **168**; 557a5:
  171; 557a7ff: **168**; 557a10ff: **171**;
  557a15: **172**; 557a18: **157**;
  557a22ff: **172**; 557b1ff: **110**;
  557b13ff: **114**; 557b25ff: **82**;
  557b26ff: **82**; 593a2: **98**; 596b14:
  151; 596b15: **159**; 596b15f: **70**;
  596b15ff: **69**; 601a4: **165**; 601a6f:
  124; 601a7: **115**; 602a26ff: **162**;
  602b28: **172**; 604b19: **91**;
  605b11: **110, 64**; 605b12: **63, 64**;
  605b17: **98**; 606a6: **38**; 609a5: **80**;
  612a34: **142**; 614b1: **96, 98**;
  622b20: **38n, 75**; 622b20ff: **38,
  59**; 622b24ff: **39**; 622b27: **40**;
  623b12: **73**; 624a34ff: **58**; 624b:
  55-6; 625a6: **63**; 625b11: **20**;
  625b17f: **61**; 625b19: **58**; 625b21:
  66; 626a8: **76**; 626a18ff: **53**;
  626a20ff: **63**; 626b1ff: **25**;
  626b10: **61**; 626b16ff: **63**;
  626b18: **64**; 626b24ff: **59**; 627:
  77; 627a15ff: **54**; 627a18f: **54**;
  627a19ff: **59**; 627a20: **61**; 627b:
  77; 627b10: **55**; 627b22ff: **79**;
  628a3ff: **78**; 628b: **79**; 628b1:
  63n; 628b1ff: **62n**; 629a31: **82**;
  633a29ff: **172**
 de incessu animalium 705b26f: **103**
 de longaevitate 466a4ff: **62n**; 467a4f:
  62n
 meteor. 382a8: **159**; 980b23: **49**
 de partibus animalium 642b3ff: **158**;
  643b2: **38**; 648a5ff: **49**; 650b24ff:
  49; 652b24ff: **22**; 652b25f: **23**;
  682a18ff: **119**; 682a25: **123**;
  682a37ff: **19**; 682a5f: **157**; 683a8:
  77; 683b2f: **19**
 Problemata 2.16 (860b): **168**
 de resp. 471b19ff: **23**; 474b31ff: **23,
  122**; 475a4f: **62n**; 475a29ff: **23**;
  478a25ff: **23**
 Rhet. 1394bf: **115n**
 de sens. 444b12: **98**
 de somn. et vig. 456a11ff: **23**
 Fragments: 288 Rose: **168n**; 372
  Rose: **93**
[Aristotle]
 Marvels Heard 147 (845b): **85**; 8
  (844b): **77**; 120 (184a): **85**; 13
  (831b): **96**; 139 (844b): **142**; 176
  (847b): **141**; 30 (844b): **143**
Arrian

Index locorum

Epictetus' Discourses 3.22.99: **62**
Indike 8.11: **62**
Artemidorus
  Oneirocr. 2.22 (p.139f. Pack): **85, 135n**; 3.6: **43**
Asclepiades
  F.Gr.Hist. 12 F.13: **164**
Athenaeus
  126A: **156**; 133B: **131**; 157A: **156**; 659A: **119**
Atra-Ḥasis
  III v 34f: **151n**
Ausonius
  Id. 11.20 (Latin): **73n**
Babrius
  fab. 28: **2n**; 84: **2n, 166n**; 107: **2**; 140: **4**
Bacchylides
  Odes 10.10: **71**
Basil, St.
  Homilies on the Hexameron 83B: **40**
Bianor
  AP 9.273 = *GP* 1707ff: **116, 128, 129**; 9.273.2 = *GP* 1708: **119**
Callimachus
  Hymn to Apollo 109ff: **69**; 110: **58, 70**
  Hymn to Demeter 102: **8n**
  Fragments: 1.29ff Pf.: **124**; 1.31ff: **124n**; 36: **124n**; 1.33ff Pf.: **126n**; 191.26ff Pf.: **15**; 260.19 Pf.: **102**; 380.2 Pf.: **76**; 551 Pf.: **135**
[Callisthenes]
  2.16.2 (p.85 Kroll): **76**
Charon of Lampsacus
  F.Gr.Hist. 262 F 12: **69, 70**
Christodorus
  AP 2.69: **71**; 2.110: **71**
Cicero
  de divinatione 1.78: **43**
  de natura deorum 3.45: **68**
Cleanthes of Assos
  fr. 515 Von Arnim (*Stoicorum Veterum Fragmenta* 1.116): **41**
Clearchus
  fr. 56 Wehrli (3.26): **127**
Clement of Alexandria
  Paed. 2.8 (1.197 Stählin): **85**; 2.10.107 (1.220 Stählin): **102, 112**
  Protr. 1.1ff (1.3 Stählin): **116, 118**
  Strom. 5.4 (2.339f Stählin): **84n**; 5.5 (2.343 Stählin): **117, 118**
Clitarchus
  Fr.Gr.Hist. 137 T10 = F14: **82-3**
Collectanea Alexandrina
  Powell p.185f. no.7: **viii-ix, 51, 56, 70**
Columella
  de re rustica 9.2.4: **66**; 9.8.12: **54**; 9.14: **55**; 9.14.3: **70**
Corpus Glossorum Latinorum
  II 259 10 and 37: **156-7**; 7.567: **146**
Corpus Medicorum Graecorum
  1.2.4 (Joly): **105**
Demetrius
  de elocutione 304: **82-3**
Democritus
  68B fr. 126 D-K: **107n**
Deuteronomy
  22:13: **51**
Didymus
  fr. 14 Schmidt: **67**
Dio Chrysostom
  orat. 32.97: **85**; 40.32: **42**; 40.40f: **42**; 48.16: **42**
Diodorus Siculus
  3.2f: **165**; 3.29: **142**; 17.75.5: **83**
Diogenian
  cent. 2.97: **96**
Dioscorides
  de mat. med. 2.6: **92**; 2.52: **142**; 2.61.1: **91**; 5.109.4 (3.81 Wellman): **82n**
  de Simpl. 1.149 (2.208 Wellman): **176n**
Epic of Gilgamesh
  XI 159-61: **151n**
Epicharmus
  Heracles (fr. 76 Kaibel): **86**
  fr. 199 Kaibel: **149**
Epictetus
  Gnom.: **116**
Epilycus
  fr. 4 (1.804 K): **131**
Epiphanius
  Panarion haer. 41.3 (2.93 Holl): **72**
  1.301c: **81**
Erucius
  AP 7.36 = *GP* 2262ff: **72**
Et. Gud.
  194.12: **162**; 1.146 de Stefani: **79n**
Etym. Magn.: **132**
  s.vv. *br(o)ukos, br(o)uchos*: **135n, 145**; *empis*: **165**; *mastax*: **135n**
Eubulus
  fr. 10 Hunter: **123, 130**; fr. 32 Hunter: **168**; fr. 107.10 Hunter: **144, 145**
Eudoxus of Rhodes
  F.Gr.Hist. 79 F4: **141**
Euenus
  AP 9.122 = *GP* 2318ff: **127**
Euripides
  Cyclops 475: **78**
  Hel. 1095f: **180**
  Hippolytus 76: **51, 65, 70**
  Scholia
  Hipp. 2.14 Schwartz: **65**

196 Index locorum

Eustathius
  Il. 395.33 (1.622 Van der Valk): **125**;
  1161.29: **162**; 1243.24: **156**;
  1243.29: **156**; 1259.41: **44**;
  1329.25: **90n**; 1928.16: **162**
  Od. 1454.25f: **152**; 1469.53: **146**;
  1496.53: **135n**
Exodus (Greek translation)
  8:16: **98**
Ezekiel
  Exagoge (*Tr.G.F.* 1 (128) 135): **98**
Fables
  (References are to Perry's Appendix to Loeb edn. of Babrius and Phaedrus) 3:3; 72: **6n**; 80: **14n**, **155**; 84: **88n**; 112: **4**; 137: **2n**; 163: **6n**; 166: **4n**; 184: **123**; 216: **4n**; 235: **3**; 241: **127**; 255: **4n**; 259: **3n**; 268: **2n**; 299: **4n, 5, 69**; 373: **4**; 397: **4n, 129**; 400: **6n**; 427: **6**; 470: **122**; 471: **170**; 521: **4**; 556: **100n**; 564: **3n**; 650: **12n**; 659: **84**; 724: **2n**
  see also Babrius; Phaedrus
Gaetulicus
  AP 7.71 = *FGE* 197ff: **76**
Galen
  19.726: **91**; 19.89: **91**; 248.18: **135n**
Geoponica
  4.10: **76**; 15.1.20: **40**; 15.2.9: **55**; 15.2.15: **70**; 15.3: **54**; DK *Vorsokratiker* 2.125 (fr. 8): **47**
Gregory of Nazianza
  carm. mor. 14.17ff: **115**
Heliodorus
  Aethiopica 10.25.2: **112**
Heraclides of Pontus
  fr. 55 Wehrli (7².22): **124**; fr. 153 Wehrli (7.45): **152**
Heraclitus
  fr. B56 DK: **171**
Hermogenes
  Scholia (Waltz, *Rhet. Gr.* (4.79 n.40)): **118, 125**
Herodas
  1.15: **155**; 1.57: **164**; 2.73: **111, 156**; 7.42: **7n**; 12.1: **160**; 12.2: **90**
Herodicus of Babylon
  fr. 494.3 *Suppl. Hell.*: **111**
Herodotus
  1.193.4-5: **82**; 2.37: **170**; 2.67: **80**; 2.75: **148**; 2.95: **165, 166**; 3. 102ff: **44**; 3.107: **148**; 3.109: **148n**; 4.109: **172**; 4.168: **172**; 4.172.1: **145**; 5.114: **51**
Hesiod
  Theogony 41:**8n**; 594ff:**52**
  Works and Days 233: **51, 57**; 304: **52**; 418: **96**; 582: **119**; 583: **115, 117**, **119n**; 583ff: **123n**; 584: **121**; 778: **40, 43**
  Fragment 205MW: **42**
[Hesiod]
  Shield 393: **119, 123, 129**; 394: **115, 129**; 395: **123**
Hesychius
  (References are to Latte's edition) 1.82: **130**; 1.89: **144**; 1.77: **79n**; 1.178: **79**; 1.284: **146**; 1.333: **72-3**; 1.335: **37**; 1.349: **145**; 1.351: **139**; 1.354: **37**; 1.416: **80**; 2.81: **165**; 2.198: **131**; 2.290: **110**; 2.370: **38**; 2.411: **176**; 2.412: **94**; 2.415: **146, 176**; 2.462: **94**; 2.464: **146**; 2.465: **131**; 2.477: **132**; 2.478: **129**; 2.494: **98**; 2.527: **177**; 2.549: **92, 157**; 2.554: **158**; 2.555: **132**; 2.596: **117**; 2.628: **176n**; 2.644: **67**; 2.682: **160**; 2.686: **37**; 2.749: **136, 144**; 2.776: **37**; 2.801: **143**; 4.408: **86n**
Hieronymus
  fr. 15 Wehrli (10.13): **117, 127, 128n**
Himerius
  orat. 48.11: **117**; 59.1: **72**
Hippocrates
  Epidemics 1.20ff: **170**
  Internal Affections: **170**
  On Regimen 1.6f. and 29.2: **105**
  On Superfetation 28.2: **108**
  T32: **93**
Hipponax
  fr. 92W: **11**
Homer
  Iliad 2:469f: **7, 15**; 2.87ff: **7, 15, 49**; 3.149ff: **122n, 126n**; 3.151ff: **8, 115, 127**; 7:177f: **180**; 11.1: **126**; 12.167ff: **7, 49, 75**; 16.259ff: **7, 75**; 16.641ff: **7**; 17.570ff: **8**; 19.24ff: **8**; 19.237: **126**; 21.12ff: **135, 140**; 21.394f: **155, 156**; 421: **155**; 24.414f: **8**; 24.532: **8n**
  Scholia on *Iliad* 1.180 (1.60 Erbse): **42**; 3.15 (1.385 E): **8n**, (1.386 E): **120**; 3.151 (*F.Gr.Hist* 4.F140): **127**; 21.12ff (5.125 E): **140-1**), (5.126 E): **135**; 21.394ff (5.219E): **155**, (5.220 E): **156**; 22.94 (5.288 E): **44**; 24.253 (5.566 E): **73n**
  Odyssey 4.130ff: **8**; 10.81ff: **162**; 13.103ff: **52n**; 13.106: **64**; 17:300: **8, 157**; 21.395: **8n, 97**
  Scholia on *Odyssey* 10.85: **162**; 17.300: **156**; 22.229: **162**
  Homeric Hymn to Aphrodite: **126**
  Homeric Hymn to Hermes: **70**
Horace

Index locorum

Odes 4.2.27ff: **71**
Hyginus
  fab. 136:**68**
Inscriptions
  IG 4²121 B 28 **173**
  2027:10 Peek: **8n, 117, 119n**
  Inscr. Délos: **151**
Isidore
  12.8.9: **144**
Jerome, St.
  epist. 22.18: **124**
Job, Book of
  4:11: **45**; 4:19: **109**
John of Carpathos
  epist. 95: **169**
Josephus
  Antiquities 18.174f: **6**
Judges
  14:8: **51**
Julian the Apostate
  Misopôgon 228C: **169**
Julian the Egyptian
  AP 9.739: **161**
Juvenal
  Sat. 9.69: **116**
2 Kings
  1:2: **152**
Leonidas of Tarentum
  AP 6.120.1f = *HE* 2521f: **115, 126**; 6.120.2 = *HE* 2522: **116**; 6.120.7 = *HE* 2527: **118, 122**; 7.13.1f = *HE* 2563f: **71**; 7.198 = *HE* 2084ff: **136, 137**; 7.198.3 = *HE* 2086: **137**; 7.198.4 = *HE* 2087: **130**; 7.408.2 = *HE* 2326: **76**
Livy
  2.32: **175**
Longus
  Daphnis and Chloe 1.9.1: **51**; 1.10.2: **138**; 1.14.4: **138**; 1.23.1: **119**; 1.25: **116, 117, 119, 127, 129**; 1.25f: **119**; 3.24.2: **119**
Lucan
  9.288f: **54**
Lucian
  Charon 15 (2.15 Macleod): **75n**
  The Fly: **150-1**; 7: **151**; 12: **156**; ad fin.: **155**
  Icaromenippus 19 (1.301 Macleod): **42**
  Ignorant Book Collector 1 (2.121 Macleod): **110**
  Iup. Trag. 31 (1.233 Macleod): **144**
  Pseudologistes: **129**
  Scholia: *The Fly* (p. 10 Rabe): **165**
[Lucian]
  Amores 18: **116**
  Philopatris 12: **149n**
Lucilius
  AP 11.265.1: **156**
Lucretius
  de rerum natura 3.11: **71**
Lycophron
  18: **124**; 181f: **78**
Martial
  1.115: **129**; 4.64: **103**; 5.18.8f: **153**; 12.59.8: **169**
Matthew, Gospel of St.
  6:20: **111**
Meleager
  AP 5.57 = *HE* 4074: **100n**; 5.151 = *HE* 4166ff: **166**; 5.152 = *HE* 4174: **166**; 5.184.6 = *HE* 4375: **46**; 5.195 = *HE* 4058ff: **138**; 195.2 = *HE* 4059: **117, 137**; 5.195.4 = *HE* 4061: **135, 137**; 5.196 = *HE* 4066: **119, 123**; 5.196.3 = *HE* 4068: **115, 122**; 5.196.4 = *HE* 4069: **129**; 5.196.5ff = *HE* 4070ff: **117**; 5.196.7 = *HE* 4072: **116**
Menander
  fr. 437 Koerte (2.154): **151**; fr. 538.5f. Sandbach: **111**
Menander Rhetor
  peri epideikt. 2.391.13: **117**
Metrodorus of Scepsis
  F.Gr.Hist. 184 F11: **93**
Mimnermus
  fr. 4 W: **126**
Mnasalces
  AP 7.192 = *HE* 2647ff: **14n, 118n, 136, 137**; 7.192.4 = *HE* 2650: **121, 136**; 7.194 = *HE* 2651: **14n, 136, 137**; 7.194.3 = *HE* 2653: **137**
Musaeus
  Hero and Leander 134: **164**
Nearchus
  Fr.Gr.Hist. 133F 19: **113n**
Neoptolemus of Parion
  fr. 9 Mette: **155**
Nicander
  Alex. 115ff: **93**; 128ff: **93**; 182: **81**; 183: **72**; 335ff: **91**; 547: **82**
  Ther. 128ff: **148n**; 740: **77**; 747: **46**; 760: **108-9**; 802: **146-7**; 806: **72**; 811ff: **76**; 812: **81**
  Fragments: 38 Schneider: **94**; 93 Schneider: **58**; 94 Schneider: **66**
  Scholia: *Ther.* 760, p.274 Crugnola: **108-9**; *Alex.* 335, p. 128 Geymonat: **95**
Nicias
  AP 2.200 = *HE* 2767ff: **115, 129**, 7.200.2 = *HE* 2768: **121**
Nonnus
  5.243ff: **51**

198   Index locorum

Origen
  contra Celsum 4.57: **84**; 4.59: **84**; 4.81: **60**
Ovid
  Ars Amatoria 1.271: **116**
  Fast. 3.741 (3.136f.): **54n**
  Metamorphoses 7.366 (291): **177**
Pamphilus
  AP 7.201.1 = HE 2839: **115, 129**; 7.201.2f = HE 2840: **117, 119**
Papyri
  see Tebtunis Papyri
Parmenio
  AP 9.113 = GP 2598f: **46**
Paulus
  AP 9.764-6: **166**
Pausanias
  1.20.7: **174**; 1.24.8f: **141**; 5.14.1: **152**; 6.26.6ff: **113n**; 7.2.11: **166**; 8.26.7: **152**; 9.40.1f: **55**; 10.5.5ff: **69**; 10.10.7: **169**; 10.28.7: **155**
Pausanias Atticistes
  s.vv. *sphêx*: **76**; *kerkôpê*: **131**; *terêdôn*: **96, 98**
Petronius
  Satyricon 56.6: **69**
Phaedimus
  AP 7.197 = HE 2931ff: **14n**
Phaedrus
  fab. 1.24: **2n**; 3.6: **2n**; 3.13: **5**; 3.16: **127**; 4.25: **4**
  Perrotti's Appendix 31: **4, 100n**
Phaennus
  AP 7.197 = HE 2931: **137**; 7.197.2 = HE 2932: **136, 137**
Pherecrates
  fr. 145.20ff (1.188K): **42**
Philip
  AP 7.405.4 = GP 2864: **76**; 9.438 = GP 2987ff: **44**; 11.321.1 = GP 3033: **111**; 11.347.2 = GP 3042: **111**
Philo
  de opificio mundi 154 (1.250 Arnaldez): **143**
  de praemiis et poenis 96: **76**
Philostratus
  epist. 71: **118**
  Imagines 1.23.2: **161n**; 2.8.6: **72**; 13.3: **75**
  Vita Apollonii 7.11: **119, 120**
Photius
  Bibl. 455a (7.174 Henry): **45**; (1.288 Theodoridis): **144**; s.vv. *mastax*: **146**; *mulabrides*: **148n**; *okornos*: **136**; *prasocuris*: **167**; *pyrolampis*: **158**
Phrynichus
  Praep. Soph. 126.8: **158**

Pindar
  Ol. 6.45ff: **67**
  Pythian 4.60: **70**
  Fragments: fr. 52, i. 60ff Snell: **69**; fr. 123.10f Snell: **69**; fr. 158: **69**; fr. 222 Snell: **110**
  Scholia: Ol. 13.130A (1.382 Drachmann): **164**
Planudean Appendix to Greek Anthology
  9:**156n**
Plato
  Apology 30E: **161**
  Ion 533Eff: **72**
  Phaedo 82b: **38n**
  Phaedrus 230C: **114, 116**; 258E: **114, 116**; 259C: **122**
  Republic 552C-537A: **62**
  Symp. 191C: **124**
Plato Comicus
  fr. 37 (1.610 K): **86, 92**
Pliny the Elder
  Naturalis Historia 2.109: **40**; 6.195: **142**; 7.29: **142**; 8.44: **25n**; 8.104: **41**; 10.75: **141, 152**; 10.190: **22n, 151**; 10.195: **165**; 10.198: **44**; 10.204: **80**; 10.206: **44**; 10.419: **44**; 11.10: **61**; 11.12: **59**; 11.19: **98**; 11.20: **54, 55, 63**; 11.22: **62, 112**; 11.28: **77**; 11.30: **56**; 11.32: **123**; 11.48f: **74**; 11.60: **53**; 11.61: **55, 76, 166**; 11.65: **110n**; 11.70: **77, 84**; 11.72: **69, 80**; 11.73: **63n, 77, 78**; 11.74: **62n, 112n**; 11.75: **72**; 11.92: **120, 128**; 11.93: **119, 120, 124, 129**; 11.94: **123, 127n**; 11.95: **115**; 11.98: **85, 158**; 11.100: **103, 160, 166**; 11.103: **143**; 11.104ff: **141**; 11.106: **141**; 11.107: **120, 135**; 11.108ff: **39**; 11.109: **40**; 11.110: **38, 41**; 11.112: **102**; 11.113: **161**; 11.114: **174**; 11.115: **172**; 11.116: **157**; 11.117: **82**; 11.118: **167**; 11.119: **159**; 11.120: **151, 157, 160**; 11.140: **127n**; 11.258: **151**; 11.266: **53, 120, 150**; 11.267: **135**; 11.279: **85**; 15.67: **76**; 15.80: **82**; 16.220: **95, 96, 98**; 17.221: **95, 103**; 17.255: **81**; 18.152: **93**; 18.252f: **159**; 18.253: **159**; 18.292: **40**; 18.364: **43**; 19.106: **152**; 23.43: **77**; 23.198: **77**; 24.52: **152**; 26.138: **174**; 27.100: **92**; 29.94: **92**; 30.30: **91, 142**; 30.49: **147, 148n**; 30.53: **98**; 30.68: **128**; 30.111: **142**; 30.123: **142**; 34.57: **128n**
Plutarch

Index locorum

Amator (moralia 767C): **124n**
Apophthegmata Laconica 8 (moralia 208E): **170**
Conjugal Precepts 44 (moralia 144D): **70**
de sera num. vind. 17 (moralia 560E): **129**
de sollert. anim. (moralia 967B): **59**
How to tell flatterer from friend 2 (moralia 49C): **168**
Isis and Osiris 10 (moralia 355A): **84, 96**; 74 (moralia 381A): **84, 96, 145**
Life of Agis and Cleomenes 29.3: **84**
Life of Cimon 18.4: **43**
Life of Solon 23 = F 62 Ruschenbusch: **52**
Life of Sulla 36.3f: **174**
Natural Questions 5.399 Bernardakis = 11.218ff. in Loeb text: **70**
Old Men in Politics (moralia 790C): **6**
On Having Many Friends 7 (moralia 96B): **75n**
On the Intelligence of Animals (moralia 967D-968B): **38**; 967F: **43n**
Quaest. Conv. 2.9 (moralia 642Bf): **172**; 8.7.3 (moralia 727E): **117, 118**
Quiet of Mind 15 (moralia 473E): **85**
moralia 611F: **102**; 710E: **85**; 727E: **127**; 874B: **93**; 967E: **41**; 968A: **40**; 1058A: **85**; 1096A: **85**
Pollux
4.10 (1.230 Bethe): **56**; 9.110: **160**; 9.113 (2.178 Bethe): **160**; 9.123 (2.181 Bethe): **160**
carm. pop. 876 P: **160**
Onomasticon 2.29 (1.89 Bethe): **168**
Porphyrius
The Cave of the Nymphs in the Odyssey 18: **64**
Posidippus
AP 12.98.1 = HE 3074: **118**
Proverbs (Greek translation)
6:8f: **42**; 12:4: **96**; 25:20: **96**
Psalms
81:16: **51**
Quintus of Smyrna
2.197ff: 141; 11.146ff: **76**
Sappho
fr. 101a V: **115-16, 121**
Semonides
7.83ff W: **59, 62**
fr. 13 W: **3n**
Servius
2.207 ed. Harv.: **66**

Sextus Empiricus
Pyrrh. 1.55: **76, 85**
Silentarius
AP 6.54.9: **119**
Simias
AP 7.193: **137**; 7.193.1 = HE 3272: **139**; 7.193.3 = HE 3274: **138**; 7.193.4 = HE 3275: **119, 136n**
Simonides
521.3f. P: **153**; 541.10 P: **14n**; 610 P: **118n, 130**
Sophocles
Daedalus (Tr.G.F. 4 F162 Radt): **86**
Ichneutae (Tr.G.F. 4 F314.307 Radt): **86**
Inachus (Tr.G.F. 4 F279 Radt): **163n**
Men of Camicus (Tr.G.F. 4 F324 Radt): **11**
Phineus (Tr.G.F. 4 F716 Radt): **10, 147**
Tr.G.F. 4 F778 Radt: **76**; 4 F879: **65**
Sostratus
fr. 10 Wellman (Hermes 26 (1891)): **161**
Speusippus of Athens
fr. 10 Tarán: **131**; fr. 11 T: **112**
Stephanus of Byzantium
s.v. akanthos: **130**
Stesichorus
fr. 240 P: **117**
Strabo
2.1.14: **51**; 6.267.2: **57**; 13.613: **97**; 13.613.64: **141**; 16.772.12: **142**; 16.774.15: **45**; 7 fr. 30: **85**
Strato
AP 12.190.3f: **98, 99**
Strattis
fr. 66.1 (1.730 K): **167**
Suda
(References are to Adler's edition) 1.76: **130**; 1.376: **129**; 3.25: **84, 85**; 3.320: **176**; 3.386: **90**; 3.596: **143**; 4.126: **112, 165**; 4.275: **158**; 4.343: **177**; 4.346: **74**; 4.60: **138**
Suetonius
Life of Nero 20.2: **118**; 46.1: **43**
Life of Tiberius 77.2: **43**
peri blasphêmiôn 5: **155**; 8: **98**
Synesius
Hymn 9.45: **123, 124**
Tebtunis Papyri
i.1902.1: **viii-ix, 51, 56, 70**
Tertullian
adv. Marc. 4.5.3 (2.270 Evans): **75n**
de anima 15.1 (p.9 Waszink): **151**
Theaetetus
AP 11.16.4: **117**
Theocritus
Idylls 1.52: **128n, 137, 142**; 1.106f:

70; 1.148: **119**; 4.16: **123**; 5.34: **119**; 5.108: **128n, 139**; 5.110f: **116, 128**; 5.114f: **90**; 7.78ff: **72**; 7.80ff: **51**; 7.138: **115n, 116, 129**; 10.18: **177**; 15.45: **44**; 16.95f: **115, 119**; 17.107: **44**; 22.40ff: **51**
Syrinx 3: **72**
Scholia: *Id.* 10.18 (p.229 Wendel): **176-7**; *Id.* 7.138 (p.110 Wendel): **116**
Theophrastus
 de Causis Plantarum: 2.9: **82**; 3.18: **82**; 3.22.3ff: **97, 103**; 4.15.4: **96**; 5.10: **103**; 6.5.1: **85**; 6.5.3: **98**
 de lapidibus 37: **167**; 49: **97**; 58-9: **158**
 de odoribus 4: **85**
 Historia Plantarum 2.4.4: **102**; 2.8.1ff: **82**; 2.8.2: **81**; 2.8.3: **98**; 3.12.8: **103**; 4.14.4ff: **103**; 4.14.5: **95**; 5.1.2: **96**; 5.4.4: **98**; 5.4.5: **95, 96, 99**; 6.10.8: **98**; 7.5.4: **149, 167**; 8.10.1: **93**; 8.10.5: **97, 103**; 8.11.2: **103**; 9.14.3: **95**
 Metaph. 29: **157n**
 Fragments: 174: **136**; 187: **122**
[Theophrastus]
 de sign. 22: **43**; 47: **78**; 54: **130**
Thucydides
 Scholion: 1.6.3 (p.8 Hude): **118**
Tiberius Ilus
 AP 9.372 = *FGE* 2062ff: **127**; 9.372.6 = *FGE* 2070: **116, 118**

Timaeus
 F.Gr.Hist. 566 F 43: **118, 120-1**
Timon of Phlius
 fr. 786 Suppl. Hell.: **111**; fr. 804 S.H.: **115, 126n**
Tragicorum Graecorum Fragmenta
 2 (adesp.) F295: **155**; 4 T 1.88ff: **71**; 4 T 109-12: **71**
 see also Aeschylus; Ezekiel; Sophocles
Varro
 de re rustica 3.16: **54, 72**
Vegetius
 Mulomedicina 2.142: **91**
Vergil
 Aeneid 4.367: **83**; 6.706ff: **65**
 Eclogues 1.54: **57**; 2.12f: **116**; 13f: **117**; 4.30: **57**; 7.37: **57**
 Georgics 1.131: **57**; 1.379: **43**; 3.328: **117**; 4.47ff: **55**; 4.49: **54**; 4.54: **59**; 4.178ff: **61**; 4.181: **58**; 4.191: **55**; 4.194: **59**; 4.197ff: **70**; 4.206: **62**; 4.219ff: **69**; 4.237: **53**; 4.403: **42**
Xenarchus
 fr. 14 (2.473 K): **119**
Xenophon
 Memorabilia 3.11.5: **155**
 Oeconomicus 7.17: **62**; 7.32: **59, 62, 69**; 7.38f: **62**
Zenobius
 cent. 1.51: **130**; 2.53: **3n**; 2.94: **177** (Leutsch-Schneidewin refs. ad locc.); 32 (4.252 Bühler): **74**

General index

References to illustrations are given by page numbers in **bold** type

abuse, *see* insult
Acrolepia assectella Zell (leekbane), 167
Aelian, 28, 29-30
  common source with Plutarch?, 39
  see also Index Locorum
Aesop, **5**, 6, 13
  fables of, 1-6
aetiology, *see* fables; myth
affection for insects, 90, 91, 128-9, 137-8
Agesilaus, king of Sparta, 170
agrios (prob. hornet), 79
agrios melissa (= wasp), 49
agrios sphêx (wild wasp), 77
akanthios (cicada), 130
akarnos (locust), 138-9, 144
akris, 135-44
  anatomy, 119, 120-2, 142
  arouraia (mantis), 176
  cicada, 117-18, 121-2, 137
  = cricket, 137-8
  epitaphs for, 128n, 136, 137
  etymology, 135
  as food, 141-2
  = grasshopper, 137-8
  identification, problem of, 135-7
  kalamaia (mantis), 176
  = locust, 138-9
  = mantis, 135, 176-7
  as pet, 128n, 136, 137-8
  sound of, 119, 121-3, 136-7, 138; *liguros* of, 117-18, 137
analogy with modern forms, ix
  kynamuia, 157
  mantis, 180

muôps, 160
prasocuris, 167
tettix, 14
ant (*myrmêx/formica*), 37-47
  in art, ii, 31, **37**
  cicada eaten by, 127
  communication, 41-2
  dead, treatment of, 39, 41
  in epic similes, 14
  epigrams on, 41
  in fables, 2, 4, 130
  in folklore, 40, 43
  food collection, 39-40, 42-3, 57
  food-traffic, 40-1
  in legend, 42-4
  moon, sensitivity to, 40
  nest, structure of, 38-9
  organisation, social, 38-40, 42, 60
  Oriental, 40, 44-5
  in proverbs, 43-4
  = *(s)knips*: Egyptian plague, 98
  waste, disposal of, 39
ant-lion (*myrmêko-leôn*), 45
anthrêdôn (wasp), 79-80
  etymology, 38, 73n, 79, 98
anthrênê (wasp), 79-80
anthropomorphicism
  ant, 39
  Aristotle, 61-2, 63
  bees, 61-2
  dung beetle, Fabre refutes, x-xi
  Vergil, 61-2
antidotes to poison, Nicander on, 15
aphrodisiac, cantharidin as, 93
Apis cerana (bee), 53
Apollo: wards off flies, 152

202 General index

Apollodorus (pharmacologist), 15
Apomuios, Zeus, 152
Archilochus (poet), 7, 76
Argus (Odysseus' dog), 8, 156
Aristaeus (hero) and bees, 65, 67-8
Aristophanes
  dung-beetles, 11-12
  flea, 149
  wasps, 75-6
  see also Index Locorum
Aristotle
  achievement assessed, xii, 16-28
  anthropocentricity, 23, 49
  anthropomorphicism, 61-2, 63
  on bees, 48-9; anatomy, 23, 53-4; dance of, 55-6; food of, 56-8; hives, observation of, 49-50
  'bloodless' of insects, 22-3
  on breathing, 22-3, 27
  classification of insects, 18-20, 23
  eggs of insects, terms for, 22
  entomon defined, 18-19
  on generation, spontaneous, 21
  Historia Animalium, authenticity of portions of, 26-7, 48, 142-3
  identification of insects, 19-20
  influence of contemporary attitudes, xii, 17-18, 24-6, 48-9
  and mean, golden, 18
  observation, individual, 16-17, 20-1, 24-5, 28, 49
  On Marvels Heard not by, 27-8
  scientific enquiry: principles, 28
  sources, 17, 24-5
  teleology, 22-3
  see also Index Locorum
armies: infestation, 9-10, 46n, 170
arouraia (mantis, praying), 176
art, 30-6
  composite figure (*Mischwese*), 35-6
  insects in: ant, 31, **37**; bee, **34, 50, 53, 57, 60, 61, 67, 68, 71**, 72; beetle, 83, 86, **87**, **93**; butterfly, 31, **99, 101, 104, 105, 106**; cicada, **114, 125**, 130; dragonfly, 31; fly, 9, 31, **150, 153, 154, 163**, 164; grasshopper, **33, 134**; locust, **139, 140, 143**; praying mantis, **178, 179**; wasp, **ii**, 9, 61, **74, 78**, 79
  parody, 36
  realism, 161
  size of insects in, 33
  see also coins; gems; jewellery; manuscripts; pottery; sculpture; vase painting; wall-paintings
askepês of bees, ix, 51-2

asses
  and dung beetle, 84
  and louse, 172
astakos (locust), 144
Athens
  beekeeping, 52
  cicada emblem of, 125-6
  plague, 9-10, 149
attakos (locust), 144
attelabos (locust), 135, 136, 144-5

Babylon
  ants, 44
  epic, 7
  fables, 1-2
basket-worm, 113
bed bug (*koris/Cimex lectularius*), 46-7
  in comedy, 12-13, 46
bee (*melissa/apis*), 47-75
  anatomy, Aristotle on, 23, 54
  in art: coins, **57, 60**, 72; gems, **50**, 65, 68-9, **68**, 72; jewellery, 34-5, **34, 53, 61**, 72; sculpture, 31; tomb decorations, 65; vase painting, 32, 66-7, **67, 71**
  attacked by other insects, 76, 166
  bougonia, 65-6
  and chastity, xii, 70
  communication by, 54-5
  dead, treatment of, 39
  diseases of, 63-4
  domesticated, 52
  drones, 5, 52, 62
  'economy', home, 59, 62
  in fables, 5-6
  in folklore, 47-8, 55
  food of, 56-9
  holiness of, 6, 48-9, 69-70
  in Homeric similes, 7
  intelligence, 49
  in legend, 66-9, 72
  life-cycle, 49, 62
  in literature, 7, 13, 15; literary works on, 15, 48-50, 60, 75
  mason, 59
  misconceptions, popular, 49, 62
  oistros =, 164
  onomatopoeia in names, 73
  organisation, social, 38, 59-62
  and poetry, 13, 70-2
  and pollen, 58
  in proverbs, 59
  purity of, xii, 69-70
  queen, 49, 62-3
  in religion and ritual, x, 48, 65, 69-70
  senses of, 54-5
  = siren, 73-5

General index

as soul, 64-5, 68-9, 74-5
sound of, 53-4
sting, 6, 52-3, 63
water, use of, 58-9
wax production, 58
wild, viii-ix, 50-2
and Zeus, 66-7
beetle/cockchafer (*kantharos/mêlolonthê*), 83-96
 in art: coin, **87**; gem, **83**; ms. illustration, **93**
beetle/cockchafer confused, 83
in religion, 95-6
see also dung-beetle
Bellerophon, myth of, 12, 164
Bembex rostrata, 79-80
bembix/bombyx, 72
Benét, Stephen: *The Devil and Daniel Webster*, xii
Blake, William, 106n
blind man's buff, 160
bombul(i)os (cocoon), 102
bombykion (bee or wasp), 73
bombylios (bumble bee?), 73
Bombyx mori (silk moth), 112
bombyx/bembix, 72-3
borers of wood, 8n, 96-9
 see also skôlêx
bormax (ant), 37
boubrôstis, 8n
bougonia (generation of insects from carcasses of oxen), 65-6
bouprêstis (beetle), 91-2
Brachiella thynni Cuv., 162
broukhos, broukos (locust), 135, 145
Browning, Robert: on cicadas, 116
bruchid from Pompeii, xi
brukhos, brukos (locust), 145
burmax (ant), 37
butterfly/moth (*psychê*), 99-114
 in art, 101; Cupid's Psyche depicted as, 107; gems, 30-1, **31**, **99**, **101**, **104**; sculpture, **106**, 107; as soul in Roman art, 102, **106**, 107; vase painting, **105**; wall painting, 36
in fables, 4
fever: linguistic connection, 110
generation and life-cycle, 102-3
in literature, 100-1
medicinal use of, 107-8
in Minoan and Mycenaean religion, 107
name, taboo on, 100n
phallus and, 105-7
Prometheus and, **106**, 107
Resurrection and, 103
semen, connection with, 104-7
soul in form of, xii, 99-100, 103-7, 108-9
symbolism and metaphor, 103-7
Byron, Lord: on cicadas, 116

Callicrates (sculptor), 31
cantharidin (blister beetle's toxin), 91, 92, 93
Cantharolethrus (place fatal to beetles), 85
'Capital' pin, 34-5
carcasses, generation of insects from, 64, 65-6, 77-8, 84
Cerambycidae, 94-5
Chalicodoma muraria (bee), 73
Chalicodoma sicula (bee), viii-ix, 51-2
chalkê muia (blind man's buff), 160
Chantraine, Pierre, ix
 see also Index of Modern Works
Chironomus (common gnat), 167
chrysokantharos, 89
chrysomêlolonthê, 90-1
cicada (*tettix*), 113-33
 anatomy, 23, 119-22, **120**
 in art: coins, 35, 125-6, **125**; gems, 72; jewellery, 130; 'Mischwese', 36; pottery, 31, **114**; sculpture, 31
 affection for, x, 117-19, 128-9
 akris confused with, 117-18, 121-2, 137
 colour of, 129, 133
 emblem of Athens, 125-6
 epigrams on, 14, 128, 129
 etymology, 113, 130-3 *passim*
 in fables, 4, 5-6, 123, 128
 in folklore, 4, 130
 as food for others, 127-9
 food of, 122, 123-4
 generation of, 124n
 grasshopper, confused with, 115n, 122, 124-5, 134
 and heat, 4, 115-16, 122
 in Homer, 8, 126n
 hunting of, 127-8
 immortality of, 124, 126
 and Muses, 8n, 117-18, 122
 in myth, 42, 117, 122, 126-7
 as nickname, 119
 as pets, 128n
 in proverbs, 129-30
 reproduction, 124-6
 silent, 118
 sound of, 116-22; *liguros* used of, 117-18, 122; reactions to, x, 116-19; source of, 119-20
classification, entomological, 18-20
Clitarchus (glossographer), 82-3, 147

204 General index

cockchafer (*mêlolonthê*), 89-91
  see also beetle
cockroach, ix, 177n
cocoons
  bombul(i)os =, 102
  of Galeriidae (moths), 64
  of *Lasiocampa otus* (silk moth), 112-14
coins, insects on
  Acragas (grasshopper), **134**
  Athens (cicada), 35, 125-6, **125**
  Caulonia (fly), **153**
  Crete (gad-fly), **164**
  Ephesus (bee), **60**
  Etna (dung-beetle), 86-7, **87**
  Hybla (bee), **57**
  Metapontum (locust), **143**
colour, words for, 129, 133
Comatas (herdsman in Theocr. *Id.*), 72
combs, structure of
  anthrênê/anthrêdôn, 80
  bees, 38-9
  wasps, 77
comedy, Attic: insects in, 11-13
  bed bug, 12-13, 46
  exaggeration, humorous, 13, 169
communication
  ants, 41-2
  bees, 54-5
composite figures, part insect; in art ('Mischwese'), 35-6, 72
contemporary ideas, influence of, viii, xii, 17-18, 24-6, 48-9
coprophagy, 88-9
Cos, silk trade, 112-13
Crecops latreilli Leach, 162
Crete
  art, insects in: bee, **61**, **71**; butterfly, **31**, **99**; dragonfly, **31**
  and bees, 32, 66-7, **71**, 72
  coins, 164
  Mallia pendant, 30, 33-4, **61**
  Minoan seals, 30-1
  religion: bees, 65; beetles, 95; butterflies, 107
cricket, 134-49
  = *akris*, 137-8
  cf. grasshopper/locust (qq.v.), 135
cucuracha (Spanish: cockroach), ix, 177n
Cyrinus (beetle), 162

Daedalus, 11, 42
damage to crops
  kantharis, 93
  locust, 141-2
Dante, 100, 167
dead
  insects' connection with: bees, 64-5, 68-9, 74-5; butterflies, xii, 99-100, 103-7; sirens, 74-5
  insects' treatment of own: ants, 39, 41; bees, 39; wasps, 39
dellis-ithos (wasp), 80
dêx (wood borer), 96
dew, 8n, 56, 57, 123-4
  as food: *akris*, 137; cicada, 123
Diogenes (philosopher) as wasp, 76
Dionysus: nurtured on honey, 67
Dioscorides (medical writer), 29n, 35, 93
'dog-fly', see *kynamuia*
dragonfly: on Minoan seals, 30, **31**
drosophila (fly), 157-8
drosos (dew/semen), 102
dung-beetle (*kantharos/Scarabeus pilularius*), x-xi, 11-12, 84-9
  in comedy, 11-12
  Etnean (*Aitnaios k.*), 86-7, **87**
  in fables, 3-4, 12, 84
  food of, 12, 88-9
  generation from carcasses, 84
  hibernation, 85
  in proverb, 85
  reproduction, 84, 90
  scents and, 11, 85, 88

earring, gold: bee on, 53
eggs, insect: Aristotle's terminology, 22
Egypt
  plagues of, 98, 157
  scarab-beetle in religion, 95-6
  emblems, local and national, 35, 57, 87, 125-6, **125**, **143**
  on coins: Athens, 125-6, **125**; Etna, **87**; Hybla, **57**; Metapontum, **143**
empis (gnat)
  = *Chironomus* (common gnat), 167
  etymology, 165
  = *hyperon*, 111-12
  = *kônôps*, 165-7
  may fly, 165
  = *muôps*, 161n
  = *oistros* larva, 165
  = *pênion*, 112
  = *(s)knips*, 98
  see also gnat
enceladus (similar to cicada), 130-1
entomon: Aristotle's term, 18
Eos and cicada (myth), 117, 126-7
ephemerôn (fly), 19, 157-8
Ephemeron longicauda (fly), 157
epigrams, Hellenistic, 13-14
epitaphs for insects: *akris*, 128n, 136, 137; ant, 41; cicada, 14, 128n, 129; grasshopper, 14

General index

Erinna (poetess) compared to bee, 71
Eros compared to gadfly, 14
Etna (Sicily), 11-12, 86-7
  etymology
  composite names, 90
  formal and popular, ix
  humorously incongruous, 133
  see also analogy; individual words
eulê (wood borer), 96
Eumenes (wasps), 73
euphemism: of vermin, 46

fables
  Aesopic, 1-6
  aetiological, 3-4, 6n
  antiquity of, 1
  dispute type, 4-6
  insects in, 1, 6; ant, 2, 4, 130; bee, 5-6; butterfly, 4; cicada/grasshopper, 4, 5-6, 123, 128, 130; dung-beetle, 3-4, 12, 84; fly, 2, 4, 155; gnat, 1-2, 3n; mosquito, 4n; ticks, 5, 6; wasp, 4, 5
  in literature, 6-7
  Oriental, 1-2, 4
  political use of, 6, 170
Fabre, Jean Henri, x-xi, 180
Fernández, Gil, ix
  see also Index of Modern Works
fever and butterfly/moth, 110
figs, pests of, 95, 115
flea (*psylla/pulex*), 149
flea, dog- (*kynoraistés*), 157
fly (*muia/musca*), 150-64
  aetiological myth (Lucian), 151
  anatomy, 150, 151
  in art, 9, 31, **150, 153, 154, 163**
  artificial, for fishing, 153
  dog-, 8, 90, 155-7
  in fables, 2, 4, 155
  fire-, 158-9
  gad-, 14, 159-64, **163**
  in Hellenistic epic, 14-15
  hippouros of Macedonia, 152-3
  in Homer, 7-9
  horse-, 159-64
  Lucian: *The Fly*, 150-1
  may-, 165
  nuisance value, 151-3
  Oriental similes on, 151
  in proverbs, 155
  remedies against, 151-2
  reproduction, 151
  swatters in temple inventory, 151
  symbolism and metaphor, 153-5
  and wasps, 76, 79
folklore
  ant, 40, 43
  bee, 47-8, 55

cicada, 4, 130
louse, 171
wasp, 78
food
  of insects, *see* individual insects
  of man: insects as source, 127-9, 141-2, 172
Formica sanguinea (ant), 41
foul brood (disease of bees), 64
fox
  and Aesop, 5
  fables, 2, 6
  cicada eaten by, 127
  and wasps, 78

gad-fly, 159-60, 162-4
  in art, **163**, 164
  bite like pangs of love, 14, 164
  in Homeric similes, 8
  horse-fly compared, 160-1
  madness, metaphor for, 164
  in myth, 163-4
Galen (medical writer), 26, 29n, 92
Galeriidae (moths), 64
Galleria mellonella or *cereana* (waxmoth), 64
Ganymede, 12, 88
gecko, ancient attitude to, 173
gems, insects depicted on, 35
  ant, **37**
  bee, **50**, 65, 68-9, **68**, 72
  beetle, **83**
  butterfly, 30-1, **31, 99, 101, 104,** 105
  cicada, 72
  dragonfly, **31**
  fly, **9, 150, 163**
  locust, **139**
  moth, **139**
  wasp, **9, 74, 78**
generation of insects, spontaneous, 10n, 21
bed bug, 46
bee, 64, 65-6
beetle, 84, 93
borers of wood, 96
butterfly, 102-3
from carcasses, 64, 65-6, 77-8, 84
cicada, 124n
gnat/mosquito, 167
louse, 171
wasp, 77-8
Geometridae (moths), 111-12
gnat (*empis*), 164-7
  bite, 166
  in fables, 1-2, 3n
  generation, 167
  locust, confused with, 164
  nuisance value, 165-7
  sound, 166-7

206 General index

see also empis
grammarians, insulting names for, 111
grasshopper, 134-49
  = *akris*, 137-8, 141-4
  in art: coins, **134**; 'Mischwese', 36; vase painting, **33**; wall painting, 36
  cicada, confused with, 115n, 122, 124-5, 134
  epigrams on, 14
  in fables, 4
  as food for man, 141-2
  sound, 122, 135
Greek Anthology, 13-14, 48
  see also epigrams; Index Locorum
  gruesome, fascination with, 175-6
Gryllidae, see crickets

Haematopinus asini (louse), 172
haemolymph, 23
Harpies and locusts, 10
hebdomadal rule, 17, 18n
hêpiolos (= moth, Aristotle), 110
Heraclitus: on soul, 105
Herculaneum: wall-painting, 36
Hermes (god) on gems, 68-9, 104
Hermes, Homeric Hymn to, 70; see also Index Locorum
Herodotus: flying snakes, 148-9
  see also Index Locorum
herpyllis (cicada), 131
Hesiod
  bees, domesticated, 52
  uses fable, 7
  see also Index Locorum
Hesperophanes (beetles), 95
hierarchy, animal, 7n, 20, 48
hippomyrmêx (ant), 38
Hipponax (poet), 11, 76
hippouros (fly), 152-3
historia (scientific method), 16
hives, bee, 49-50, 52
  diseases and infestations, 63-4
Homer
  insects in, 7-10, 75, 126
  and louse in anecdote, 171
honey
  in fables, 155
  as food: for babies, 76; for bees, 56-7
  ritual use of, 47, 48, 64
  source of, 56-8
  -thieves, in legend, 66-7, **67**
honey-dew, 8n, 56, 57, 123-4
hormix (ant), 37
hornet (*sphêx agrios/anthrênê*), 79
horse-fly (*muôps*), 159-64
hyperon (moth), 111-14

Iamus: nurtured on honey, 67

ibis and flying snakes, 148-9
identification, problems of, vii-ix, 19-21
infants nurtured by bees, 72
infestation see hives, vermin
influence of contemporary attitudes on scientists, viii, xii, 17-18, 24-6, 48-9
'insect': definitions, xi, 19
instruments, optical, 20
insult, insect names used as
koris, 46
kynamuia, 8, 155-6
mantis, 177
parnôps, 143-4
sês, 111
(s)knips, 98
tettigonion, 120n
Io myth, 163-4
ioulos (millipede?), 81
ips (wood borer), 96, 97, 99
irascibility, wasp as type of, 75-6
Isomachus (in Xenophon), 40, 59
ix (wood borer), 96, 97

jewellery, insects in, 33-5, 36
ant, **37**
bee, 30, 33-5, **34**, **53**, **61**, 72
cicada, 130
fly, **154**
scarab rings, 84, 96
Julian the Apostate: on lice, 7n, 169

kalamaia (praying mantis), 176
kalamaion, see *kerkôpê*
kampê
  = butterfly grub/larva, 102-3
  = *kantharis*, 93
kantharis (beetle), 92-3
kantharos (beetle), 84-9
  k. Aitnaios, 86-7
kar, karnos (louse), 176
kara(m)bus (beetle), 94
karnos
  = locust, 138-9
  = louse, 146, 176
kentrinês (wasp), 81
kêphênes (drones), 73-4
kerambêlon (beetle), 94
kerambux (beetle), 94
kerastês (beetle), 95
kerka (locust), 113, 146
kerkôpê (cicada), 131-2
kikous (cicada), 132
killos (cicada), 129
kis (wood borer), 96
kixios (cicada), 132
klêros (moth or beetle), 63-4, 110
knips (wood borer), 97-8, 99

General index

kôbax (cicada), 132
konis (nit), 176
kônôps (mosquito), 165-7
  = *bombykion*, 73
  etymology, 165
  hyperon and *pênion* similar to, 112
  = *oinopota cellaris*, 165
koris (bed bug), 46-7
Kornôpion, Heracles, 141
kornôps (locust), 135, 138-41
kynakris (locust), 146
kynamuia (dog-fly), 155-7
  abuse, as term of, 8, 155-6
  etymology, 90, 155-6
kyno-prêstis (beetle), 92
kynoraistês (dog-flea), 157

lacetas (cicada), 132-3
Laertes (ant), 44
lampyris (fire-fly), 158
larvae, Aristotle on, 22
Lasiocampa otus (moth), 102, 112-13
leekbane (*prasocuris*), 167
legend, *see* myth
leirioeis (epithet of cicadas), 8
Leonardo da Vinci, 26
ligantôr (cicada), 117, 133
liguros: epithet of
  akris, 118n, 137
  cicada, 117-18, 122
Linnaeus: classification system, 19
lipokentros (of bees), viii-ix, 51
literature, insects in, 6-7
  see also individual authors and insects; poetry
locust, 134-49
  in art, 32, **139, 140, 143**
  confused with: cicada, 122; cricket and grasshopper, 135
  damage to crops, 139, 141-2
  as food, 141-2
  and Harpies, 10
  medicinal use, 142
  remedies for, 140-1
  and scorpions, 142
  in similes, literary, 140-1
  and snakes, 142-3
  see also akris; mantis; mastax; okornos
louse (*phtheir/pediculus*), 168-76
  anecdotes involving, 170-1
  animal, 171-2
  body, 169-70
  in comedy, 12-13
  etymology, 168
  in folk-tale, 171
  generation, 102, 171
  hair, 168-9
  phthirophagy, 172-3

phthiriasis, 173-6
  and plague, 9-10, 169-70
  remedies for, 173
  ubiquitousnes, 7, 168-9
  in war, 9-10, 46n, 169-70
  'wild', 171
  winged, 176
Lousiad, The (Walcot, J. (pseud. Peter Pindar)), 6
Lovelace, R. (poet), 115, 130n
Lucanidae (beetles), 94
Lucian: *The Fly*, 150-1
Lytta (Cantharis) vesicatoria (Spanish-fly), 93

malaria, 166n
Mallia pendant, 30, 33-4, **61**
mantis
  = *akris*, 135, 176-7
  = locust, 146
  = praying mantis, 11, 176-80
mantis, praying (*mantis/mantis religiosa*), 11, 176-80, **179**
  in art, **178**
  'Evil Eye' and, 176-7
  like praying seer, 177, **178-9**, 180
  modern analogies for name, 180
  name used as insult, 177
manuscripts, illustrated, 35, 92, **93**
marine shipworm, 98
mason-bees, 73
mastax (locust), 10, 135, 146-7
mean, golden: Aristotle, 18
medicine: use of insects in
  bed bug, 47
  beetles, 93
  butterfly, 107-8
  locust, 142
Melanophila acuminata de Geer (fire-fly), 159
Melissa, Melisseus (Cretan legend), 67
melissa: etymology, 47
  see also bee
melissae (nymphs), 69
Melissaeus, of Zeus, 67
Meliteus: nurtured on honey, 67
Meloe variegatus Donov. (beetle), 91
mêlolonthê (cockchafer), 89-90
membrax (cicada), 133
menstruation: and pests, 93, 103
microscopes, 20
Milton, John, 43, 57-8
millipede, 81
'Mischwese' (fantastic combination of different creatures), 35-6
Mnaseas of Patara, 69
moles: locusts eaten by, 141
mosquito (*kônôps*), 164-7
  bite, 166

General index

in fables, 4
generation, 167
gnat, confused with, 164
and malaria, 166n
nets, 165, 166
nuisance value, 165-7
sound, 166-7
see also kônôps
moth (*psychê*), 99-114
in art, **139**
clothes-, 110-11
silk-, 112-13
muia: etymology, 150; *see also* fly
Muiagros (god), 152
muinda (blind man's buff), 160
muôps (horse-fly), 159-62
etymology, 160
and *kynamuia*, 156-7
in metaphor, 161-2
and *oistros*, 160-1
Muses
and bees, 72
and cicadas, 8, 72, 117-18, 122
Mylabris (beetle), 92
Myrmecides (sculptor), 31
myrmêkeion (insect that mimics ant), 46
myrmêko-leôn (ant-lion), 45
Myrmeleontidae (predators of ants), 45
myrmêx (ant), 37-47
etymology, 37-8
see also ant
myrmêx (type of boxing thong), 44
Myrmidon legend, 43
myth and legend
aetiological, 122
ants, 42-3
bees, 66-9
cicada, 42, 117, 122, 126-7
fly, 12, 151, 163-4
Myus (Ionian city), 166

nectar as source of honey, 56
nekydallos (pupa), 100, 102
Nero and cicada, 118
nets, mosquito, 165, 166
Newton, Isaac, 18n
Nicander of Colophon
on bees, 48
illustrated mss. of, 35
remedies against insects, 15, 92
nit (*konis*), 176
nuisance value
fly, 151-3
gnat/mosquito, 165-7
wasp, 76-7
nursery rhymes, 92

observation, individual, viii-ix
in Aristotle, 20-1, 28, 49
and optical instruments, 20
oinopota cellaris, 165
oistros, 14, 159-60, 162-4
= bee, 164
etymology, 162
identification of, 162
larva of = *empis*, 165
and *muôps*, 160-1
see also gadfly
okornos (locust), 10-11, 144
On Marvels Heard (wrongly attributed to Aristotle), 27-8
onomatopoeia in insect names
bee, 73
cicada, 113, 132-3
fly, 150
locust, 147
reduplication, expressive, 81
oracles, bees and, 69-70
organisation, insects' social, 38
ant, 38-40, 42, 60
bees, 59-62
wasps, 77
owl: eats cicada, 127

painting, *see* vase painting; wall-painting
Parnôpios Zeus and Apollo, 141
parnôps (locust), 135, 136, 138-41
parody involving insects in art, 36
Pasteur, Louis, 21
Peck, A.L., 17n, 18, 26, 27
see also Index of Modern Works
Pelopaeus (Sceliphron) spirifex (wasp), 80-1
pêlourgos (of bees), ix
pemphrêdôn (wasp), 81, 133
pênion (moth), 111-14
Pennella filosa L (parasite of sword-fish), 162
petêlis or petênis (locust), 147
phalaina (moth), 108-9
pets, insects as, 90
akris, 137-8
chrysomêlolonthê, 91
cicadas, 128n
mêlolonthê, 90
Pherecrates (comic poet), 42
Pherecydes: *phthiriasis*, 174
Phidias: insect sculpture, 31
philosophers and insects, 12n, 112, 149, 169, 174
philosophy and science, vi
Phrynichus (poet) cf. bee, 71
phtheir (louse), 168-76
etymology, 168
see also louse

General index

phthiriasis (alleged disease), 173-6
phthirophagy, 172-3
Phthirus pubis (louse), 171
Pindar and bees, 71, 72
pins, Peloponnesian gold, 34-5
plague
   Athenian, 9-10, 149, 169-70
   Egyptian, 165-6, 157
Plato
   cicada myth (*Phaedrus*), 122
   nurtured by bees, 72
   see also Index Locorum
Pliny, elder, xi, 28, 29
   see also Index Locorum
Plutarch, 30, 39
   see also Index Locorum
Poe, E.A., 175-6
poetry
   didactic, 15-16
   epic, 6-10, 14-15
   insects in: bees, 70-2; cicadas, 8, 72, 117-18, 122; sirens, 74; wasps, 76
   see also epigrams
poisonous creatures: Nicander on, 15
Polistes (wasp), 80
'political' of insects, 38
pollen, 58
Polyidus myth, 68-9
Pompeii, insects found at, xiii
Pompilidae (wasp), 80-1
Pope, Alexander, 76
pottery: cicada, 31, 114
pranô (locust), 147
prasocuris (leekbane), 167
preconceptions and scientists, viii, xii, 17-18, 24-6, 48-9
prejudice, anti-female, 63
priestesses and bees, 69-70
Prometheus and butterfly, **106**, 107
proverbs, insects in
   akris, 144
   ant, 43-4
   bee, 59
   cicada, 129
   dung beetle, 85
   fly, 155
   louse, 168
   moth, 109, 110-11
   wasp, 76
psên (wasp), 81-2
psôra (moth), 109
Psyche
   caterpillar of (basket-worm), 114
   depicted as butterfly, 107
psychê, 99-101
   see also butterfly
psylla (flea), 149
pyraustês (moth), 64, 109-10

pyrolampis (fire-fly), 158-9

Real-Encyclopädie der klassischen Altertumswissenschaft: inaccuracies in, xii
   see also Index of Modern Works
Réaumur, R.A.F. de (naturalist), 62n
Redi, Francesco, 21, 172
reduplication, expressive, 81, 114
remedies against insects
   bed bug, 47
   beetle, 92, 93
   fly, 151-2
   locusts, plagues of, 141
   louse, 173
   wasp, 76-7
reproduction of insects, see Aristotle; generation; names of individual insects
Resurrection and butterfly, 100, 103
Rhoecus legend and bee, 69
rings, finger, see jewellery
romos, romox (wood borer), 96

Sappho compared to bee, 71
sarcophagi, butterfly on, **106**, 107
sathrax (louse), 168
satyr plays, 86
Saussure, H.B. de (naturalist), 21
scabies, 171, 175
Scaevola, Mucius: *phthiriasis*, 174
scarabs, see gems
scarab-beetle (*Scarabeus sacer*), 84, 95-6
science
   influence of contemporary ideas upon, viii, xii, 17-18, 24-6, 48-9
   and philosophy, vi
scientific method, 16, 28
scorpions and locusts, 142
sculpture, 31, **106**, 107
seals: Minoan, 30-1
   see also gems
seirêdon (bee or wasp), 73n
seirên/siren (bee or wasp), 73-5
semen and butterfly, 102, 104-7, **104, 105**
Seriphos, old woman of, 176-7
sês (clothes-moth), 96, 110-11
Shakespeare, W., 83, 90-1, 109, 111
shield devices, **ii**, 32-3, **33**
Shelley, P.B., 111
sigalphos (cicada), 133
sigion (cicada), 133
silk trade, 112-13
similes using insects
   in *Argonautica*, 14-15
   in Homer, 7-8, 51, 140
   Oriental, 151

210 General index

in tragedy, 10-11
sirens, mythological, and *siren/seirên*, 74-5
size of insects
　in art, 33, 35
　and fables, 1-4
　and identification, vii, 20
　in proverbs, 44
sknips (wood borer), 97-8, 99
skôlêkôsis (disease, alleged), 175n
skôlêx (larva of wood borer), 96, 99, 120-3
　etymology, 38
skolopendra, 81
slang, *see* euphemism; insult
snakes
　and ants, 43
　flying, 148-9
　and insect venom, 77, 93
　and locust, 142
　and wasp (fable), 4, 77
snow and spontaneous generation, 21
social life of insects, 38
　ants, 38-40, 42, 60
　bees, 59-62
　wasps, 77
Sophocles and bees, 71, 72
soul in form of insect, xii
　bee, 64-5, 68-9, 74-5
　butterfly, 99-100, 103-7, 108-9
Spallanzari, Lazzaro, 21
Spanish-fly, 93
Spenser, E. (poet), 100
Sphaerella nivalis (alga), 21
Sphecidae (wasp), 80-1
sphêx (wasp), 75-83
　etymology, 38, 75
　sph. agrios (hornet), 79
　sph. ichneumôn (wasp), 38
Sphinx euphorbiae L. (moth), 108
sp(h)ondulê (beetle), 95
'Sphinx' pin, 34
spider: eats cicada, 127
staphylinos (beetle), 91
sting
　bee, 6, 52-3, 63, 66-7
　wasp, 76-7
stitthon (locust), 147
Stratiomys (fly), 152-3, 162
Strömberg, R., ix
　see also Index of Modern Works
Sulla (dictator), 170, 174, 175
superstitions, x, xii-xiii
　see also folklore
swallow feeds young on cicada, 127
Swammerdam, Jan (Dutch microscopist), 62
Swift, J.: *Pastoral Dialogue*, 169
Synagris (wasp), 73

Syrphus (fly), 162

taboos on names, 100n
teleology, Aristotle's 22-3
tenthrênê/tenthrêdôn (bee), 82-3
　etymology, 38, 82, 98
tephras (cicada), 133
terêdôn
　pest in bee hives, 64
　wood borer, 96, 98
Tettigoniidae (grasshoppers), 135
tettigonion: of cicadas and prostitutes, 120n
tettix (cicada), 114-33
　etymology, 114
　see also cicada
tettix (grey colour), 129
Theophrastus (philosopher), 27, 28-9
thêrion used of insects, 7, 46
thrips (wood borer), 96, 99
Thompson, D'Arcy Wentworth, vii
　on Aristotle's achievement, 24-5
　biography of, 138n
　identifications of insects, vii-viii
　see also Index of Modern Works
Tiberius (Emperor), 6, 43
ticks in fable, 5, 6
Tithonus, legend of, 8
tithumallis (moth), 108
tomb decorations, bees as, 65
tragedy, insects in, 10-11
Trichodes (Clerus), apiarius (pest of bees), 64
trixallis (cricket/locust), 148
trôx (cricket/locust), 148
trôxallis (cricket or locust), 147
Trygaeus (Aristoph. *Peace*), 11-12
vase painting
　Aesop and fox, **5**
　insects in, 32-3; bee, 32, 66-7, **67, 71**;
　butterfly, **105**; grasshopper?, **33**,
　locust, 32, 139, **140**; wasp, **ii**, 32, 78-9
mantis, **178**
painters: Amasis, **32**; Nicosthenes, **33**; Roundabout, **ii**; of Yale lecythos, **178**
venom, insect, 44, 77, 93
Vergil, *Georgics*, 15, 48, 60, 61-2
vermin
　in army, 9-10, 46n
　in comedy, 169
　in Homer, 8
　philosophers and, 12n, 149, 174
　wars and, 9-10, 46n, 169-70
　see also bed bug; flea; louse
Vesuvius; wall-painting, 36
von Frisch, Karl; dance of the bees, 55-6

Walcot, J. (pseud. Peter Pindar): *The Lousiad*, 6
wall-paintings of insects, 36
wars
  First World, 9-10, 46n
  Peloponnesian, 9-10
  Trojan, 10
wasp (*sphêx/vespa*), 75-83
  in Aristophanes, 76
  in art, **ii, 9,** 61, **74, 78,** 79
  and bees, 75, 76
  combs, structure of, 77
  damage by, 76
  dead, treatment of, 39
  in fables, 4, 5
  feeding of young, 78
  and flies, 76
  generation in carcasses, 77-8
  hibernation, 78
  in Homer, 7, 75
  and honey-dew, 57
  ichneumon, 80-1
  nuisance value, 76-7
  in proverbs, 76
  remedies for, 76-8
  reproduction, 77-8
  as shield device, **ii**
  and snakes, 77
  social life, 38, 77
  solitary, 73
  sting, 76-7
  as type of irascibility, 75-6
  as weather portent, 78
weather prophets
  ants, 40, 43
  bees, 55
  wasps, 78
weevil, strawberry (from Pompeii), xi
wood, decaying: and spontaneous generation, 21
wood borers, 8n, 96-7
  see also skôlêx

xylophagus bous (wood borer), 94

Yeats, W.B., 85

Zeus and insects
  ants, 42-3
  bees, 66-7
  dung-beetle, 3
  flies, 152, 163-4
  locusts, 141